D1414559

ESSAYS IN
INTELLECTUAL HISTORY

AMS PRESS
NEW YORK

Essays in
Intellectual History

═══

DEDICATED

TO JAMES HARVEY ROBINSON BY

HIS FORMER SEMINAR STUDENTS

═══

1 9 2 9

HARPER & BROTHERS PUBLISHERS

NEW YORK *and* LONDON

Library of Congress Cataloging in Publication Data
Main entry under title:

Essays in intellectual history.

    CONTENTS: Muzzey, D. S. Toleration.--Smith, E. P.
The philosophy of Anthony, third Earl of Shaftesbury.
--Brehaut, E. Occupational development of Roman
society about the time of the elder Cato. [etc.]
    1. History--Addresses, essays, lectures.
2. Robinson, James Harvey, 1863-1936. I. Robinson,
James Harvey, 1863-1936.
D6.E85 1973   901   78-126677
ISBN 0-404-05369-6

Reprinted from the edition of 1929, New York and London
First AMS edition published in 1973
Manufactured in hte United States of America

AMS PRESS INC.
NEW YORK, N. Y.   10003

CONTENTS

---

[v]

[vi]

FOREWORD

THE essays in this volume have been written by former students of Professor James Harvey Robinson for presentation to him upon the occasion of the delivery of his address as president of the American Historical Association.

Their immediate publication is made possible by the generous coöperation of a publisher who shares with the authors in this tribute to the life and work of a great teacher of history and to the profound influence of his scientific criticism upon the outlook of thoughtful people outside the academic world.

It would be utterly out of keeping with the attitude of mind which Professor Robinson impressed upon and exacted from his seminars if either the objective quality of these studies should be affected by the circumstance which calls them out, or the choice of subject should be limited by retrospective interests. The volume, therefore, has not been edited down to any single theme; each author has been free in both choice of subject and method of treatment. The result is a miscellany which may seem formless and puzzling to those who conceive of history as the repository of neatly fitting events arranged in the logic of cause and effect.

To those who studied under Professor Robinson the wide variety of these themes has another meaning. It offers a reminder, however slight, of his mastery of criticism of the reconstruction of accepted perspectives and of the pragmatism that rests upon fundamental objectivity.

JAMES T. SHOTWELL

TOLERATION

by

David Saville Muzzey

I

TOLERATION

THE immemorial custom of dedication has suffered strange vicissitudes. Originally it had the quality of supplication. It was a prayer to the powers above to be graciously pleased to dwell in a sacred edifice:

> O Thou, whose own vast temple stands
> Spread over land and sea,
> Accept the house that mortal hands
> Have raised to worship Thee;

or an invocation to the muses to inspire the mind and endow the pen of the poet with the divine efflatus. The transition from the solicitation of heavenly aid to the appeal to the powerful ones of this earth was natural. Might not more immediate and tangible benefits result from the favor of mundane millionaires than from mythical muses? So far had the mania of literary captation developed in the Roman Empire that the tart Martial satirized it in an epigram addressed to his latest composition: "Hasten, little book, to choose a proper patron for thy dedication, lest thy leaves find their way into some vile kitchen to be used to wrap a tuna fish in or to serve as a cornucopia for the pepper and spices." But Martial's ridicule had no effect upon a custom which promised to earn for author, painter or musician the benefactions of the rich, and to enhance the value of his work by the reflected glory of a great name. Thus, to its culmination in 17th century France and England, grew the habit of profitable dedication. Treatises on philosophy were cast in the form of "Letters to a Noble Lord"; paintings were limned for a powerful patron—with his portrait somewhere on the canvas; odes were composed in honor of princes. Even a Francis Bacon, in a groveling dedication to James the First, would fain have the reader of "The Advancement of Learning" believe that the light of his wisdom was derived from the spluttering candle of the Stuart monarch's intellect; and the radio-active mind of Voltaire could dally with flatteries to the most debased court in Europe in order to promote his chance to become the royal historiographer. Dignity, disinterestedness and truth have all been gainers from the modern and growing habit of the silent commendation of works of literature, science and art to the judgment of the competent critics of today and of an anonymous posterity. And dedications, if they still appear on the title pages, are generally complimentary and gratuitous expressions of friendship or affection. "To my wife," "To Ernest, Bob and Sally," "To my beloved teacher, J. W. M."

Nevertheless, there is a kind of dedication which has none of the quality of that sort of gratitude which has been defined as "a lively sense of benefits to come," nor is merely a conventional gesture of esteem; but is the recognition of a special competence in some art or science and of a ready sympathy with every contribution thereto. Such is the spirit in which the pages of this book are dedicated to you, my dear "Robbie." The other contributors have written historical and critical essays which will doubtless both enlist your interest in the subject presented and reflect in the method of treatment the stimulating influence of your teaching. Will you permit me in a more informal way to "converse" with you, albeit in a monologue, on a principle which has ever been of directive force in your thinking, and for the furtherance of which you have been a consistent protagonist through your writings, your discourse and your example.

[4]

Toleration is too often thought of as an amenity. In reality it is an arduous and exacting discipline. It is the chief element of progress in all cultural advance, as distinguished from the inventions and discoveries that have steadily augmented our material civilization. Even the latter, too, have depended for their successful exploitation far more often than is commonly realized upon the growth of political and religious toleration. Poets and philosophers have sung the praises of freedom as the mother of progress. Freedom is, of course, a noble state, the only state befitting a responsible human being. No sane man would deplore the growth or depreciate the encomiums of freedom. When it is invaded in the political sphere, men tend to become sycophants or rebels; when it is denied in religion, hypocrites and atheists are bred. But freedom, after all, is only a condition, although the most indispensable condition, of progress. It is negative, like opportunity. It furnishes in itself no guide or principle for action. It can be frightfully abused, as well as nobly used. Freedom is at most a guaranty that men shall not be unduly interfered with in the pursuit of their ideals; it furnishes no guaranty of discrimination between the quality of those ideals. A man is as "free" to spend his whole day on the golf links and his whole evening in the club lounge, if he can afford it, as he is to devote his waking hours to the improvement of his mind or the service of his fellows. He is as free to acquiesce in the stagnant conventions and standpat orthodoxies of society as he is to exercise his birthright of spiritual independence. The flapper is as free in her empty flapperism as a Jane Addams in her noble humanitarianism. Therefore freedom alone is not, and cannot be, the mother of progress. Like Edith Cavell's patriotism, it is "not enough."

Neither is enthusiasm alone enough. If freedom, as a mere condition of progress, lacks the criterion of impelling motives, enthusiasm often lacks judgment in the direction of these motives. Freedom, indeed, is the element in which the ship of progress moves and enthusiasm is the wind which drives it. But history is replete with instances of disaster due to the want of wise pilotage—ships stranded on the sand-bars of shallow prejudice, valuable cargoes wrecked on the rocks· of bigotry. It was not without good cause that the rationalists of the 18th century repudiated enthusiasm as a religious aberration and a social nuisance, although they threw out the child in emptying the bath that was muddied by intolerance and persecution. For man cannot live on the thin diet of rationalism alone. He is a creature of varied emotions, of desires that quicken the blood, of devotions that ignore the calculations of logic, of curiosities that refuse to be stilled by the veto of agnosticism, of aspirations that transcend even the expectation of fulfilment. He persists in the surmise, at least, that these non-rational elements in his experience are just the most significant and basically human part of it, and will not see them sacrificed to a syllogism. *"Naturam expellas furca, tandem usque recurret."* The key to cultural progress, therefore, in a milieu of freedom, must be found in a principle which, after the Hegelian formula, synthesizes the thesis of enthusiasm and the antithesis of rationalism. It is the age-long and arduous problem of how to purge the mind of its persistent illusions, prejudices and irrationalities, without impairing the vitality of the affectional and aspiring qualities in human nature.

There is no other way, it seems to me, to the solution of this problem than along the patient path of toleration—understanding by that word not the passive and often disdainful endurance of opinions, beliefs and customs differing from our own, but the positive sympathetic effort to comprehend their cause and appraise their value. Toleration thus being the social virtue par excellence, the solvent for the most

[6]

grievous quarrels that have vexed mankind, and the indispensable factor in the direction of thought and action toward enduring cultural gains, it cannot be amiss to inquire into the history and nature of this virtue.

From the many treatises written on toleration, with their irrefutable proofs of its reasonableness and their cumulative evidence of the baneful effects of its violation, one would think that the case should have been long ago completely won. But the student of anthropology, psychology and sociology comes to wonder rather how such moderate progress as we have achieved in toleration has been accomplished. For unnumbered centuries rigid custom ruled our remote ancestors. To depart from the ritual prescribed for hunt or harvest, to violate the tabus which embodied the awful sanctions of supernatural power, was to endanger the very existence of the tribe. At the entrance to every path of independent thought or individual action stood the angel with the flaming sword in his hand. The stranger was *eo ipso* the enemy, the protégé of hostile divinities and the practiser of destructive arts. In the course of time, by ways and from motives of which we have no recorded knowledge, some anonymous heroes with hearts of "triple bronze" dared to break through the sacred bounds of custom—else we should still be living in caves and huts. But the vast majority, with little courage and less discernment, went to swell the mass of blind conformity. Realizing, as we now do, that the few original and innovating minds have had to drag through the centuries the dead weight of complacent custom, as the small heads of the prehistoric monsters dragged their huge bodies through swamp and slime, we may wonder that mankind was not permanently mired in intellectual stagnation.

Furthermore, it is to be doubted whether anyone, without the severe discipline of reason, would incline toward toleration. Our own views seem to us right, or they would not be our views. How readily we warm to a person who agrees with us in a judgment or an argument, even though his opinion be far less entitled to respect than that of our opponent. We hanker for confirmation, because of the subtle flattery it brings to our self-esteem. Hobbes' characterization of mankind as a "race of unmitigated egomaniacs" may be a bit severe, but it is nevertheless true that one of the most difficult things in the world is to wean a mind from the precarious self-assurance on which it has been fed by centuries of custom and conformity.

Institutions have supervened to confirm and conserve. They have been established by and for men of like belief, like speech, like blood, like habits, to strengthen their religious, patriotic, racial and social convictions of the superiority of these institutions to those of people of other beliefs, speech, blood or habits. Toleration has never been a charter article in the planting of churches, states and schools. And if, in very recent years, it has made any way in these institutions, it has been by dint of strenuous efforts and by virtue of developments (to be noticed later) alien to their original purpose. The church, for example, until the most recent days and except in a few of its branches, has been not a forum for free discussion of baffling religious questions, but a close corporation guarding the faith delivered to the fathers against the inroads of intellectual inquiry and "science falsely so-called." "He who is gifted with the heavenly knowledge of faith," say the decrees of Trent, "is free from inquisitive curiosity." The state still is, with the uproarious approval of nearly "a hundred per cent" of its citizens or subjects, the embodiment of perfection: supreme in power, unimpeachable in its righteousness, unapproachable in its culture. Let a minister take a high tone of menace to a foreign government, and the press of the country resounds with applause. The arch-chauvinist Mussolini seems to be as much admired in democratic America as he is venerated in Italy. Join the circle discussing politics over their coffee and cigars at the club, and it will not be long before you hear some solid citizen announce with an air of finality: "What we need in this country is a Mussolini." What are such trivial incidents, or accidents, of citizenship as free parliaments, liberty of teaching and uncensored publications compared with the surge of pride symbolized by the forward thrust of fifty thousand black sleeves! It is so comfortable to be a member of a society which is securely fixed on the bed-rock of national egotism, so flattering to vanity to be on friendly terms with omnipotence, so much easier to believe than to reason, to conform than to reform. Were it not for the proscribed and often persecuted few who have persisted in the ungrateful Socratic task of keeping the lamp of reason alight amid the gusts of conflicting dogmas, there would be no toleration in the world, and without toleration there would be no progress.

Whether the Greeks and Romans were the shining exemplars of toleration they were represented to have been by the philosophers of the 18th century is open to question. Voltaire in his celebrated *"Traité sur la Tolérance,"* written in defense of the name and family of Jean Calas, victim of bigoted ecclesiastical injustice, made an elaborate argument for the tolerant attitude of classical antiquity, and even of the early Christians, as a foil to the persecuting orthodoxy of his own day. And Gibbon's famous encomium of the age of the Antonines may be somewhat too highly colored as a contrast to the era of dogmatic quarrels which was ushered in with the triumph of imperial Christianity. In a recent magazine article Mrs. Gerould speaks of toleration as a "lost pagan virtue." But even Athens in the glorious days of her enlightenment, the "eye of Hellas," would not tolerate the speculations of Anaxagoras or the interrogations of Socrates or even the virtues of Aristides. The Athenians as portrayed by Aristophanes and Euripides have little resemblance to the high-souled and sane-minded citizens of Pericles' immortal oration. Mr. Wells may be nearer the truth than his protesting critic, Ernest Barker, in surmising that the average of the Athenian people, in spite of their privilege of attending the edifying tragedies of Æschylus and Sophocles at the expense of the state, were neither more cultivated nor more liberal-minded than the audience of a London music-hall. As for the Romans, Cato the Censor was certainly no champion of toleration; and if the imperial policy permitted the free exercise of a multitude of cults, indulgence ceased abruptly when any of them refused the supreme worship of the "genius" of the Emperor as the symbol of Roman world supremacy. When "lèse-majesté" is a mortal heresy it is a mockery to speak of toleration. That such enlightened and humane rulers as Trajan and Marcus Aurelius sanctioned the persecution of men whose conscience would not allow them to pay divine worship to enthroned earthly power is a more damning evidence of fundamental intolerance than the raging of a hundred bigoted inquisitors.

However, to question the extravagant claims made for the toleration of the Greeks and Romans as a "lost pagan virtue" is in no wise to condone the intolerance of the Christian church, once it had survived the ordeal of persecution and become the imperial institution without whose pale there was no salvation. The monopoly not only of religion but of the whole field of secular interests (so far as they existed) established and maintained by the mediæval church was naturally hostile to the propagation of toleration. There was plenty of intellectual acumen, but it was directed into channels inexorably marked by the dogmas of apostolic, patristic and scholastic orthodoxy. Social status was unalterably fixed by the ordering of God, and the political state was a subordinate and obedient sphere of jurisdiction in the ecumenical economy of the *Civitas Dei.* The basic factor of constructive thought, discrimination in the nature of evidence, was lacking, because the evidence was complete in a supernatural revelation which was to be acknowledged on pain of temporal and eternal punishment. Honest doubt was dealt with as impious rebellion; speculative restlessness as Satanic suggestion. Moreover, the befogging mediæval virtue of spiritual transport obscured not only the improbity of slovenly and lethargic thinking, but the far more serious inhumanity of systematic persecution. Thought could not be free in the midst of constant fear that its conclusions might entail loss of goods in this life and in the life to come eternal torment. There were, to be sure, in every generation some undaunted spirits who risked these perils for the sake of intellectual and moral integrity; but the promptness and thoroughness with which they were suppressed by civil and ecclesiastical authorities alike, with the general approbation of the multitude, is proof of the sinister influence of power unchecked by conscientious opposition. "We have enough religion to hate and persecute," wrote Voltaire, "but not enough to love and succor." Perhaps the church, as Professor Sumner remarked, "has never been on the level of the best *mores* of any time." The appeal to the baser passions in God's name has always met with a ready response. "Do I not hate them, Lord, that hate thee?" is a text more honored than the Christian injunction, "Love thine enemies." If the true saints of the middle ages, of whom Francis of Assisi will always be the adorable example, made earnest with the precepts of Jesus, it was rather because an inextinguishable love for all creation possessed them than because of any reasoned sympathy with the tolerant maxim that the wheat and tares must grow together till the harvest.

The explanation of such measure of toleration as has been

achieved in modern times is to be found in a complex and cumulative set of circumstances whose uniform trend has been toward the emergence of secular interests from their long eclipse by mediæval dogmatism. When a new earth was revealed by Columbus, Vespucius and Magellan, and a new heaven by Copernicus, Kepler and Brahe, the thoughts of men could not but be widened with the process of the suns. Could this little world, displaced from its fixed and major majesty at the center of the universe, really be the absorbing concern of Omnipotence? Furthermore, in spite of the manifest shortcomings of humanism in general, and of Italian humanism in particular—its servile imitation of classical models, its moral indifferentism, its literary "preciousness" and artistic dilettantism—it is incontestable that the Renaissance, by its rediscovery and rehabilitation of man's creative powers, contributed much to redress the balance which had been excessively weighted in the scale of otherworldliness for a millennium. If the works of man were admirable, then his mind must be estimable. One by one the various fields of human activity—politics, finance, philosophy, art, letters, education, law, medicine, commerce, diplomacy, drama, diet—were cut off from the all-inclusive domain of theology and subjected to intensive cultivation by mundane instruments. When men woke to the realization that there were more things in heaven and earth than were dreamed of in the mediæval synthesis, the rule of authority based on inadequate knowledge and buttressed with question-begging argument was doomed. The best minds turned from the defense of tradition in ponderous *Summae* to the patient task of the detection and correction of error step by step. Sir Thomas More was a staunch defender, even to death on the scaffold, of the papal church. Yet it is highly significant that in his "Utopia," which Wingfield-Stratford characterizes as "a merciless analysis of the selfishness, waste and muddle of the professedly Christian politics of contemporary Europe," he constructed an ideal state "without any appeal to the authority of mediæval dogma or the approval of the Roman Church."

"Those who take few factors into consideration," said Francis Bacon, "arrive at conclusions quickly." The proximate recourse in argument to an unarguable thesis, like the divine right of kings, the final perfection of a constitution, a 100 percent chauvinism, or a revealed dogma, shuts the door of the mind on toleration. It is the insistent crowding of new knowledge about that door in the centuries since Francis Bacon, rather than any spontaneous welcome of the human mind itself, that has opened it, if only ajar as yet, to sanity and reason. The mere enumeration of these new factors of knowledge would be a chapter index to the history of modern thought and culture. Conspicuous among them have been the realization of the futility of the religious wars which devastated Europe in the 16th and 17th centuries; the discoveries of science, which multiplied the evidences from experimentation and inductive reason in their challenge to the arbitrary and untested "explanations" of sanctified tradition; the expansion of trade and commerce which refused to draw a "cordon sanitaire" around the shores of an heretical country or to sacrifice a prospective customer on account of his theological opinions; the efforts of the English Deists and the French *Philosophes* to recover a "natural religion," consonant with the mental integrity and moral dignity of man, out of the welter of mutually persecuting sects which flourished in the fertile soil of the Protestant revolt; the growing respect for human life and freedom, under the increasing agencies for the refinement of manners and the enhancement of personality, which gradually abolished scores of death penalties, replaced savage inquisitors by considerate juries, and relegated the witch-

[13]

hunt, the torture-chamber, and the sadistic horrors of public executions to the limbo of barbarism; the Industrial Revolution, which, by the very evils that it created in sweating slums and slavery to the machine, partially provided the antidote by directing the attention of philanthropists and reformers to the improvement of social conditions through factory legislation, health crusades, organized charities, free education, parks and recreation centers.

When Voltaire remarked that "toward the middle of the 18th century men ceased to speculate about free grace and began to speculate on the price of grain," he stated the basis of modern toleration with his accustomed epigrammatic exaggeration. Of course, men had been concerned in all the centuries before the 18th with their food supply; and they continued and still continue to be interested in their salvation. But the important point is that in the "ages of faith" all mundane affairs were referable to and controlled by a fundamentally intolerant system of doctrine, whereas in the modern "harmonizing" of religion and science it is religion which, by concession, interpretation and judicious reticence, adjusts itself to the essentially tolerant, because provisional, attitude of science. The philosophers or scientists of today who feel any concern to demonstrate their religious orthodoxy (if they have it) to the world are probably as few as the clergymen who are not anxious to seem and to be in sympathy with the modern trends of secular thought. If toleration is still for some the Abbé Houterville's "dogme monstrueux" or the New England Puritan's deadly cocatrice's egg from which all human vice is hatched, the weapons of persecution have been taken out of the hands of the inquisitor. In advanced and highly integrated communities the infidel is as free to publish his opinions as the believer, the socialist as the conservative, the innovator as the traditionalist. The long and bitter battle for the "liberty of prophesying" has been won. It remains to be seen whether the liberty won, which, be it remembered, is an opportunity only and not a program, is to be frittered away in the indulgence of an aimless hedonism or gratefully accepted as an invitation to examine and discuss, without fear or forfeit, any pattern of thought, or plan of action put forth in the promise of enhancing the moral, mental or material value of life.

But some will ask whether toleration can exist with conviction. Is not the moral earnestness which gives purpose and courage to life sapped by the admission of contrariety? Can the artist tolerate sloppy work, the musician discord, the scholar charlatanism, or the preacher sin? This is a serious practical question which deserves respectful consideration. For undoubtedly intolerance in all ages has been due rather to the dictates of conscience than to a positive lust for persecution. The inquisitor Torquemada is said to have been a man of kindly nature; but heresy was a deadly contagious disease which had to be stamped out if men were to be saved from eternal perdition. The New England Puritans were not devoid of gracious amenities and deep affections; but, under the relentless scrutiny of the "great taskmaster's eye," they felt themselves bound in the Lord to exercise an equally relentless censorship over the beliefs and behavior of their neighbors, in order, as Cotton Mather said, "that the Devill should not spoil the vinyard that God had planted." Thus conscience doth not "make cowards of us all." Of many it makes zealots and fanatics, who erect their inhibitions into standards to which they seek to make others conform, as formerly at the point of the sword, so, in these less sanguinary days, at the behest of legislatures or various organizations for the maintenance of the social lockstep.

That the praiseworthy motive of genuine conviction has so often worked to the prejudice of the equally desirable quality of toleration is due to certain misconceptions of the true meaning of both terms. First of all is the mistaken idea, so widely held, that convictions are immune to education. A conviction is, etymologically, something that holds one in a bond. The "convict" is in the clutches of the law. The convinced person is held in the grasp of an idea: "Woe is me if I preach not the gospel." But the mere fact of being possessed by an idea is of itself no warrant for the validity or wholesomeness of that idea. Conviction *per se* is as little worthy of respect as the vagaries of an opium eater. Immature or arrested minds are notably strong in their convictions. Our lunatic asylums are filled with people who are convinced that they are Julius Cæsar or Napoleon Bonaparte. And there is a strain of lunacy, on some subject, in most of us. Moreover, when we consider the number of ardent convictions which we have outgrown in the process of our intellectual and emotional education, it ought to warn us of the truth of Renan's remark that a man's opinions tend to become fixed at the point where he stops thinking. If men would only realize that just in the measure that they are privileged to demand respect for their views they are also obligated to study to make their views worthy of respect, and would subject their own convictions to the same tests of historical criticism and rational analysis to which they find it perfectly natural to subject the convictions of those who differ from them, toleration would be a normal concomitant of conviction instead of a suspected competitor. "Every one, of course, must think his own opinions right; for if he thought them wrong they would no longer be his opinions. But when he views opinions in the aggregate, when he reflects that not a single being on the earth holds collectively the same, when he looks at the past history and present state of mankind, and observes the various creeds of different ages and nations . . . the notions once firmly held which

[16]

have been exploded, the prejudices once universally prevalent which have been removed, and the endless controversies
which have distracted those who have made it the business
of their lives to arrive at the truth . . . he cannot help the
obvious inference that in his own opinions it is next to impossible that there is not an admixture of error, that there
is an infinitely greater probability of his being wrong in
some than right in all." It would be well if these words of
Samuel Bailey, written over a century ago, were read today
by men who allow their zeal to master their reason, and
stigmatize the convictions of others as obstinacy while they
dignify their own as faith.

Finally, toleration is often conceived in a way which seems
to threaten to undermine genuine conviction, being identified with lethargic spiritual indifference. "Much that passes
for a benign tolerance for the opinions of others," says John
Morley in his essay on "Compromise," "is in truth only a
pretentious form of being without settled opinions of our own
or any desire to settle them." The fallacy of this Laodicean
complacency lies in the pernicious dilemma that if I do not
wish to force my opinions on my neighbor I must abandon
them myself. To urge this is to ignore the basic factor in
true toleration, and, under the guise of magnanimity, to
treat another's opinions as shabbily as one treats one's own.
For how can a man weigh evidence when he has thrown away
the scales, or evaluate conclusions when he has never taken
the pains to form any? It is not toleration, but indolence
and timidity, that weaken conviction. "The fault is in ourselves, dear Brutus." Toleration is a function not of forming,
but of realizing our opinions. It is a counsel of patience. Its
method is persuasion, not force; education, not regimenta-
tion. Its attribute is humility. Its quest, "more light." Even
the most cursory reading of history should suffice to show to
any fair-minded person that the evil consequence so often

predicted as the inevitable result of innovation in state, church or society have been largely chimerical. The debates of Congress abound in vain prophecies that the adoption of this or that measure will sound the death-knell of the American republic. Appeal to the timidity and indolence of the populace has ever been the chief support of intolerance. It is highly probable, however, that not one tithe of injury to the public weal has resulted from the advocacy of radical ideas that has come from the determination at all hazards to preserve the *status quo*. Some measure of error is inherent in human progress. "Es irrt der Mensch so lang er strebt." If all the world slept for twenty years, like Rip Van Winkle, it would awake to no marvels. Beacons will be hailed which prove to be flickering will-o'-the-wisps, prophecies uttered that are but "cock-crowings at midnight, announcing no dawn." But to shut the eyes and stop the ears on that account is to risk missing the stars and the voice of God.

THE PHILOSOPHY OF ANTHONY, THIRD EARL OF SHAFTESBURY

by

Emma Peters Smith

II

THE PHILOSOPHY OF ANTHONY,
THIRD EARL OF SHAFTESBURY

I

IT IS one of the ironies of history that the gracious and high-minded nobleman who spent most of his life in the study of virtue and in the "*business* . . . of learning how to be an honest man and friend"[1] should have been villified by those in sacred office and been classed as an "enemy of religion" and a scoffer at holy things. To be a "good" man according to these divines meant not only to believe their creeds but to uphold the doctrines and practices of the ecclesiastical organization, whatever its record might be. Any too-searching criticism of these seemed to justify an attack, sufficient to cast a shadow on the name of the offender even in the eyes of supposedly thoughtful men.[2]

That lover of virtue for its own sake, the amiable Earl of Shaftesbury, was one of the first to disassociate religion and morality and to pay his fellow-creatures the compliment of believing them able and willing to lead lives of the highest integrity without the assistance or the threats of supernatural

---

[1] Letter to John Locke, Sept., 1694. Written when he was but twenty-three, this letter indicates how early Shaftesbury turned his attention to those philosophical speculations which occupied him throughout his life. *Life, Unpublished Letters and Philosophical Regimen of Anthony, Earl of Shaftesbury,* ed. B. Rand, London 1900.

[2] In a sketch of Shaftesbury's life by his son, the fourth earl states that his purpose is "by giving the character and sentiments of the author of the *Characteristics* as they really were, to take off some of the ill impressions which well-meaning persons may have received from the many calumnies which have been cast on him." *Op. cit.* An account of his critics is given by Fowler, *Shaftesbury and Hutcheson,* London 1882.

powers. That by thinking too well of man, he was assumed to think too little of God cast small credit on a theology which appeared to depend on the continued depravity of man and his consequent need of redemption.[1]

Shaftesbury had a fundamental confidence in the goodness and possibility of human nature. He rejected alike the mediæval conception of man's sinfulness and perversity and the Calvinistic picture of his helplessness and corruption. He opposed at many points the "materialistic" philosophy of Hobbes and refused to accept his theory of narrow self-interest as the ruling motive of the world. He had no sympathy with Hobbes' low estimate of man prior to the beneficent effects of civil government in curbing his naturally vicious tendencies. He makes some pertinent comments on the difficulty of determining, in a long series of natural processes, just when a "state of nature" may be said to have set in. The goodness and honesty necessary to maintain the "social contract" after its adoption, must, he urges, have existed previously and been the very cause of its voluntary acceptance. The noble qualities of man are not due to the restraining power of princes but are inherent in man himself.[2]

[1] *The Characteristics of Men, Manners, Opinions, Times,* etc., containing all of Shaftesbury's essays which he intended for publication appeared in 1711. A second edition was carefully prepared by him just before his death in 1713. Eleven English editions were published before 1790, while a complete French translation appeared in 1769 and a complete German translation in 1776-79.

[2] *The Moralists,* Pt. II, sec. 4, and *Essay on Wit and Humor,* Pt. II, sec. 1. In a letter to his protégé, Michael Ainsworth, Shaftesbury disagrees with the philosophy of his "old tutor and governor," Locke, who by rejecting innate ideas seemed to him to "throw all order and virtue out of the world." The question, he says, is not the "time the ideas *entered*" but whether the "constitution of man be such that . . . sooner or later the idea and sense of order, administration and a God will not infallibly, inevitably . . . spring up in him." He points out that "all the free-writers now-a-days have espoused those principles which Mr. Hobbes set-a-foot in this last age . . . and that Mr. Locke . . . did go in the self-same tract and is followed by the Tindals and other free authors of our time." In *Life, Unpublished Letters,* etc.

[22]

Shaftesbury questions the common assumption that religion and morality are "inseparable companions." For, he says, there are many who profess to have religious convictions who display a lack of common humanity in their behavior, and are even degenerate and corrupt; while others who pay little regard to religion—and often so-called atheists—live lives of the highest rectitude. Indeed, in everyday practice, moral considerations carry so much more weight than religious pretensions that when we are told that a man is religious we still wish to know something of his morals. While on the other hand if we know him to have honesty and integrity we seldom inquire further as to his religion. This leads us to ask how far morality is influenced by religion and whether an unreligious person may not be entirely virtuous.

The basis of morality, Shaftesbury finds not in the authority of a church nor in the teaching of the Scriptures, but in the "moral sense." The knowledge of right and wrong, good and evil are revealed to us as clearly by this inner sense or faculty as are forms and colors to the eye. As the eye and ear distinguish shapes and sounds, so the mind discovers the beautiful and ugly, the honest and corrupt in human behavior. "It feels the soft and harsh, the agreeable and disagreeable in the affections; and finds a foul and fair, a harmonious and dissonant as truly here as in any musical numbers or in the outward forms . . . of sensible things. Nor can it withhold its admiration . . . its aversion and scorn any more in what relates to one than to the other." Morality is therefore a characteristic of rational creatures who are not only able to form notions of things and beings but of actions themselves. And so "there arises a new trial or exercise of the heart which must either . . . affect what is just and right, and disaffect what is contrary, or . . . affect what is ill and disaffect what is worthy and good." [1]

Virtue, which is an affection for and a deliberate choice of the good finds its highest expression in benevolence—that is, in love towards mankind and a devotion to its welfare. This devotion to the good of the whole of which he is a part, Shaftesbury calls the *natural affections*, as distinguished from self-affection which seeks the interest of the individual as its end. Natural affection, or moral rectitude, is to the advantage of every one, for to have "just, kind and generous" affections towards others is to have the chief means of enjoyment and the highest happiness in life. Thus "virtue is the good and vice the ill of every one."

What effect then can religious belief have on morality? Shaftesbury maintains that the knowledge of right and wrong and the attitude towards them are developed long before one is capable of having any definite or "settled notions" about a Deity. Morality is therefore antecedent to and independent of religion and more fundamental in our lives. Religion, he says, is capable of doing great good or harm but atheism "nothing positive either way." At least atheism will not be the occasion of setting up a false species of morality by esteeming anything fair and noble which is in reality the contrary. On the other hand, "corrupt religion or superstition" may cause many things "unnatural and inhuman . . . to be received . . . as good and laudable." . . . "If there be a religion which teaches the . . . love of a God whose character it is to be captious and of high resentment, subject to wrath and anger . . . revenging himself, when offended, on others than those who gave the offence; and if there be added to the character of this God a fraudulent disposition, encouraging deceit and treachery amongst men, favorable to a few . . . and cruel to the

[1] *Inquiry concerning Virtue or Merit*, Bk. I, Pt. II, sec. 3.

rest, 'tis evident that such a religion . . . must of necessity raise even an approbation and respect towards vices of this kind and breed a suitable disposition, a capricious, partial, revengeful and deceitful temper . . . so that where one worships a supreme Being who is other than truly just and good . . . there must ensue a loss of rectitude . . . honesty will be supplanted by zeal . . . when one is thus unnaturally influenced and rendered immorally devout." [1] While false religion may impair the sense of right and wrong, a "perfect theism" is conducive to virtue for it "raises the affections" towards the qualities of a supreme being who is represented as worthy and good, benevolent and just.

Men obey a deity, he asserts, either because of a belief in his power and for the advantage that will result from keeping his commands, or on account of their idea of his excellence. In the first case there can be no virtue, for obedience is mere servility. Shaftesbury rejects the whole theory of rewards and punishments which formed so essential a part of both natural and revealed religion. If virtue, he says, "be not really estimable in itself, I can see nothing estimable in following it for the sake of a bargain." He deprecates a system which emphasizes "the grace and favor which result from well-doing" and where so little is made of the worth of virtue itself. It tends, he urges, to encourage the pursuit of self-interest and so to lessen the affection toward public good. Moreover, it causes God to be loved as "an instrument of pleasure" and thus results in a diminution of piety which is to love God for his own sake. "Virtue is something in itself, not constituted from without and dependent on custom, fancy or will; not even on the supreme will which can in no way govern it." . . . It is only when good is fol-

<hr />

[1] *Inquiry*, Bk. I, Pt. III, sec. 2.

lowed for itself alone that a man can be deemed truly virtuous.

A far more important element affecting conduct than rewards and punishments is "good taste," for nothing charming or delightful can be accounted for without the pre-establishment of a certain taste. "It is not merely moral principles but a taste which governs men." They may know what is right, expedient and wise but if their fancies and appetites are set the other way their conduct will be decided by their preferences. "Even conscience, such as is owing to religious discipline" will be of little avail when the desires are opposed.[1] Shaftesbury concedes that with the "vulgar" the fear of a devil and hell may be operative, but with the educated and liberal such threats amount to little. As conduct is determined by our affections, so the affections are governed by our taste. Morality thus becomes a form of æsthetic appreciation.

In art and music we acknowledge standards of perfection and are eager to cultivate an understanding of the best. We find that this is achieved, however, only after long and patient study, practice and experience. " 'Tis not instantly we acquire the sense by which these beauties are discoverable." Is then "science or learning necessary to understand all beauties else and for the sovereign beauty [virtue] is there no skill or science required?" For "there is nothing so divine as beauty which belonging not to body nor having any existence except in mind and reason, is alone discovered and acquired by this diviner part."[2] When, however, we learn to discern those qualities which constitute the "decorum and grace" of things "will it not be found that what is beauti-

[1] Elsewhere Shaftesbury defines conscience as the apprehension of moral deformity; religious conscience being commonly terror of the deity. *Inquiry*, Bk. II, Pt. II, sec. 1.
[2] *The Moralists*, Pt. III, sec. 2.

ful is harmonious and proportionable; [1] what is harmonious and proportionable is true; and what is at once both beautiful and true is of consequence agreeable and good?" Here Shaftesbury comes to the very purpose of all his writings which he himself says is "to assert the reality of a beauty and charm in moral as well as natural subjects and to demonstrate the reasonableness of a proportionate taste and determinate choice in life and manners." [2]

II

In his well-known letters on the English Deists, Leland says: "it gives me a real concern, that, among the writers who have appeared against revealed religion, I am obliged to take notice of the noble author of the *Characteristics*." [3] There is great reason to apprehend that not a few have been unwarily led to entertain unhappy prejudices against revealed religion and the authority of the scriptures, through too great an admiration for his Lordship's writings." [4] The easy classification of authors into groups on the ground of similar opinions often proves misleading; for in emphasizing certain ideas which they appear to hold in common, other ideas are neglected which the authors themselves would have regarded as far more fundamental and important. One cannot but think that the noble lord who devoted his retirement to philosophical speculation would have been not a little surprised to find his name associated with that group of miscellaneous writers known as the "deists."

The deistical writers of the late seventeenth and eighteenth centuries in England differed greatly in personality, ability and temperament as well as in many ideas. Yet they were

[1] There is a footnote to this passage which says that "this is the *honestum, the pulchrum*" on which the author "lays the stress of virtue and the merit of this cause in all his works." *Miscellaneous Reflections,* III, ch. 2.
[2] *Miscellaneous Reflections,* III, ch. 2.
[3] *A View of the Deistical Writers,* London 1754. Letter V.
[4] *Op. cit. Letter* VI.

all agreed that religion needed to be rescued from the ways into which it had fallen and a new relationship established between God and man independent of the teachings of traditional theology. They sought not only to rehabilitate man but to create a nobler conception of God and advocated a religion whose simple truths should be based on reason and be discoverable by all men without the assistance of supernatural revelation. The main tenets of this *natural religion* which were early formulated by Lord Herbert of Cherbury, were simple and few in number. "That there is one supreme God; that he ought to be worshipped; that virtue and piety are the chief parts of divine worship; that we ought to be sorry for our sins and repent of them; that divine goodness doth dispense rewards and punishments both in this life and after it." [1]

There is no doubt that Shaftesbury shared the spirit of rational inquiry which animated the Deists in their questioning of accepted ideas and their rejection of the evidences of revealed religion. In view of his ethical theory, however, it is interesting to inquire how far his philosophy was in accord with the assumptions of *natural religion* and at what points it diverged.

Shaftesbury repeatedly acknowledges the existence of a supreme principle or mind by whose providence the universe is regulated and maintained. It is natural that man should admire him for his excellence and desire to imitate his perfections.[2] He does not conceive of the Deity, however, as desiring or demanding praise. "Is the doing of good for glory's sake so divine a thing?" This he maintains is one

[1] *De Religione Gentilium* published posthumously in 1663; Eng. transl. 1705, chap. 1.

[2] Shaftesbury uses both forms Theist and Deist which in the *Moralists* is called the "highest of all names." The question here is not that of Shaftesbury's theistical philosophy, but how far he deserved to be classed as a "Deist" in the derogatory sense in which the name was employed by Christian apologists and in which it lingered in the popular mind as a bad name bordering on atheist.

of the unworthy ideas which man, owing to his own limitations, has of God, that he thinks of him as taking delight in
lavish commendation and the ignorant applause of men.[1]
Shaftesbury also deprecates the "wretched effect within" of
"vulgar prayers and addresses to the Deity." It is needless to
say how distasteful a form of worship prayer, in the sense of
petition, would have seemed to one who throughout his life
desired neither preferment from man nor recompense from
God. While he would have agreed with Lord Herbert that
virtue was the highest good and the greatest happiness of
man he did not view it as a form of obedience to God. No
other incentive to morality is necessary than the love of virtue for itself. "For if virtue be to itself no small reward and
vice in a great measure its own punishment we have a solid
ground to go upon." With the elimination of the theory of
rewards and punishments some uncertainty is inevitably cast
on the future state where these are assumed to be administered. To meet the objection that his philosophy precluded
the possibility of immortality, Shaftesbury replies that exalt-
ing virtue does not necessarily prove a disbelief in a future
state, but that "by building a future state on the ruins of
virtue, religion in general and the cause of the Deity is betrayed, and by making rewards and punishments the principal motives to duty, the Christian religion in particular is
overthrown and its greatest principle, that of love, is rejected and exposed." [2] Although he does not deny a future
state he nowhere avows any confidence or hope in a life to
come.[3]

As for the fifth of Lord Herbert's *notitiae communes*, the
necessity of repentance for sins, this seems to be clearly a

[1] *Letter on Enthusiasm.*
[2] *The Moralists*, Pt. II, sec. 3.
[3] *Cf.* A letter To a Friend, Dec. 1704, in which Shaftesbury comments on
a farewell message which Locke before his death had sent to Anthony
Collins. Given in *Life, Unpublished Letters*, etc.

hold-over from the very theology which the Deists were endeavoring to escape. With the idea of obedience it perpetuates the traditional conception of authority as against the freedom and sufficiency of the individual. Shaftesbury does not mention sin nor the need of atonement for misconduct. He offers no corrective except within man himself in the misery which he suffers when he realizes that he has committed a vicious act.

While the passages in his Lordship's writings which seemed most dangerous to Leland were those concerned with the doctrine of rewards and punishments, he objected also to Shaftesbury's advocacy of ridicule as a criterion of truth and found "many other things" which seemed "evidently calculated to cast contempt on Christianity." Shaftesbury had asserted that all sorts of superstitious notions are perpetuated under the guise of solemnity which if subjected to ridicule would be discovered as impostures.[1] It was for this reason, he argued, that enthusiasts and zealots feared ridicule far more than attack. Leland though free from the vindictiveness of many of his fellow-apologists, nevertheless tends to give a wrong impression of the purpose of Shaftesbury's criticisms of Christianity which were illustrative rather than the main theme of his essays.

Yet in dealing with false and harmful notions, Shaftesbury's quiet irony cut deep and proved more effective than angry argument and assault. His method was that of exposition rather than attack. He abhorred the ugliness and abuse characteristic of the controversial writing of his day, which he declared was profitable only to book merchants. The "infinite replies, defences, rejoinders, replications" of authors who wrote in "learned Billingsgate" he believed

[1] "Gravity is of the essence of imposture," he says, so easily does it run into formality. The attitude of gravity is often the result of unreality in ourselves and in this mood we are unable to distinguish between what is truly serious and what ridiculous. *Letter on Enthusiasm.*

"have been long since paying their attendance to the pastry cooks." [1]

Shaftesbury shared the attitude of the Deists towards the vast accumulation of unexamined beliefs and practices which constituted an essential part of traditional Christianity. He was convinced, as were they, that many of these outworn ideas and "things indifferent" had served not only to discredit religion but were responsible for endless dissension and persecution in the past. He perceived the need of a great simplification in religion and advocated complete freedom of inquiry and the toleration of every form of belief. It was this spirit of toleration which led him to look indulgently on the superstitions of the vulgar and to urge that they be laughed at rather than violently suppressed. It also led him to conform with graciousness to an established church with which he could have had little real sympathy.

"What a wretched kind that is which we call *free-talking* about matters of religion and the established rites of worship. What the effect is, when we oppose or impugn such opinions as those, especially if it be done after a certain manner . . . if it be not still with a certain economy and reserve; if it be done vehemently; if it be acutely, and as showing wit; if it be ridiculingly and with contempt." . . . Why should we "be concerned about these wrong notions of the Deity? . . . Remember to respect the rites whatever they be, which others have within their own minds erected to the Deity, as well as those other rites which they have publicly erected and in other outward temples." [2]

While he realized that the national church played a useful part as a "public leading" in religion, it must not, he contends, invade the privacy of men's minds and attempt to regulate their beliefs or suppress by violence the "natural passion of enthusiasm." It should not even seek "to ascertain it and reduce it to one species." The ancients wisely tolerated both philosophy and superstition and so being let alone

[1] *Miscellaneous Reflections,* I, chap. 2.
[2] In *Life, Unpublished Letters and Philosophical Regimen,* pp. 28, 29.

"superstition never raged so as to occasion bloodshed, wars, persecution and devastation" as it later did in Christian countries. "But a new sort of policy which . . . considers the future lives and happiness of men rather than the present has made us leap the bounds of natural humanity, and out of a supernatural charity has taught us the way of plaguing one another most devoutly." [1] The remedy is not uniformity of opinion, he argues, in religion any more than in science or mathematics. "If honesty and wit cannot save us 'tis vain for the government to interfere." If we are but granted liberty, he declares, we shall have as much wit to save ourselves in religion as in temporal affairs. Those "enthusiasms" which have been permitted to go their own way have declined, so that "crusades, the rescuing of holy lands and such devout gallantries are in less request than formerly." The reason that the "soul-rescuing" spirit still remains is that we have not learned to meet religious zeal with tolerance and good humor.

Like the Deists, Shaftesbury questioned the evidences of revealed religion, disposing lightly of prophecy. Miracles seemed to him an inconclusive form of revelation, for he held that God could not witness for himself in any other way than by revealing himself to men's reasons. . . . The contemplation of the universe, its laws and government . . . is the "only means which could establish the sound belief of a Deity." In the *Moralists*, Philocles accuses the defender of miracles of "laboring to unhinge Nature, whilst you are

[1] *Letter on Enthusiasm.* Shaftesbury speaks bitterly of those who through superstition and fanaticism would interfere with true liberty of thought. " 'Tis to them . . . we owe the . . . abuse of those naturally honest appellations of free-livers, free-thinkers, latitudinarians or whatever other character implies a largeness of mind and generous use of understanding. Fain would they confound licentiousness in morals with liberty in thought and action and make the libertine . . . resemble his direct opposite. . . . 'Tis thought dangerous for us to be over-rational or too much masters of ourselves in what we draw by just conclusion from reason only. . . ." *Miscellaneous Reflections,* V, chap. 3.

searching heaven and earth for prodigies and studying how to miraculize everything you bring confusion on the world, you break its uniformity and destroy that admirable simplicity of order whence the one infinite and perfect principle is known." It is a "preposterous system," he claims, "which teaches one to seek for deity in confusion and to discover Providence in an irregular and disjointed world." [1]

The difficulty of accepting the scriptures as an infallible authority and guide, he argues, is that "there are so many originals, texts, glosses, various readings, styles, composi- tions, manuscripts, compilements, editions" and publications that it needs careful study to determine "what of this col- lection of ancienter and later tracts" can be properly com- prehended under the title of Scriptures; "whether it were the apocryphal or the more canonical? The full or the half- authorized? The doubtful or the certain? The controverted or uncontroverted?" [2] . . .

Besides there are the difficulties as to meaning. "There are," he says, "innumerable places that contain great mys- teries, but so wrapped in clouds or hid in umbrages, so heightened with expressions or so covered with allegories and garments of rhetoric, so profound in the matter or so altered and made intricate in the manner, that they seem to have been left as trials of our industry and as . . . op- portunities for the exercise of mutual charity and toleration rather than as the repositories of faith and furniture of creeds." [3]

Like the Deists, Shaftesbury criticises the standards of ethics displayed in the Old Testament, finding it hard to follow the ways of Jehovah.

"There is a certain perverse humanity in us which resists the divine commission though ever so plainly revealed. The wit of the best poet is not

[1] *The Moralists*, Pt. II, sec. 5.
[2] *Miscellaneous Reflections*, V, sec. 3.
[3] *Ibid.*, V, sec. 3.

sufficient to reconcile us to the campaign of a Joshua or the retreat of a Moses by the assistance of an Egyptian loan." Nor can he make "that royal hero appear amiable in human eyes who found such favor in the eye of Heaven. Such are mere human hearts that they can hardly find the least sympathy with that only one which had the character of being after the pattern of the Almighty's. 'Tis apparent . . . that the manners, actions and characters of sacred writ are in no wise the proper subject of other authors than divines themselves. They are matters incomprehensible in philosophy; they are above the pitch of the mere human historian, the politician or the moralist." . . .[1]

Shaftesbury's reputation as a Deist seems to rest on his criticisms of revealed religion rather than on an entire agreement with "deistic" philosophy. Although he rejected the traditional theology of organized Christianity he did not advocate any form of natural religion. Whether merely critical of the old, or constructive in the search for a new Christianity, the Deists were, after all, occupied with religion. As Professor McGiffert says: "the difference between them and the avowed apologists was far less than has commonly been supposed. . . . They were upon opposite sides in the religious controversy not so much because of any great disagreement in religious beliefs and in ethical ideals as because of a difference of attitude toward the ecclesiastical establishment and the ecclesiastical authorities." [2] The Deists appealed to reason sometimes against ideas which they disliked and sometimes in support of assumptions which were congenial in the old system.

Shaftesbury on the other hand was not primarily concerned with religion but with moral philosophy. His ethics were not sought in religion but his religion was rather the result of his ethical theory. "We begin," he says, "at the wrong end when we would prove merit [virtue] by favor and order by a Deity." While to the Deists, religion seemed no longer necessary as a "power unto salvation" or a light of truth to

---

[1] *Advice to an Author*, Pt. III, sec. 3.
[2] *Protestant Thought before Kant*, New York, 1910, chap. x.

guide, it remained as an incentive and sanction of morality. Man might know his duty but he needed to be stirred to its performance by God's commands and to be rewarded for meritorious conduct in a life to come. What then is the function of religion when man no longer looks to God as the rewarder of them that diligently seek him, but establishes his own divinity within himself by doing right because he loves right? In taking conduct outside the realm of religion, Shaftesbury created a philosophy of life in which religion had ceased to be indispensable either as a solace or a guide. In his philosophy the Deity exacts no tribute from man, nor bargains with him as to his behavior. Freed from the consciousness of sin and the need of reconciliation with God, man has achieved a true liberty in which he is free to emulate that divinity of which he feels himself to be a part. To live therefore, according to Nature, and not in the fear of God, is to him the good life.

III

That Shaftesbury was deeply affected by the writings of the later Stoics and himself had made a substantial contribution to Stoical philosophy was not appreciated until nearly two hundred years after his death. In 1900, his philosophical meditations, hitherto unpublished, were made available for the first time. These reflections—"exercises," he calls them—were written down in his note books and were intended solely for his own use.[1] They are invaluable to an

[1] *The Life, Unpublished Letters and Philosophical Regimen of Anthony, Earl of Shaftesbury.* The mss. of these note books are among the Shaftesbury Papers in the London Record Office. According to the editor, the earliest writing is dated Holland, 1698, and the latest, Naples, 1712, thus covering nearly the whole period of his literary activity. In form the "exercises" are a series of reflections on philosophical topics such as Deity, Character, Nature and Life. The editor has chosen the title of *Philosophical Regimen* because, as he says, the term is frequently used by Shaftesbury in reference to them and because it best describes their purpose and character as a code of life. The *Philosophical Regimen* exceeds in length the *Inquiry concerning Virtue* and *The Moralists* combined.

[35]

understanding of his philosophy and attitude towards life.

"Nor were there" . . . he writes, "any more than two real distinct philosophies, the one derived from Socrates, and passing into the old Academic, the Peripatetic and Stoic; the other derived in reality from Democritus and passing into the Cyrenaic and Epicurean. . . . The first . . . of these . . . philosophies recommended action, concernment in civil affairs, religion. The second derided all, and advised inaction and retreat. . . . The first maintained that society, right, and wrong was founded in Nature, and that Nature had a meaning . . . [was] well-governed and administered by one simple and perfect intelligence. The second again derided this. . . . The first therefore, of these philosophies is to be called the civil, social, Theistic; the second, the contrary." [1]

Philosophy has been used to serve many purposes. To some it has been a source of intellectual entertainment, a form of what Veblen calls "idle curiosity"; to others it has been an aid in a more serious inquiry into the "nature of things"; or it has been employed to make fine distinctions and prove favorite hypotheses. To still others it has meant a way of life. In this sense it may be said to be those general conclusions about God, man and the world by which a man believes and acts, hopes and fears. It serves him as a kind of "religion."

Although religion and philosophy are ordinarily regarded as two distinct provinces of thought between which there must necessarily be a "border warfare," it is possible, as Cornford suggests, "to think of them as two successive phases, or modes, of the expression of man's feelings and beliefs about the world." For philosophy has "inherited from religion certain great conceptions . . . which continue to circumscribe the movements of rational thought and in some measure determine their main direction." [2]

The later Stoical doctrines approximated in many respects a religion. According to Cleanthes' division of Stoical philos-

[1] Letter to Pierre Coste, 1706. In *Life, Unpublished Letters,* etc.
[2] Cornford, F. M. *From Religion to Philosophy,* London, 1912.

ophy, Physic also embraced Theology. While Ethic was founded on the nature of man, it was intimately connected with Physic (the nature of things) and Theology (the nature of the Deity). It is not difficult to see how a philosophy of a universe perfectly ordered and wisely governed for the good of all by a benevolent Deity offered a sense of security and relief to the frail and sensitive Shaftesbury. His temperament was religious rather than scientific. Not that he accepted a body of outworn and traditional beliefs, but in so far as he embraced a philosophy that was "civil, social, Theistic" he displayed a sense of "religious" responsibility rather than a spirit of scientific detachment towards life.[1]

To him a philosophy which led to an understanding of nature and himself had "preëminence above all other knowledge." "By this science," he says, "religion itself is judged . . . the sole measure and standard being taken from moral rectitude and the discernment of what is sound and just in the affections."[2] The purpose of philosophical speculation was not the "examination of those ideas [such as space, extension, solidity] which [one] may be the best versed in of any man in the world and yet of all men be the farthest from tranquillity." Rather is it the work of philosophy to "fortify the mind," to teach one "how self is to be governed. How far and in what am I to be concerned . . . how to free myself from contradictory passions . . . to calm my anger,

[1] No philosopher better exemplified his theories in his life than Shaftesbury. He spent his failing strength unsparingly in his short Parliamentary service until developing consumption forced him to retire. He met the many responsibilities of his high position and estate, even during his illness, with unfailing courage and sweetness of temper. The Fourth Earl writes: "His life would probably have been much longer if he had not worn it out by great fatigues of body and mind which was owing to his eager desire after knowledge, as well to his zeal to serve his country." He spent not only the whole day but "the great part of the night in severe application which confirmed the truth of Mr. Locke's observation on him that the sword was too sharp for the scabbard." In *Life, Unpublished Letters*, etc.

[2] *Advice to an Author*, Pt. III, sec. I.

quell resentment . . . how to bear with accidents and support the common chances of the world." [1]

The peculiar interest and charm of the philosophical reflections is that for the first time we come, through them, to know the real Shaftesbury. All the formality and restraint of the essays intended for the public are laid aside and with perfect freedom he converses with himself about the values of life, the vanity of seeking, or being occupied by, power, riches and honor; how true peace and serenity are achieved; what it is to live according to nature and fulfil the end of man. He discusses character and conduct, friendship, the passions, appearances and fancies, how one maintains a love for mankind by expecting neither his good nor ill from them; who is the truly "wise" man; and what it is to be a "citizen of the universe." We see that in the search for the good and virtuous life he draws his inspiration from classical rather than Christian ideals. The *Philosophical Regimen* contains no references to the Bible, the Christian fathers, or to Catholic or Protestant writers. Only ancient authors are quoted and so far as the religious outlook is concerned it might readily be credited to a classical philosopher.

In the light of these philosophical meditations we begin to perceive a coherence in all Shaftesbury's writings and many passages in the *Characteristics* take on a new significance. The theistic philosophy of his essays is in perfect agreement with the Stoical conception of a supreme mind governing the universe according to its perfect design. As a part of nature, man's duty and greatest happiness is to live in harmony with her laws. Man is not, as in Christian theology, at odds with the world as a place of evil from which he longs to escape. It is his realization of his place in nature and his exalted view of the Deity which may be conducive to virtue. If all is arranged for the interest of the whole

[1] In *Life, Unpublished Letters,* etc. Under "Philosophy."

[38]

there can exist no real ill in the world and as to those things which may befall him he is utterly indifferent. "Despise the things not in thy power." Man approaches the Greek conception of a rational creature free and capable of self-control before he was weighed down with the corruption laid upon him by mediæval theology. The love and service of mankind which to Shaftesbury is the highest form of virtue is also a Stoical doctrine.

The *Philosophical Regimen* shows not only how completely Shaftesbury embraced the teachings of Epictetus and Marcus Aurelius but how sincerely and earnestly he addressed himself to the task of perfecting his life according to Stoic ideals. Of the purpose of his "exercises," he writes:

"Memorandums for what? about what? a small concern, perhaps a trifle; for what else can it be? Neither estate, nor money matters, nor policy, nor history, nor learning, nor private affairs, nor public. These are the great things. In these are great improvements. How many memorandums, how many common-place books about these. Who would think of any other memorandums? Would one dream of making any for *life?* Would one think that this were a business to improve in? What if this should be the thing of all others chosen out for a pocket book and memorandums? But so it is. Remember then, the memorandums as truly such and for such use . . . Is there really such a science as the perfection of life? If so, how is it in other arts where improvement is looked for? . . . Begin therefore, and work upon this subject. Collect, digest, methodise, abstract. How many codes, how many volumes . . . how much labor and what compiling in the study of other laws. But in the law of life, how? . . . But remember, he says, as Epictetus counsels these exercises are for yourself, not for others. It is your business to improve by them, "not publish . . . profess or teach them." . . .[1]

While like those of Marcus Aurelius', Shaftesbury's meditations were set down for his own use, they form more connected discourses and are more eloquently stated than the

[1] *Life, Unpublished Letters,* etc. Under "Improvement."

brief and often obscure paragraphs of the Roman emperor. Though every page reveals his devotion and indebtedness to his Stoic masters, the *Philosophical Regimen* remains a unique and independent expression of Stoicism modified inevitably by the intellectual heritage and outlook of an eighteenth century philosopher.

"Happy he whose faith in Deity, satisfaction, assurance, acquiescing, rejoicing in Providence and in the universal administration and order of things depends not on any history, or tale, or tradition or wonder amongst men; not on man himself or any set of men; not on any particular schemes or systems or solutions of the phenomena of the world, no not even on that great solution by a futurity; but who leaving the present things to be as they are and future ones as they are to be, committing all this to Providence to be or not to be, as to that seems best; knows, feels and is satisfied that all things are for the best; nothing ill-made, nothing ill-governed, nothing but what contributes to the perfection of the whole." [1]

It is unnecessary to point out that some of Shaftesbury's ideas have been superseded and that the ancient ideals which he cherished seem no longer adequate in coping with a modern and ever-changing world. Yet his contribution to the development of free thought remains a real one. By insisting on the necessity of a free and impartial inquiry into every subject, however sacred, and maintaining that liberty in this direction cannot go too far, he advocated the only means by which existing evils can be detected and overcome. By rescuing man from his helpless dependence on external agencies, asserting his inherent worth and his ability to "work out his own salvation"; by showing that the responsibility for his conduct and its improvement rested on himself alone, Shaftesbury turned man's face from the past and pointed the way towards a future of progress and the indefinite perfectibility of mankind.

[1] *Life, Unpublished Letters,* etc. Under "Deity."

OCCUPATIONAL DEVELOPMENT OF ROMAN SOCIETY ABOUT THE TIME OF THE ELDER CATO

by

Ernest Brehaut

III

OCCUPATIONAL DEVELOPMENT OF ROMAN SOCIETY ABOUT THE TIME OF THE ELDER CATO

THE earliest general statement as to the occupations open to a Roman citizen who wished to make money is contained in the introduction to Cato's *De Agricultura,* a work noted for its business-like conciseness and fidelity to hard fact. In this introduction Cato's brevity is so extreme and his point of view so alien that his words must be read and considered with unusual care. The translation runs as follows: [1]

"It is true that sometimes it would be better to seek a fortune in trade, if it were not so subject to risk, or again, to lend money at interest, if it were an honorable occupation. But our fathers held a belief which they enacted into a law to this effect, that, while a thief was compelled to repay double, one who loaned at interest had to repay four-fold. From this one may judge how much worse than a thief they thought the fellow-citizen who lent at interest. And when they were trying to praise a good man, they would call him a good farmer and a good tiller of the soil. The one who received this compliment was considered to have received the highest praise.

[1] It is evident from this passage as well as from Livy, VII, 42; Appian, *bella civ.* I, 54; Tacitus, VI, 13, 3, that the Romans believed that there had been a time when the lending of money at interest was absolutely forbidden by law. Declareuil, *Rome the Law Giver,* p. 259, remarks that the older conception of a loan "as a philanthropic contract whose nature it was wrong to change by seeking to make a profit out of it" did not give way until the end of the Republic to the newer one of "a loan at interest as a form of hire." The opinion of interest held by Cato is to be regarded as characteristic of a society not yet fully embarked on a money economy or of an individual who idealized that stage of social development. As a matter of fact the law referred to and the beginning of coinage at Rome are both attributed to about 350 B.C. See Hugh Last in *Cambridge Ancient History* VII, pp. 477, 545.

"Now I esteem the trader who is active and keen to make money, but, as I have said before, he is exposed to risk and absolute ruin.

"Moreover it is from among the farmers that the sturdiest men and keenest soldiers come, and the gain they make is the most blameless of all and the most secure and the least provocative of envy, and men engaged in this pursuit are the least apt to be disaffected."

In this passage, as in the *De Agricultura* in general, Cato is at no pains to make clear his point of view. He makes his statements abruptly and lets it go at that. We may infer, however, that in his introduction to a book in which he describes a system of capitalistic farming conducted by the aid of slaves and with a slave overseer, his purpose is to refer to the alternative lucrative occupations in which a prospective farmer of this class might engage, i.e., we have here the occupations which a Roman, probably of the ruling class and certainly with money at his command, might consider.

These occupations are three in number, and expressed in modern terms are banking, wholesale trade and farming. Cato's attitude toward banking is rabid, probably political, but undoubtedly sincere. Wholesale trade, which is trading in ship cargoes on the Mediterranean, is turned down, not on moral grounds, but because it is *periculosus et calamitosus*, i.e., exposed to unjustifiable risks. A single approved occupation is left, namely, farming of the sort described above. Here it is worth noting that Cato has attached the virtues of the small working farmer, among whom he himself was classed in his earlier years, to the slave-exploiting, capitalistic farm owner.

To convince ourselves that Cato is speaking in his usual matter-of-fact way and is really affording us a valuable glimpse into the interior of Roman social psychology we should read a parallel passage [1] on "trades and occupations"

[1] From *De Officiis* I, 150-1. Though this work of Cicero *On Duties* is mainly of Greek origin, being based on a similar work, not extant, of the

from Cicero, written a century later and treating of the same subject from a wider point of view.

"As to trades and occupations we have the following beliefs as to which are to be considered worthy of a free man and which are mean and contemptible. First, those occupations are disapproved which incur the dislike of mankind, such as those of customs-house officers and money-lenders. The occupations of all wage-earners are slavish and contemptible when it is their labor and not their skill which is purchased; for in their case the very wages they receive constitute a badge of servitude. Those who buy from wholesale merchants to peddle out are likewise to be rated as contemptible, for they would get nothing by their business unless they lied, and indeed there is nothing more debasing than falsehood. All mechanics are engaged in a contemptible occupation, for a workshop can have nothing worthy of a free man about it. The least respectable of all trades are those that minister to pleasure, such as, (to quote Terence), 'fish-dealers, butchers, pastry-cooks, poulterers and fish-peddlers,' to whom we shall add, if you please, dealers in perfumes, dancers and all theatrical performers.[1]

"The occupations in which a greater intelligence is necessary and a greater service is rendered, like medicine, architecture and the higher education, are respectable for those to whose rank in life they are appropriate.[2] Merchandizing on a small scale is despicable; but if it is extensive and imports commodities in large quantities from all the world and distributes them honestly, it is not so very discreditable; no, it rather seems rightly creditable, after the merchant, satiated, or rather I should say satisfied, with his gain, has made the safe harbor of a landed estate.

Stoic Panaetius of Rhodes, there is much illustration in it from Roman life, and this chapter appears to be based on the Roman scale of values for occupations. After discussing the question whether Cicero was serious in rating agriculture so highly, H. Blümner concludes: *Allein Ciceros standpunkt ist damals der allgemeine; auf anständige Weise kann nur der Gutsbesitzer Geld verdienen. Die Römischen Privataltertümer,* s. 536, note.

[1] Compare Livy 7, 2, 12: "It is a fixed tradition that performers of Atellan plays are not disfranchised, but serve in the army as though they had no connection with the stage." Loeb trans. by B. O. Foster.

[2] I.e., they are not appropriate as occupations for a Roman citizen. Cicero placed all intellectual activities on a lower plane than those characteristic of the life of a Roman citizen. In *De Off.* 1, 19, speaking of intellectual interests and mentioning astronomy, mathematics, logic and civil law in particular, he says: "All these professions are occupied with the search after truth; but to be drawn by study away from active life is contrary to moral duty." Loeb trans. by W. Miller.

But of all gainful occupations none is better than farming, none more productive, none more agreeable or worthy of a free man."

Such a substantial agreement as that shown by Cato and Cicero on a matter of common observation is a strong evidence of fidelity to fact. Both turn down banking with almost equal vigor and both have a very qualified attitude toward wholesale trade. Cicero condemns all other commercial pursuits absolutely, all forms of industry and also such professions as he mentions. For both, farming remained the only unexceptionable occupation in which the Roman citizen who desired the respect of his fellow-citizens could make a living.

For the ordinary plebeian Roman, farming no doubt meant an active occupation, but for the Roman of the ruling class, in Cato's day as in Cicero's, it was no longer an occupation but merely the owning and desultory management of a farm that was worked by slave labor and managed by a slave foreman, that is, really, an investment. The days in which such men could work on their farms with their own hands were gone. Such a Roman, then, was restricted to a single occupation and that an occupation that had lost its content; he had no economic occupation at all in the modern sense.

To look at another aspect of this situation, let us glance at the services that are usually first differentiated from the mass in a primitive society, services in political office, in the army and in what we term the professions—religion, law and medicine. We find that these, where existing in the Roman society of the time, offered practically no remuneration. Political office-holders in Cato's time, and generally under the Republic, served without pay and were sometimes even expected to devote large sums from their private means to the entertainment of the people. As for service in the army, it was done in the earliest days without pay and the soldier had to furnish even his weapons, food, and clothing; and although in Cato's time there was a fixed allowance for soldiers and officers, the pay in itself was not sufficient to raise this service out of the class of burden. Furthermore, as to the professions, they were non-existent for the Roman as specialized, career-offering, lucrative occupations. Service in religious functions was done without reward by ordinary citizens selected for the purpose. There was no legal profession, the pleaders in the courts and the advisors on points of law being men of ability who served in the capacity of friend of the client and got their reward in political advancement.[1] Cato and Cicero were among the greatest of these. Neither was there any medical profession. As Pliny tells us, the Romans got along without physicians for six hundred years i.e., down to about 150 B.C.[2] Their conception of disease and its treatment was simple enough to be satisfied with a folk medicine which included simple remedies and magic practices and called for no separate class of medical men.

All these characteristics of Roman society seem primitive; they seem to be marks of a society which has made little progress from an undifferentiated state. All signs of a normal occupational development are lacking.

[1] Payment of an advocate was forbidden by the Lex Claudia (second century B.C.). The amateur working of the legal profession is illustrated by Polybius' account of his friend, Scipio Africanus the Younger. Scipio, then eighteen years of age, is represented as saying to Polybius, "I am considered by everybody, I hear, to be a mild effete person, and far removed from the true Roman character and ways, because I don't care for pleading in the law courts. And they say the family I come from requires a different kind of representative, and not the sort I am. That is what annoys me most." (xxxii, 9.) In another passage we are told that "the time that other young men spent in the law courts and formal visits, haunting the Forum and endeavoring thereby to ingratiate themselves with the people, Scipio devoted to hunting; and by continually displaying brilliant and memorable acts of prowess, won a greater reputation than others, whose only chance of gaining credit was by inflicting some damage on one of their fellow-citizens—for that was the usual result of these law proceedings. Scipio, on the other hand, without inflicting annoyance on anyone, gained a popular reputation for manly courage, rivalling eloquence by action." (xxx, 15, Schuckburgh translation.)

[2] At about this time Greek physicians appeared in Rome. See Natural History, 29, 11.

Though the Roman state and the city of Rome had developed gradually through several centuries and Rome in Cato's later days was the mistress of the Mediterranean world, a center of wealth and large population, yet, if we believe Cato and Cicero, there was only one approved gainful occupation, and that the one which had prevailed when Rome was a village. And now, as we have seen, this occupation of the primitive Roman, namely farming, had become fossilized as far as the Roman of the ruling class was concerned; it had changed from an occupation to an investment. This was a case not merely of arrested development but of actual atrophy. And therefore as an economic person the Roman of the ruling class was without visible means of support.

Here, however, we meet with another difficulty. From the evidence as to the remunerative occupations open to the Roman citizen he should be a poor man. But the opposite was the case. The wealth of the Mediterranean which began to converge on the city of Rome after the defeat of Hannibal did not find a lodging especially in the treasury of the state or in the private fortunes of traders, manufacturers and bankers,[1] but in the coffers of those very citizens who were so restricted in their methods of acquiring wealth. The mere possession of landed estates such as Cato describes, or even much larger ones, could not account for so large and rapidly increasing a concentration of wealth. For if we follow Cato's description of how these estates were bought, developed and

---

[1] The general situation in commerce and industry is indicated by these passages from Tenney Frank's *Economic History of Rome:* "We do not know of any very large fortunes actually made in commerce, banking or manufacturing at Rome." (p. 258); "The machinery of banking also developed more slowly in the Republic than the growth of the state would seem to require." (p. 287); "Can it be that Rome after all had not yet entered either the commercial or the capitalistic field that her armies had opened and that only those peoples who were already upon the high seas profited from the *pax Romana* and the 'freedom of the seas' that followed the expansion of the Roman rule?" (p. 291).

equipped it is clear that on the contrary they themselves required much outside capital.

How then is this gap between the wealth of the Roman citizen and the practical absence of any lucrative occupation for him to be filled? What set of influences brought about the comprehensive series of inhibitions against the ordinary ways of making a living that is exhibited in the words of Cato and Cicero? In what direction should we look for an hypothesis that will throw some light on this matter?

The primary outstanding fact about Roman society is that it was a military society. In the early days, at least, the state was the army and the army was the state. To the end of the Republic the sovereign assembly, the *comitia centuriata*, was a political reflection of the Roman army. In this assembly the membership was graded into classes according to wealth, and service in the army was reserved for grades above the lowest.[1] So that it seems hard to resist the suspicion that if citizenship was a privilege, as it undoubtedly was, service in the army was a somewhat greater privilege.

The Roman citizen who was subject to military service, or privileged to it, could be called upon for twenty campaigns in the twenty-nine years between eighteen and forty-six inclusive, and as the Roman state was always at war and as there was even a regular provision for the enrollment of soldiers who had served more than the required number of campaigns, it seems likely that during the years of physical strength the Romans spent more time in the aggregate as soldiers than they did in any other occupation whatever. Furthermore for the Roman of the ruling class, who was equally subject with the ordinary citizen to military service and who was obliged to serve ten campaigns as a preliminary to the lowest political office, the combination of service in the

[1] This holds to the time of Marius.

army and in political office served as an engrossing career which excluded all other interests except as subordinate.

It is therefore within the area of his characteristic activity that the puzzle of the economic life of the individual Roman citizen must be solved.[1] The effort to explain him economically apart from his political and military activities seems on the face of it an impossibility. The suspicion at once arises that Roman society, not merely in its manifestation as a state but more intimately in its structure, i.e., in a way that could influence the range of occupations for its members, was essentially predatory.

Such a suspicion indeed would be legitimate from the objective evidence and entirely apart from any interpretation of the limitation of occupations for Roman citizens. The passages bearing on military plunder and other modes of exploitation of the conquered are numerous in Latin literature.

Polybius, for example, a contemporary and qualified observer and the best authority we possess on the history of the Romans in the second century B.C., tell us what conquest by the Romans meant:

"Those who surrender themselves to the Roman authority, surrender all territory and the cities in it, together with all men and all women in such territory or cities, likewise rivers, harbors, temples, tombs, so that the Romans should become actual lords of these, and those who surrender should remain lords of nothing whatever." (xxxvi, 4.)

This is of course a sweeping statement and the application

---

[1] The causal connection between the military activities of Roman society and its low rating of industry is expressed by H. Blümner, *Die röm. Privatsaltertümer*, s. 599, as follows: "Die servianische Ordnung, die den Heerdienst, der zwar Last, aber auch Ehre war, auf diejenigen Gewerbe die für den Krieg speziell geeignet waren, die Zimmerleute, Kupferschmiede und gewisse Klassen von Spielleuten, beschränkte, sie hat wohl, wie Mommsen vermutet, den Anfang gebildet zu der späteren sittlichen Geringschätzung und politischen Zurücksetzung der Gewerbe. Es kam daher auch in der Republik nicht zur Bildung eines unabhängigen Handwerkstandes, so wenig wie es eine anständige Kaufmanüschaft gab.

of its details always yielded to practical considerations, but it is to be noted that with this theory behind their control of a conquered territory and its population much at least of their wealth would speedily pass to the Roman state and in various ways and in large measure to its individual citizens.

This is what happened in the case of Syracuse (plundered in 212 B.C.) when Polybius comments: "To sweep the gold and silver into their own coffers was perhaps reasonable; for it was impossible for them to aim at universal empire without crippling the means of the rest of the world and securing the same kind of resources for themselves. But they might have left in their original sites things that had nothing to do with material wealth." (ix, 10.) Again, referring to the time after 167 B.C., Polybius speaks of "the immense difference made, both in public and in private wealth and splendor, by the importation of the riches of Macedonia into Rome." (xxxii, 11).

How the wealth arising from conquest was distributed according to the various claims made upon it is a question of the highest importance for an understanding of the economic development of Roman society but no definite attempt to answer it has ever been made. All that is certain is that at all times the chief parties at interest, the state, the individuals of the ruling class and the private soldier, received enough to keep them functioning as parts of the machine of conquest and at various times considerable surplus came to all.

As the party most likely to suffer, it is worth while to glance at the position in this matter of the private soldier.[1] His economic interest in the campaign lay in the plunder (*praeda*), including movable property, domestic animals and

[1] How he might suffer is shown by a surviving fragment of one of Cato's political speeches: "Never have I divided the plunder among a few friends of my own, neither the actual booty taken from the enemy nor the money received from it, so as to defraud the man who took it. . . . Never have I divided among the members of my staff and my friends the money given as largess, and I have not made them rich to the general disadvantage." H. Jordan, *M. Catonis praeter librum de re rustica quae extant,* 1860.

captives. That this was not a momentary but a continuous interest and also one that was recognized and regulated is well shown by the oath in relation to booty which Roman soldiers took at the beginning of a campaign, the substance of which was that all should share in the booty in an equitable way.

There were two main sources of booty, the open country and the walled city, the former representing the everyday earnings of the industry of war and the latter the extra dividend. In each case the looting was systematically done, and in Polybius' account of "the Roman method of procedure in the capture of cities" we have a view of a hard-headed, business-like, disciplined performance by the Roman army which is a testimony alike to the importance of the booty and to the thoroughness and equity with which it was assembled and distributed. It even gives rise to the suspicion that the famed Roman discipline was to a considerable extent founded on intelligent self-interest.

"Now the Roman method of procedure in the capture of cities is the following: sometimes certain soldiers taken from each maniple are told off for this duty, their numbers depending on the size of the city; sometimes maniples are told off in turn for it: but there are never more than half the whole number assigned to the work. The rest remain in their own ranks in reserve, sometimes outside, at others inside the city, for taking such precautions as may be from time to time necessary. . . . All who are told off for plundering carry all they get each to his own legion; and when this booty has been sold, the Tribunes distribute the proceeds among all equally, including not only those who were thus held in reserve, but even those who were guarding the tents or were invalided, or had been sent away anywhere on any service. But I have spoken fully before, when discussing the Roman constitution, on the subject of the distribution of booty, showing how no one is excluded from a share in it, in accordance with the oath which all take on first joining the camp. I may now add that the arrangement whereby the Roman army is thus divided, half being engaged in gathering booty and half being drawn up in reserve, precludes all danger of a general catastrophe arising from personal rivalry in greed. For as both parties feel absolute confidence in the fair dealing of each in respect to the booty—the reserves no less than the plunderers—no one leaves the ranks, which has been the most frequent cause of disaster in the case of other armies . . . There is nothing about which leaders ought to exercise more care and foresight than that on such an occasion all may have an absolutely equal prospect of sharing in the booty."

From this and countless other passages [1] in the Roman historians it is evident that the taking of the enemies' movable property was a primary objective of the Roman soldier and it is evident also that it was an item of importance. In the only study of military plunder that has been made with any detail, that of Arnold Langen,[2] published in 1882 and confined mainly to the first century B.C., are such conclusions as these: "By the foregoing evidence I think I have made it clear that through the plundering of the conquered lands, which was the usual practice, large sums of money must have come into the hands of the Roman soldiers" (p. 20) and again: "If one reflects that these magnificent donatives [distributions of money by a general usually at the end of a campaign] were accompanied by the continual gains

---

[1] Livy, for example, puts these words in the mouth of a Roman consul of 295 B.C.: "I have in mind to enroll no more than 4000 foot and 600 horse. I will take with me those of you who give in their names today and tomorrow. I am more concerned to bring all my men back with their purses filled than to wage war with many soldiers." (x, 25.)

[2] *Die Heerespflegung der Römer. III Teil. Ueber Beute und Donativa.* The treatment covers preceding centuries briefly but finds the same conditions. See this study for references to plunder. They are especially abundant in Livy.

which the soldiers were able to make by plundering on their own account not merely from the enemies' country but from friendly territory as well, and even from Italy, it can no longer appear surprising if even common soldiers arrived at the possession of considerable wealth"; and, "From the evidence that has been given it is clearly revealed that the soldier who allowed himself to be recruited, went to war chiefly to win wealth for himself." (p. 18.)

There is certainly ground for suspicion that the ordinary Roman campaign of the age of expansion was to a considerable extent a speculative undertaking, which must often have yielded a rich dividend to all concerned, perhaps eclipsing the modest gains from any trade or occupation and thus effectively preventing the natural occupational evolution of Roman society.

If this interpretation is correct, the occupational development, or interior structure, of Roman society is shown to be in harmony with the career of conquest of the Roman state. The restriction of the citizen to the one occupation of farming as the approved way of making a living does not indicate the economic superiority of this occupation but is merely evidence that when the career of conquest began the Romans were universally small farmers. At this time Roman society was "set," constant war being the determining factor, and the body politic received a lasting form that suffered little modification during the republic. Commercial and industrial Rome developed as an alien growth, almost as a tumor, on this body politic, played no essential part, and received no honorable recognition. Roman imperialism, of this period at least, had no feature of commercial and industrial expansion but was an imperialism of direct appropriation, in the machinery of which individual citizens and classes of citizens received such immediate benefit that the structure of society was fundamentally influenced.

SPENGLER

by

James T. Shotwell

IV

SPENGLER

THE serious student of the intellectual history of our time must sooner or later come to grips with Spengler's *Untergang des Abendlandes*. This would remain true whatever may ultimately be thought of the intrinsic worth of the contribution of the book itself, for its reception by the German people in the post-war years constitutes an historical event in itself. Under any circumstances the immediate sale of one hundred thousand copies of a scientific or learned treatise would be notable enough, but the original text of Spengler's work had greater obstacles to overcome than the natural apathy of the reading public. It was published in a country and at a time when financial and economic chaos forced the common citizen to the utmost rigorous economies and only the keenest sense of intellectual need could account for the fact that practically the entire cultured world of Germany made it a point to secure in some way or other this ponderous work.

The explanation is surely not to be found in either the style of the author, on the one hand, nor a quickened interest upon the part of its readers in world history—which is its ostensible theme. Although, as we shall see, there is more than a trace of genius in the presentation of the material, the author has distinctly shunned the field of literature in the ordinary sense of the word and has made no concessions to the populace in tricks of style. The opening sections of the book are, if anything, more abstruse and difficult to understand than those which follow. Theories of mathematics ordinarily make little appeal to readers of history, and yet, this book plunges at once into discussions of this kind. One wonders what would have been the fate of Mr. H. G. Wells' *Outline of History* if before laying out its historical perspective the author had indulged in a sort of Einsteinian discussion of the relativity not merely of events but of the whole scheme of time and space in which the events occur. Moreover, the text is even more erudite than it is philosophical. It is filled with unexplained allusions to phenomena in almost every field of knowledge, from the history, art and religion of the ancient East to the most recent theories of science in the West, and the reader is supposed to know enough about each of these widely diverse subjects to appreciate a novel synthesis built up out of a new coördination of these varied elements of culture. If the author injects at times the charm of a poet's fancy, yet so massive is the framework of this survey of world history that the explanation of its appeal must be sought in something else than in the form of expression.

A much more natural explanation lies at hand in the German interest in history itself. One might very well imagine that here we have the parallel to what happened in Germany in the opening of the nineteenth century, that in a larger and maturer way the thoughtful public of Germany was recasting its historical perspectives as it did in the days when German historical criticism denied the legends of antiquity, both sacred and profane, and recast the facts of history and all principles of historical writing. But a closer study of both Spengler and of Germany today shows that this analogy is utterly superficial. Not only is there no historical renaissance yet visible in post-war Germany similar to that which a hundred years ago resulted in the disciplines of the historical seminar and the vast output of document and narrative, but there has been, if anything, a definite decline in the taste for history itself. This, at least, is the judgment of one of the most distinguished scholars of Germany, Dr. Carl Becker, Prussian Minister of Education, in a thoughtful study published in 1927, calling attention to the relative decline of the historical seminar and, more especially, to that interest in historical literature which is in Germany an almost equal index of the intellectual output. According to him the thought of the new age is less and less of the purely scholarly type and more and more pragmatic. Although the German seminar still applies the precepts of Ranke, historical research has suffered something like an eclipse in the country which played so large a part in making that research scientific. The detached curiosity concerning the human past is making way for an interest in the present and the future. When we add to Dr. Becker's observation the fact that the controversy over the question of German war guilt has, without the reproof of any outstanding German historian, violated the canons of historical criticism at almost every turn, we find it still more difficult to attribute the German interest in Spengler to any profound stirring of genuine historical interests.

As a matter of fact, the explanation of the appeal which Spengler's work has made to the German mind—and to the minds of many readers of the English text as well—is not the historical appeal in the proper sense of the word. It is a performance that must be judged by different criteria than those of the historical seminar. This is true of content, purpose and method. As to content, it is not a history but a comment upon history; as to purpose, it does not seek to orient us with reference to the past but rather with reference to the present and future, and as to method, it violates boldly and openly at every turn the most elementary precepts of historical scholarship. The fundamental appeal to the public, therefore, must lie in its destructive criticism and in its almost prophetic synthesis; for Spengler speaks with the assurance of a Nietzsche and with equal vigor of assertion and denial. For a society shattered, as his had been, by the tragedy of the war and the chaos which followed it, there was surely an intellectual comfort to be found in a survey of civilization which boldly dared to ignore the passing evils of his day. If the *Untergang des Abendlandes* was a creation of the war, it remained, nevertheless, a monument of intellectual defiance not only to it but to all purely temporary events. In a way it recalls such creations as those of Beethoven in Vienna during the disastrous fall of the Holy Roman Empire, or of Goethe looking calmly at the disturbed world of a revolutionary era. It is perhaps this detachment from the contemporary history of Germany during the World War which furnishes the first clue to its great appeal.

The Decline of the West seems at first sight to be a collection of separate essays or monographs. It deals with the field of social and intellectual evolution, not chronologically but topically. The chapters of Volume I bear such strange titles as "The Meaning of Numbers," "Physiognomic and Systematic," "The Destiny-Idea and the Causality-Principle," "Makrosmos—The Symbolism of the World Picture and the Problem of Space," "Faustian and Apollinian Nature Knowledge." Those of Volume II are somewhat more concrete, but are still far removed from the ordinary chapter headings of history. The lower cultures are preceded by a survey of "Origin and Landscape" dealing with plant and animal life, "Being and Waking-Being," and the "Mass Soul." The problem of Arabian culture bears the title "Historic Pseudomorphoses." The volume ends with two great chapters on the "Form-World of Economic Life" in two divisions, "Money," and "The Machine."

When one compares these subject groupings with the arrangement of any general manual of world history, one sees at once that, however suggestive and thought-provoking these monographic chapters may be, they have little to do with the ordinary concepts of history. The purpose of the historian is to reproduce the past as it actually happened, reducing the subjective element to a mere editorial task of deciding whether to devote more or less attention to this or that event, but, upon the whole, intent upon rescuing for knowledge phenomena which have interest in themselves. Spengler's purpose is of an entirely different kind. It is an artistic interest in the formation of a great synthesis, a world philosophy. The incoherent past is to be made articulate and no longer meaningless by stating it in terms of symbols which in themselves have an art-meaning for the author. He is "convinced that it is not merely a question of writing one out of several possible and merely logically justifiable philosophies, but of writing *the* philosophy of our time, one that is to some extent a natural philosophy and is dimly presaged by all."

Now this effort to write "*the* philosophy of our time" is not history in the true sense of that word, but rather the denial of it. It is, as Spengler himself states in the preface to the revised edition, the "intuitive and depictive" arrangement of phenomena for the purpose of illustrating other things, and the whole synthesis is frankly in the subjective world of the thinker. It addresses itself solely to readers "who are capable of living themselves into the world-sounds and pictures as they read"—which means that it is addressed to those who can fit their imaginations into the imaginative creation and attitude of the writer himself. This is myth making; it is poetry. In the hands of Spengler it becomes ultimately massive and splendid poetry because the structure of his thought is architecturally magnificent, powerful in outline and beautiful in detail. Nevertheless, it is a dream structure and should not be mistaken for reality.

The title itself suggests the trend of the narrative. Western civilization is on the threshold of an inevitable and all-embracing decline. In this prediction the author falls back upon a theory of history which arranges events according to a series of cultures which have each their childhood, youth, manhood and old age. There have been eight such ripe cultures, the Chinese, the Babylonian, the Egyptian, the East Indian, the Greco-Roman, the Arabian, the Maya of Yucatan and Mexico, and that of "the West." Each of these cultures lasts for about a thousand years and then decays. The sign of decay is when a culture passes into a civilization, that is, when spontaneous, energetic and creative life exhausts its creative impulses and grows mechanical; when the skeptic denies and the dilettante toys with the things that have been sacred and stimulating to feeling as well as thought. The outward form of this change from culture to civilization is seen in the growth of cities and the socializing process which city life imples. There is no sign of a directing divinity, as in Hegel, no meaning that inspires with confidence or hope, but a recurring cataclysm when the dead nerves no longer respond to impulse and the keen impressions that make the joy of living are burned out, leaving only the ashes of a worn and empty world. It should be said that the emptiness that follows upon disaster receives none of that stressing which it would be given by a moralist.

Spengler is interested in the great and tragic drama which he depicts and wastes little idle sympathy upon the victims of the recurring night. And it is in this depiction of the process that the writer is carried along through a world of suggestion and by ways that open up history in new perspectives. The two huge volumes are packed full with varied data of all kinds of interest, artistic, scientific, political and philosophical. It is a rich and ever stimulating collection of historical detail placed in the strangest juxtaposition, like some vast museum in which things from different eras have apparently been mixed by some irresponsible fancy and yet when studied more deeply one sees a design running through what seems at first mere willful medley.

It is obviously wrong to judge this book as an historical manual or even as history. There is in part the suggestion of a prose Goethe with a range of sensibility that is as capable of lyric outbursts as it is of the enjoyment of abstract formulæ. Take the opening paragraphs of Volume II for instance. They are worth quoting, and fortunately the English translator has rendered the full beauty of the original —which, by the way, may be said of the whole translation, and saying this is a high tribute to the translator:

"Regard the flowers at eventide, as, one after the other, they close in the setting sun. Strange is the feeling that then presses in upon you—a feeling of enigmatic fear in the presence of this blind, dreamlike, earth-bound existence. The dumb forest, the silent meadows, this bush, that twig, do not stir themselves; it is the wind that plays with them. Only the little gnat is free—he dances still in the evening light, he moves whither he will. A plant is nothing on its own account. It forms a part of the landscape in which a chance made it take root. The twilight, the chill, the closing of every flower—these are not cause and effect, not danger and willed answer to danger.

"They are a single process of nature, which is accomplishing itself near, with, and in the plant. The individual is not free to look out for itself, will for itself, or choose for itself. An animal, on the contrary, can choose. It is emancipated from the servitude of all the rest of the world. This midget swarm that dances on and on, that solitary bird still flying through the evening, the fox approaching furtively the nest—these are *little worlds of their own within another great world*. An animalcule is a drop of water, too tiny to

[63]

be perceived by the human eye, though it lasts but a second and has but a corner of this drop as its field—nevertheless is *free and independent in the face of the universe.* The giant oak, upon one of whose leaves the droplet hangs, is not."

This is a lyric approach to the problem of the "Cosmic and the Microcosm." It is pure poetry, but leads one from the elements of life and nature to the formation of those "inspired mass units" which become coherent in terms of social or national action. Thus in a few pages we are carried from gnats to the psychology of crowds—"noisy and ecstatic at Eleusis or Lourdes or heroically firm like the Spartans at Thermopylæ . . . they form themselves to the music of chorales, marches and dances, and are sensitive like human and animal thoroughbreds to the effects of bright colors, decorations, costume and uniform." Thus Spengler sweeps from "the hours at eventide" to the streets of Paris in 1789, when "the cry, *'A la lanterne!'* fell upon the ear."

The whole book is written with this imaginative freedom, and the marvel of it—for it is a marvel—is that the vigor of the imagination has not been cramped or wearied by the vast scope of the survey. Few books are more learned than this, reaching as it does from Oriental culture through the antique world and medieval thought into the science of to-day; nevertheless, one feels generally that the author has entered sympathetically into the thinking of these civilizations which in the upbuilding of his scheme of philosophy he moves backward and forward across the ages so as to place Cromwell along with Pythagoras and Mohammed and Buddhism along with Stoicism and Socialism. To be able to move these massive forms and yet to give each age a touch that is almost like a caress is something that makes Spengler's prose the kind of thing that Heine described in the *Nibe-*

lungenlied, which has Gothic proportions that, however, do not distort the realism of detail.

Nevertheless, we must repeat, this poem is not history. The use of historical data should not blind us to the fact that the architectural method employed in building up the synthesis is the very opposite of that which the historian uses. A series of analogies furnishes the pattern according to which this rich pageantry of the imagination is given its design.

Spengler divides world history into four cycles of civilization: the Indian, beginning about 1800 B.C.; the antique, dating from about 900 B.C.; the Arabian, which includes the foundation of Christianity and Islam, and the Western, which began about 900 A.D. Each cycle has its *Spring, Summer, Autumn* and *Winter.* The Western cycle is now depositing its harvest as the Winter of a dark age presses upon us once again. This synthesis is allegorical in character and is akin to that type of thinking which dominated the early Christian Fathers when they had a similar problem to that which Spengler has undertaken, namely, the effort to fit into a single whole the recalcitrant data of life and the world which seemed to be running at cross purposes to the divine plan. They found unity by insisting that not all reality was equally real, but that some phenomena existed for the purpose of foreshadowing others. Thus the primitive Jewish past could be made contributory to the Christian era. Spengler has another synthesis, but his method is substantially the same; the elements of the past are compared with the elements of the present in a vast human allegory, the key to which is a perception of what he calls "the cosmic beat" of life itself.

Now the historical fallacy in this philosophy is that the law of growth is only uniform for civilizations which are uniform in character, and modern civilization, that of today, is not uniform with any that has ever gone before. The drawing of analogies from the Indian and the antique past is a prejudging of contemporary civilization according to standards inappropriate to it. The external resemblances that lie in Cromwellian and Mohammedan world-outlook furnish no criteria as to the contribution made to the world by Cromwell on the one hand and Mohammed on the other. Cromwell may have thought in the accents of Islam, but his work was one that made for human liberty although he himself was impatient of its claims.

But there is a deeper fallacy in Spengler's work than that which consists of the violation of the comparative method. One does not come upon it until the very close of the second volume. While the ultimate aim of the whole work is, as the title points out, to demonstrate the inevitable decline of Western civilization, he, nevertheless, has failed to see that the scientific world of today presents entirely new phenomena which cannot be understood by any analysis of civilizations that have seemed superficially analagous to it. Spengler, it is true, brings in invention and scientific discovery in the closing chapter of his book with a penetrating characterization which seems to promise an understanding of its meaning. But so obsessed is he by the general scheme of his thought that he fails to see that the age of applied science with its conquest of time and space is not merely unlike the civilizations of the past but is undoing the very bases upon which they rested. Winter followed Autumn in the past because life was repetitive and was passed within limited areas of self-contained economy. Intercourse between societies was more predatory than stimulative because mankind had not yet discovered the means to maintain culture without an unjust dependence upon those who had no share in its material blessings. From the savage raid and slavery down to the industrial problems of today, the recurring civilizations have been largely built upon false economic forces backed up by equally false moral and religious casuistry. The civilizations that have come and gone have been inherently lacking in equilibrium because they have built upon the injustice of exploitation. There is no reason to suppose that modern civilization must inevitably repeat this cataclysmatic rhythm. In any case, we can assert with a confidence equal to that of Spengler that the decline —*Untergang*—of Western civilization can be avoided by the application to the social and political organizations of today of that same intelligence which in the physical sciences is enabling us to escape from the routine limitations of time and space.

There is therefore another perspective than that of Spengler, one which sees the present not as the end of the process but as the first beginning of the passing of the barbarian world. The conclusion lies not in disasters, Cæsarism and *Machtpolitik*, but in the equilibrium which bears the name of justice and finds its embodiment in the institutions of democracy.

This is not an idealistic conclusion but the simplest statement of historical realism, for in the free play of democratic institutions, there is the widest possible stimulus to the activities of life itself. The achievement of social justice instead of stultifying culture brings into play an ever-increasing reservoir of energy. And so instead of merely repeating the tragic episodes of the past, it seems more likely that we are at the dawn of an era as new in its potentialities as it is different from any that has gone before.

THE THREE ARNOLDS AND THEIR BIBLE

by

Walter Phelps Hall

V

THE THREE ARNOLDS AND THEIR BIBLE

TO ENLIGHTEN the understanding and to advance the cause of liberalism one could not do better than to write a history of the Bible. The influence of the Book of Books upon our civilization has been profound. It stands in a category by itself, the most important single written landmark in the intellectual history of the western world.

Liberalism and biblical lore, it is true, are not usually associated, and between theology and the modern world the nexus is not always clear. A history of the Bible which plunges into biblical exegesis is not needed. We cannot say that there is any immediate and imperative demand for further light upon the original documents which constitute the Bible. We know a good deal, as it is, concerning the canon of the old testament and of the new, and the same holds true of the various translations of the scriptures.

What is lacking in our knowledge of the Bible is a synthetic account of its influence, its effect not simply on codes of conduct, laws and the externals of life but also on the imagination, sympathy and general mental attitude of people affected by it.

A history of the Bible from this point of view might properly emphasize a growing tendency to regard it as other books. "The Holy Bible," "The Sacred Page," "The Word of God Incarnate"; these are phrases which formerly were taken literally. The taboo, the magic, the *sacra* which they connote are now less in evidence than in the past. The thunder which reverberates from Sinai is no more, or at least it is more distant. Armageddon and the end of all things is indefinitely postponed.

To those who take the Bible as a written sign and symbol of God's will in human affairs this is a tragedy. To others it is an augury of a better day. They hold the Bible a treasure trove of song and story, stretching all but endlessly into the past, revealing life and poor humanity in all its grossness, hopes and passions, a humanity to which we belong, which we inherit and which we must guide, free from direction imposed by priest-magician.

The process of this transformation from the revealed wisdom of the Eternal to the stumbling experience of finite man may be studied to advantage in the writings of the Arnold family. This family represented Victorian tradition at its best. It was serious, influential and cultured; its point of view was broadminded, liberal and intelligent; it stood in the vanguard of the intellectual life of its day, yet not so far in advance as to be detached from it. Dr. Arnold of Rugby, his son, Matthew, poet and critic, and his grand-daughter, Mrs. Humphrey Ward, the novelist, all were devoted to the Bible. They studied it with care and understanding; from it they drew their major inspiration; and their conclusions in regard to it may be considered as coming from a friendly source, more eager to conserve than to destroy.

Dr. Thomas Arnold, Headmaster of the Rugby School —the little pen of Mr. Strachey to the contrary—was a man of character and intelligence. He may not have revolutionized the face of education in England; but he began the process with his introduction of the prefect system and of new studies such as French and history. His point of view in regard to politics and economics may seem oldfashioned now and slightly antiquated; but to many of his contemporaries it was alarmingly radical. He was a staunch upholder of the Reform Bill and a supporter as well of state intervention on behalf of the factory operatives. He approved heartily of the French Revolution of 1830, quarrelled vigorously with the conservative trustees of Rugby, and even thought at one time of transferring himself and his family to the supposedly freer air west of the Atlantic.

In matters of religion the doctor was a liberal. He was the founder of the broad church movement of nineteenth century England. His ecclesiastical policies and programs were notable for their inclusive and comprehensive character. Stout churchman though he was, his ideas in these directions were so generous, so progressive, as to meet with slight approval in his own day. Only by the vigor of his personality and the strength of his character was he able to hold at bay those within the establishment who would gladly have squelched him if they had dared.

In regard to the Bible he was not narrowminded. "Faith without reason," he wrote, "is not properly faith but power-worship." Truth to the doctor was relative in character and not absolute. Practical ethics were of more importance than theological abstractions. The Bible, he considered, should be studied as presenting a series of practical lessons in life rather than as a proving ground for dogma. The latter should be few in number and broad in character. Almost everyone in England he thought entitled to belong to the national church. For the time being he entered a caveat in regard to Quakers and Unitarians. But even these varieties of religious folk he was confident might be won over by the proper study of the scriptures. The doctor wanted a democratic church with a large moiety of lay control. The church should belong to all the people. The peculiar form in which the Bible was written made it unavoidable that differences should arise in regard to its interpretation. "The contending parties," he affirms, "while alike acknowledging the judge's authority persist in putting a different construction upon the words of his sentence." Since this was so it behooved all Christians to work out a common denominator, a common basis of belief, to which all might subscribe. And this should be done by the people working together. It was not a matter for priests. In the words of Jesus: "Be ye not called rabbi, for one is your master, even Christ." In Dr. Arnold's opinion no special or sacred prerogatives were reserved for the ministers of the Church of England or for the ministers of any church.

The doctor's liberalism, however, never led him to criticise one thing—the authority of the *Holy Scriptures*. They were for him the final depository for God's revealed will. From Genesis to Revelations the Bible was not as other books. Holiness and sanctity were attached to it. There was no doubt about that. The learned doctor accepted quite simply the story of the fall—"man's disobedience and the fruits thereof." Evil first entered the world, he was convinced, because Adam ate the forbidden fruit. Sin and suffering from Adam to 1840 followed as a result of this error. The corruption in our natures, he believed, was the reason why population tended to outstrip the food supply. Here was the explanation, in his opinion, for all manner of hardships, even those borne by women in childbirth.

Only by belief in the atoning blood was there any hope. The prophets of the old testament made clear the coming of the Son of Man and the miracles which he performed attested to his divinity. St. Paul explains how and why we must believe, and in Revelation is described the judgment. Concerning all of the above Dr. Arnold was quite certain.

He was willing to admit, however, that not *all* of the Bible was directly inspired. It consisted of inspired sections and of historical sections. Even the revealed portions of

Holy Writ were not always as clear as they might be. It was evident to Arnold that Jesus never intended to pass spiritual authority down the ages through any priestly caste. He was quite certain of that. On the other hand there were obscure passages even in the revealed sections, such as those which prophesied the end of the world. The doctor was a bit puzzled at the unanimity of opinion in the early church that it was close at hand, and he hinted darkly that it might soon arrive. But one should not try to be too exact in such matters. The doctor believed in common sense. He wanted to concentrate on the positive aspects of faith. That they were about the same to him as to Luther or St. Thomas Aquinas, it is evident—no salvation except through the death of God on Calvary. As an old pupil of his wrote: "In the Bible he found and acknowledged an oracle of God, a positive and supernatural revelation made to man, and an immediate inspiration of the spirit."

Conservative as these ideas seem now they were not so in the early days of Victoria's reign. Even men of science did not go much beyond them. Whewell, the astronomer, in *The Bridgewater Treatises* of 1836 seemed to be completely in accord with Paley's argument from design as elaborated in the latter's *Natural Theology*. The length of days, the seasons, even the moon, all alike were peculiarly useful for the purposes of man. Sir Charles Lyell, in his *Elements of Geology*, published in 1837, opposed the idea of evolution. "The succession of living beings," he wrote, "appears to have been continued not by the transmutation of species, but by the introduction into the earth from time to time of new plants and new animals." Dean Buckland, another geologist, quickly invented the six periods of time to take the place of the six days mentioned in Genesis as the period of creation. Cardinal Nicholas Wiseman in *Twelve Lectures on the Connection between Science and Revealed Religion* (1837) set out to "bring theology somehow into the circle of the other sciences by showing how beautifully it is illustrated, supported and adorned by them all; to prove how justly the philosopher should bow to her decisions, with the assurance that his researches will only confirm them; to demonstrate the convergence of truths revealed with truths discovered." The ramparts breached by the eighteenth century philosophers had been repaired by 1837, so it was assumed.

During the middle years of Victoria's reign the situation was different. The Queen of the Sciences, upon making her début in the middle of the nineteenth century, immediately caused trouble. Biology in popular parlance came to mean evolution, and the latter brought into our thinking a new dimension, time. The three dimensional world of Sir Isaac Newton, thus suddenly enlarged by ideas of growth, change and transmutation, became four dimensional; and the old garments of theological speculation, no matter how patched and enlarged, seemed a misfit.

It was not, however, simply the discoveries of Darwin and Wallace and Marsh that led to a new view of the Bible. Equally important, and more so from the point of view of the Arnold family, were investigations carried on in the fields of anthropology, Assyriology and biblical criticism. The suspicions of the existence of the sub-human Neanderthal man grew into strong probability as the alluvial drifts located at Cro-Magnon, Grimaldi and Solutré were opened. Furthermore, with the development of anthropology came a tendency to compare the folklore of the Jews and their tribal history with that of other primitive folk. The Iliad, the Bible and the Vedas were placed in the same category. George Smith in Mesopotamia came upon tablets from the royal library of the Assyrian kings containing legends which ran parallel to those in Genesis. In Germany a searching investigation of the New Testament documents was under way. Internal evidence, too strong for refutation, showed that the gospels were not written by four independent eye-witnesses of Jesus' life; and here and there, among radical scholars, the claim arose that the fourth gospel was not a true account at all of Jesus' life but a spurious work written by a Greek philosopher at swords' points with St. Peter, and bent on discrediting him.

In such an atmosphere grew up the son of Dr. Arnold. The young man was precocious; and because of his attainments in the realm of poetry and literary criticism the fame of Matthew Arnold has become widespread. The literary critics lament that in his maturer years he plunged into biblical controversies. They think that good poetry was sacrificed for quasi-ephemeral and non-authoritative books about the Bible. They were, one thinks, mistaken. Poetry may have suffered somewhat; but that can not be proved. Upon the other hand we owe much to Matthew Arnold in other ways. He widened perceptibly the intellectual horizon of his own day; the influence of his ideas about the Bible has been and still is profound; to the historian interested in the intellectual background of our own life his name is a landmark.

It must be admitted that there is much about Matthew Arnold which is exceedingly annoying. Like Ruskin, he continuously assumes an air of unconscious superiority. For a person who has little use for dogma Arnold is extraordinarily dogmatic. He is exactly certain concerning what St. Paul and St. John meant to say. He knows what faith is and what God is and what religion is, and how it originated; and he does not hesitate to tell us in emphatic language.

Furthermore, Arnold repeats over and over again his most cherished and original definitions. Certain of these are not particularly felicitous. His definition of God as the "the not ourselves which makes for righteousness" may be excellent; but the phrasing is neither poetic nor graceful. Arnold was in some ways not only conceited but childlike. His sense of humor was rudimentary. The bishops of Gloucester and Winchester having unfortunately expressed the wish to "do something for the honor of the Lord's Godhead," Arnold would not let the bishops alone. He jeered at this somewhat occult ecclesiastical ambition over and over again. Before finishing *Literature and Dogma* the reader begins to like their lordships better than he does the author.

For the latter, in the last analysis, was a good deal of a snob. He disliked dissenters and never missed an opportunity to jibe at them. The professed aim of his religious books was to restore the Bible to the common people of England. Since this is so, it is unfortunate that one finds so little trace in his writings of "the sweet reasonableness of Jesus," a reoccurring and arresting phrase which one meets with in his pages.

Despite these criticisms *Literature and Dogma,* and its sequel, *God and the Bible,* are invigorating and thoughtful books. They approach the Bible from a new and fresh point of view which appeals to the intelligence. The essence of it is Arnold's idea that the Bible is a literary book which uses literary terms, and that it should never be considered a scientific account of man's spiritual history. The difference between literature and science, as he defines it, is that literature deals with poetry and eloquence in "terms thrown out, so to speak, at the not wholly grasped object of the speaker's consciousness," whereas science deals with exact and ascertainable knowledge.

Now the trouble with the Bible is that people have been taught that it has to do with exact knowledge, that it is to be taken literally. And since its literal meaning is obscure, abstruse reasoning has been applied to it by persons learned and acute enough in logical ability but not "conversant enough with the many different ways in which men think and speak so as to be able to distinguish between them, and to perceive that the Bible is literature; and that its words are used, like the words of common life, of poetry and eloquence, approximately, and not for the terms of science, adequately."

In other words, the "pseudo-scientific language of our creeds," has little to do with either Jesus or the Bible. Arnold would reject all three historic creeds of the church as "an inadequate and false science." "What is called theology," he tells us, "is in fact an immense misunderstanding of the Bible due to the junction of a talent for abstract reasoning combined with much literary inexperience." If we will only approach the Bible trained in literary criticism we can readily differentiate between the simple ascertainable values inherent in religion and the vast theological superstructure which is a figment of the imagination.

It is his desire to put the Bible on a real experimental basis. Conduct, he holds, is four-fifths of life; and to the eternal glory of the ancient Hebrews they thought more about conduct than their contemporaries. They thought so much about it that they associated it with a power outside themselves which made for righteousness, namely God. By experience they derived help from this power, strength and joy. Their morality became touched with emotion; they became religious. Not content with this demonstrated value they added many extra-beliefs, *Aberglaube,* as he calls them, fairy-tales, such as those to be found in the book of Daniel about the establishment of a Jewish kingdom of might and glory.

Jesus, steeped in rabbinical lore, saw clearly the faults of his inherited religion as well as its virtues. His teachings consisted in two major principles; the necessity for inward-

[79]

ness, or intuition, the "know thyself of the Greeks," and the value of self-renunciation, or the sacrifice of individual ambition if man desired peace.

The first of these teachings Arnold calls the method of Jesus and the second his secret. Both the method and the secret were practiced before his time. He, however, combined both method and secret; "cleanse the inside of the cup,"—his method; and "whosoever would come after me, let him renounce himself,"—his secret, the necessity as Faust puts it of going without.

> "Entbehren sollst du, sollst entbehren,
> Das ist der ewige Gesang,
> Den unser ganzes Leben lang
> Uns heiser jede Stunde singt."

The Old Testament, then, teaches righteousness and the New Testament teaches us how to attain righteousness. Herein lies the message of the Bible. In the same way as the Hebrews added to their ascertainable truth much fancy embroidery of the imagination so did the early Christians. The latter also had their extra-beliefs, their *Aberglaube*. The original simple motive "became a mixed motive, adding to its first contents a vast extra-belief of a phantasmagoral advent of Christ, a resurrection and judgment, Christ's adherents glorified, his rejectors punished everlastingly." The thing to do is to return to the original well-spring of inspiration, the method and the secret of Jesus. A large part of what is known as religion is "a kind of fairy-tale which a man tells himself, which no one, we grant, can prove impossible to turn out true, which no one also can prove certain to turn out true."

Arnold dismisses briefly those two props of the orthodox, prophecy and miracles. Concerning prophecy he states: "It can hardly be gainsaid that, to a delicate and penetrating criticism, the chief literal fulfilment by Christ of things said by the prophets was the fulfilment such as would naturally be given by one who nourished his spirit on the prophets and in living and in acting their words." As for miracles, but a few pages of *Literature and Dogma* are devoted to them. The author points out their comparative insignificance as indicative of the worth of Christ's message, sketches in the general atmosphere of credulity extant at the time, and implies that Christianity would have been better off without the rumor of their occurrence. "To profit fully by the new testament," he tells us, "the first thing to be done is to make it perfectly clear to oneself that its reporters could and did err. . . . To know accurately the history of our documents is impossible, and even if it were possible we should yet not know accurately what Jesus said or did. . . . Jesus was over the head of his reporters."

Literature and Dogma, of which the above is a synopsis, made a stir. Such a strong combination of biblical scholarship, polemic assertiveness and authoritative authorship England had not enjoyed since the publication of *Essays and Reviews* (1860). The hosts of conservatism at once dashed to the attack, nor was it simply the conservatives who were anxious to demolish Arnold. The Westminster Review was as scathing in its remarks as was the Quarterly Review. The Spectator joined forces with them. On the continent as in England outraged Christians vied with one another in the eagerness of their onslaught.

To Arnold this proved inspiring. The attacks were so numerous and so well-aimed that they gave him the opportunity to reply in a new book.

God and the Bible is less well-known than *Literature and Dogma*, but in many ways it excells it. The argument is closer and more cogent. The painful reiteration of bright sayings is less in evidence, and the nicety of scholarship more so. Finally, the thesis in regard to St. John's gospel, contained therein, is so brilliant and well-sustained that today, over half a century since it was written, it is still held in esteem by scholars.

In regard to miracles of every description Arnold holds his own stoutly. There is no use, he says, in going over all the old ground in regard to them. "To engage in an *a priori* argument to prove that miracles are impossible against an adversary who argues *a priori* that they are possible is the vainest labor in the world." Arnold refuses to engage in such. He does compare the story emanating from Damascus of Jesus after his death calling aloud to St. Paul with the story in Herodotus of the woman hovering over the Greek fleet at Salamis to show that both are improbable. The Greeks, he says, were just as critical as the Jews and just as acute. We believe neither the one story nor the other. "Miracles simply do not happen."

Then, turning on his enemies, Arnold complains of the want of seriousness on the part of lovers and defenders of Christianity. "They accept all kinds of stories in regard to the Bible that they would refuse all credence if met with elsewhere. Science makes her progress, not merely by close reasoning and deduction but also, and much more, by the close scrutiny and correction of the commonly received data." But for some reason or other it is assumed "that whoever receives the Bible must set out with admitting certain propositions, such as the existence of a personal God, the consubstantiality of Jesus Christ with this personal God who is his father, the miraculous birth, resurrection and ascension of Jesus. Now the nature of these propositions is such that we cannot possibly verify them."

The only concession which Arnold will make in regard to miracles is to admit that they have not been as damaging to Christianity as metaphysics. The former, at any rate, have "given comfort and joy to thousands." But the latter "have convinced no one, they have given rest to no one, people have fought over them. . . . No one has really ever understood them." And the Christian creeds Arnold would include in the category of metaphysical impossibilities.

But if Arnold despises metaphysics he does not despise scholarship. With that of Strauss, Volkmar, Tischendorf, Bauer and others he is thoroughly acquainted, and concerning textual criticism, authorship, dates and the reliability of documents he knows much. This is abundantly shown by his interpretation of the fourth gospel which is to him, as to Luther, the head-gospel.

Bauer had demonstrated to the satisfaction of most radical scholars that St. John's gospel was of little value in comparison with the synoptics. With this conclusion Arnold takes issue in delightful fashion. No historian could better his analysis of this historic document, his ability to disentangle the *logia* of Jesus from the Greek philosophy in which it is planted, and his triumphant conclusion that the *logia* in question are of the utmost importance for the purpose of understanding the teachings of Jesus. Arnold is here at his best.

Like his father, however, the headmaster of Rugby, he was in advance of his generation. Furthermore, he had no popular appeal. It takes a certain quantum of culture to appreciate Matthew Arnold. He had scorned the mob and the mob ignored him.

Not so, however, did his favorite niece, the daughter of his older brother and the grand-daughter of Arnold of Rugby. Mary Augusta Arnold Ward, to use her full name, was a novelist; she was also something of a socialist and very advanced in her religious ideas, so many thought. One of her novels, *Robert Elsmere*, worried Mr. Gladstone a good deal. He never could understand the Arnolds. Dr.

Arnold, the elder, had attacked Gladstone's first deliverance on the subject of religion. Matthew Arnold irritated Gladstone greatly; and now came Mrs. Humphrey Ward with more disturbing thoughts. The old statesman replied to them at length in kindly fashion in the *Nineteenth Century* and spent several hours in conversation trying to wean Mrs. Ward from her heresies.

Mrs. Ward was not only a radical; she was a rebel. And the audacity of her rebellion (paper though it was) made her proposals more alarming than the closet-philosophy of her uncle. Mrs. Ward wanted action. If the church would not listen to reason and purge itself, then brave men must save the church by walking out of her doors and establishing a new one. This was her first solution for the modernist problem.

In her first religious novel the hero, Robert Elsmere, clergyman and banner bearer for the Arnold tradition, falls under the influence of a learned but sceptical squire. His wife, Catherine, is saintly to an unpleasant degree. She is fond of George Herbert and takes the admonition of the latter seriously to heart—"Thy savior sentenced Joy." Catherine combats the influence of the squire. Elsmere is torn between his love for his wife, his work in which he is successful, and his conscience which will no longer permit him to officiate as a beneficed clergyman. In a moment of anguish he decides to resign his living. At the crisis Jesus is seen standing before him on the hearth, "not in the dress of speculations which represent the product of the long past, long superseded looms of thought, but in the guise of common manhood, laden like his fellows with the pathetic weight of human weakness and human ignorance." It is not an orthodox Lord who speaks but he comforts Elsmere. The latter resigns, opens a church for workingmen and draws huge crowds; but tuberculosis seizes the preacher and all is soon over.

Robert Elsmere aroused enormous interest. It was held under the ban in many of the best families in England and America; it created an even greater furor than did the attempted importation of Voltaire's *Candide* into the port of Boston in 1929.

Mrs. Ward never forgot her first hero and desired to recreate him. Twenty-two years later she did so in *The Case of Richard Meynell*, her second religious novel in which she advocates fighting for modernism from within the fold.

Again we have a modernist clergyman, Meynell, in love with Mary Elsmere, daughter of the deceased Robert. Meynell finds himself less isolated in his heresies in 1910 than did Elsmere in 1888. His ideas are the same as those of Matthew Arnold which in turn bear a striking resemblance to those of Dr. Fosdick. Thousands of Englishmen are behind Meynell, and he and his friends refuse to leave the national church to which they are attached. They demand toleration and comprehension within her borders, ideas approved by Arnold of Rugby, but never to his mind held applicable to those who denied the deity of Jesus.

Meynell believes in otherworldliness and the voice from within: but he rejects the creeds, the councils, and the deity of Jesus. His predecessor, Elsmere, holding similar doctrines, left the church. Meynell and his friends decide to stick it out and make a fight. They form a league, draw up a ritual omitting the historic creeds and whatever seems to them unintelligent. The church authorities take alarm. Meynell is summoned before them and is confronted with one of his own books in which he delicately intimates that the importance of the resurrection stories is purely symbolic. He is requested to modify this statement, and upon refusal he is tried for heresy.

[85]

All England is now aroused. The cause of the reformers is lost. The engine of things as they are triumphs. But before this takes place in a cathedral in the north of England Meynell preaches to the rebels and the new liturgy is used.

In the study of Cardinal Newman after his departure from Oxford hung a picture of his beloved university. Newman had written beneath: "Can these dry bones live?" These words were taken by Meynell as the text of his sermon. It contained one memorable sentence. "The sons of tradition and dogma have no monopoly in the exaltation, the living passion of the cross."

How far do the ideas of the Arnold family stand the test of time? The one common denominator possessed by all three, the broad church idea, seems on the surface to have fared rather badly. A great controversy is now raging in the Church of England, it is true; but for the most part it relates more to Catholic practices than to modernistic beliefs. Sound though the latter may be they do not appeal as yet to the mass of the people.

In regard to the ideas more peculiarly held by Matthew Arnold the twentieth century student of religious thought readily discovers points of adverse criticism. His theory that religion originated as a result of men thinking seriously about conduct cannot be substantiated. Rather would one say: "the potency of the mysterious is the fundamental historic basis of religion." Man did not become religious because he exalted righteousness. He was religious long before.

We might also question somewhat Arnold's calm assumption that the Bible is the one great source and fountain head from which we derive our ideas of good and evil. Put it to the pragamatic test, he asserts, "take a course in the Bible first and then a course in Benjamin Franklin, Jeremy Bentham, Horace Greeley, and Mr. Herbert Spencer; see which has the most effect, which satisfies you most, which gives you the most power." One would like to revise this list. Let us keep Benjamin Franklin's autobiography, add to it Plato on the death of Socrates, More's *Utopia*, Huxley's *Evolution and Ethics* and almost any minority opinion of Mr. Justice Holmes. One would not be as dogmatic then in asserting the overwhelming and unique predominance of Holy Writ in this matter.

Since the days of Matthew Arnold and Mrs. Humphrey Ward there has arisen a new heresy in the land, that of the humanists. It is a heresy not easy to define since between the right-wing humanists and religious liberals like Dr. Fosdick the line of demarcation is somewhat hazy. If, however, we compare the ideas of certain modern writers, loosely classified as humanists, with those held by Matthew Arnold, a certain point of cleavage becomes clear.

Let us take three books of recent vintage, Whitehead's, *Science and the Modern World*, Branford's *Science and Sanctity* and Lippmann's *A Preface to Morals*. In all three one finds an atmosphere distinctly religious. Professor Whitehead, primarily interested in the relations of science to philosophy, explains how the theory of relativity has "struck a heavy blow at the classical scientific materialism," and again he argues that "a thoroughgoing evolutionary philosophy is incompatible with materialism." Mr. Branford, looking at life from the point of view of the historian and sociologist urges a rebirth of the ideal of the cloister. Mr. Lippmann advocates disinterestedness as the keynote of his higher religion, and his tempered yet glowing praise of self-renunciation and sacrifice is as thoroughly religious in spirit as anything to be found in St. Thomas á Kempis.

None of these three books is bibliocentric. None is distinctly Christian, if that adjective implies that Jesus was God or that he was a perfect man. Are we to conclude then from this fact that the religious ideas of the three writers in question are alien to the Arnold tradition and to the evolution of Christianity?

The answer is not necessarily in the affirmative. Dr. Arnold of Rugby made the significant admission that the Bible was only in spots the revealed word of God. His son asserted that in a literal sense the Bible was not the word of God at all, but that tested by experience it provided in its broader aspects all guidance that was needed. But the humanists write as though the Bible were like any other book. They quote it as they do Aristotle, and neither the one nor the other as authoritative. They look to art, to business, to science, to philosophy, to poetry, to government to find the path which leads upward.

It is a dark path at best and no clear light shines upon it. The important thing, however, is that there is a light. The direction from which it comes does not matter. The light is the same whether it emanates from Bethlehem or from a biological laboratory. Surely it is idolatrous to worship either a manger or a laboratory. Possibly we may not have any inclination to worship anything. But obedience to the light is a higher form of worship whether we acknowledge it or not. It is not irreverent to write that Jesus is not the exclusive source of that light. Inasmuch as the humanists inspire other people with renewed courage, hope and kindliness it would seem rather unchristian to denounce them as irreligious. Because one may no longer accept the old ethics of supernaturalism and authority it does not follow that one must adopt the procedure of hogs and hyenas.

THE CONQUEST OF ALGERIA—
A CASE OF HISTORICAL INERTIA

by

M. M. Knight

VI

THE CONQUEST OF ALGERIA— A CASE OF HISTORICAL INERTIA

"Le Dey réclame, on le vole; il se plaint, on l'insulte; il se fâche, on le tue."—Alexandre de Laborde, 1830.

THOUGH three decades of the synthesis movement, in Europe and America, have not unified the aims of history, or even carefully defined them, we have at least come to expect more than chronological arrangement and guarantees of authenticity from those in possession of the facts. Even narration is impossible without selection, which is itself a form of interpretation. Having recognized that interpretation is unavoidable, historians have begun to see that it involves aims, and attempts to formulate these have led to the discovery that people do not agree about them. History might be defined as an attempt to measure the inertia of past institutions, ideas and methods. But for what purpose? Even if it is safe to adopt the working principle that all history is introductory, it does not necessarily follow that the sole object is to explain existing institutions or situations. A definitely past and completed event has a solidity all its own. However difficult to establish, its origins, circumstances and outcome represent accomplished facts, whereas the effects of a present situation—the most important things about it—are matters of conjecture or prophecy. History makes its appeal to those interested in the process of change itself, so to speak, as well as to those directly concerned with either the past or the present.

A past event, like a present one, involves the application

of an inherited social, intellectual and physical equipment, outdated and incongruous in varying degrees as one fragment or another is considered, to a situation without an exact duplicate among its predecessors. The element of deliberate reason in making these myriads of adjustments—many of the most complicated in a great hurry—is inevitably small. One of the most important tasks in the interpretation of any historical crisis, therefore, is to see how radically the situation differed from those which had furnished the precedents for handling it, and how much time there was for adapting the one to the other. Before we pin long ears to our pictures of departed statesmen, it is well to appraise the degree of irrationality to be expected in the nature of the case.

Colonial history is singularly rich in situations muddled by borrowing procedure which has worked well enough under conditions superficially similar but at bottom quite different. This is particularly true of an oversea empire which is one of exploitation rather than of settlement, like the new Greater France of the nineteenth century. Geographic differences which seem slight are oftentimes of tremendous significance in practice, especially if accompanied by the subtler ones of social organization, including religion. The very word "policy" implies a consistency in time which may be rendered absurd by a shift of objectives in space. An exotic country like Algeria, with a tenacious old civilization of its own, was bound to present maddeningly unexpected obstacles to the conquering Frenchmen of 1830-1847. The historians who later tried to make the struggle intelligible—or palatable, as the case might be—to people who had no conception of the human geography or the circumstances, were able to sneak around hurdles which the conquerors had been obliged to get over or crawl home defeated. History too often suggests the Wall Street lawyer's definition of an academic idea as "one there's no money up on."

Verisimilitude is largely a question of the audience. In time there appeared a group of scholars claiming Africa as their land of birth or adoption. The need for exhortation had passed, and with it the faith and interest in the spotless heroes of the earlier epics. Professor Gautier of Algiers was hardly criticized, even in the post-war France of 1920, for describing the conquest as a by-product of an adventure for which he used the figure of a bull in a china shop, remarking that colonization sprang up in spite of governmental policies rather than on account of them in the solitude behind the invading armies.

Practically all the good earlier history is the work of men familiar with the country they wrote about. The good revisionists of the past quarter of a century have also been "Africans," but vitally interested in some kinds of facts which did not greatly concern their predecessors. Alfred François Nettement, whose *Histoire de la Conquête d'Alger* appeared in 1856, had the advantage of working before the death of many of the leading actors in the drama, the disappearance of a great deal of written material, and an evolution of Algeria which has made the conditions of 1830-1847 increasingly difficult to visualize. Camille Rousset wrote his first small volume almost a quarter of a century later, covering the capture of the city of Algiers by the punitive expedition of 1830. Though he was the official custodian of the historical archives at the War Ministry, Rousset rarely referred to a document. His *Conquête d'Alger* is a tremendously dramatic piece of hack work, written mainly from a chronicle prepared for the purpose by a group of Army staff officers. Most of these knew their Africa, however, and whoever ignores Rousset does so at his peril. The great Aulard himself (in the *Revue Fran-*

[93]

çaise in 1923) expressed gratuitous surprise at the neglect of the consular reports on the fly-whisk episode which precipitated the break with Algeria in 1827. These, it happens, had been quoted in full by Rousset in one of the occasional lapses from his apparent disdain for the papers in his custody.

Rousset, and much worse writers who later followed his epic at second to sixth hand, did not quite gloss over an uneasy suspicion that the conquest of Algiers, exactly in the middle of the year 1830, was a separate adventure from the conquest of Algeria as a whole. Between lay a July Revolution which was a pure historical accident as far as the North African colonial empire it made possible is concerned. The roots of the punitive expedition go back to the French Revolution; but the beginnings of deliberate policy after the July Revolution resume the threads of eighteenth-century imperial history. In the background of the conquest of Algeria the fall of Algiers was only one item.

All the simplicity of the "insult" to the French consul, Deval, in 1827 disappears upon close examination. This half-Oriental Frenchman of Levantine upbringing and ways had played an ambiguous rôle in Algeria for years. The other consuls shunned him personally because of certain aspects of his mode of life which need not be discussed here. As early as 1825, his nephew, newly appointed vice-consul at Bône, caused the French trading posts there and at La Calle to be fortified. The Dey claimed that this was contrary to the terms of the long-standing concessions, had the works razed, and ridiculed the assertion that these places had "belonged" to France for four centuries. That he was still technically sovereign over the land is certain. The other side of the picture is that strict legality applies only under an effective reign of law, and that in fact French trading rights had been violated repeatedly, accompanied by the destruction of property and even bloodshed. Dey Hussein and Deval could hardly endure each other's presence after the above incident. They quarreled almost every time they met, without either being able to get at the other, and the French Government ignored requests for the consul's recall. Nobody but his superiors in Paris trusted Deval. The Chamber of Commerce of Marseilles refused to have any dealings with him. As for the Dey, he was passionately certain that the consul was in the pay of the exiled Jew, Bacri.

Bacri had a claim upon the French Government, dating from the earlier years of the Revolution. As the revenues from organized piracy and the ransoms of European captives had become precarious with the rise of powerful states, the Deys had gradually turned their financial affairs over to a group of Leghorn Jews resident in Algiers. Busnach and Bacri were the leaders at the time of the French Revolution. Busnach, known as the "King of Algiers," was killed there in an anti-Jewish riot of 1805. During the French Revolution, Bacri and Busnach had furnished grain to various armies in France and Italy, for which payment had not been made when the Dey broke with France over Napoleon's expedition to Egypt. Besides the ancient grievances against Algiers as a nest of pirates, kidnappers and tribute-takers, there were French counter-claims because of the destruction of trading posts on the occasion mentioned above, and of Bacri's private debts to French citizens.

Talleyrand, described in Bacri's letters as "the lame fellow," made repeated efforts under the Directory, the Consulate, the Empire and the Restoration Monarchy to get this account settled. That the noted French diplomat was among those bought off is stated in almost so many words in the Jew's correspondence. The heated and persistent interest of the Deys in the affair, from 1799 on, was not an impersonal one. Hussein maintained that Bacri owed him two and a half million francs, certainly the price of diplomatic aid. Bacri allowed the accumulated debt, with interest, to be scaled from nearly fourteen millions of francs to seven. Of this sum, the French Government withheld two and a half millions until certain private claims against it in France could be examined. Bacri, who was still in Europe, made no move to pay Dey Hussein, or to return to his jurisdiction. Hussein then demanded any balance which might remain from the impounded two and a half millions, and pressed the French to hurry the claims through the courts. As the matter dragged on for years and the Dey received evasive answers or counter-claims in reply to his letters, he finally arrived at the conviction that his old enemy, Consul Deval, had been bribed by Bacri. He accused Deval of receiving two millions for his services in paring down the principal and working for a settlement which would leave the Dey out in the cold. A final, personal letter to the French Government demanding the balance was not formally answered, but the well-hated Consul was instructed to convey a rejoinder orally—practically a list of counter-grievances. This infuriated Dey Hussein, who accused Deval of withholding a communication and publicly insulting him by intimating its contents.

At this inopportune juncture, Deval seized the occasion of the ceremonial breaking of the fast of Ramadan, April 27, 1827, to inform the Dey that a Roman ship in the harbor was under French consular protection, and to complain of procedure already under way. Hussein reproached the Consul for tormenting him with a minor and strictly non-French matter when no response had been made to a letter of the Dey to the King about the personal question of a large and just debt. In the exchange of invective which followed, Hussein stood up, ordered Deval out of the room, and accompanied his excited words with taps from the handle of his fly-chaser. Deval's Government accepted his interpretation of this undignified interview, which went down into history as the famous *coup d'éventail*. The Consul was withdrawn in June, Hussein had the French trading posts destroyed, as usual, and the French Government began an expensive and fruitless three-year blockade.

There is no evidence of any serious design of taking Algeria, or even Algiers, at that time. An indemnity was hinted at, and the idea rejected with scorn by the Dey, who considered that he had already been cheated out of two and a half millions. French warships were lost on this treacherous coast. The *Provence*, a parley ship bearing a flag of truce, was fired upon, apparently contrary to Hussein's orders. At any rate, he had the artillerymen bastinadoed. The French wanted the formal right to fortify their trading posts, and hoped to get moderate extensions of the territories and privileges mentioned in their ancient concessions. Although the Dey was known to possess considerable treasure, no serious historian has claimed that the French expected a large cash indemnity.

It is evident from the correspondence collected by Serres and Esquer that the British Government had no intention of allowing an actual French invasion without ample guarantees as to its restricted aims. Nominally, the Turkish Sultan was still the suzerain of the Dey of Algiers. France was in a particularly delicate position in any matter concerning Turkey and England after the battle of Navarino in the fall of 1827, and especially after the outbreak of the Russo-Turkish war a year later. It will be remembered that France played almost the rôle of a friendly neutral in the evacuation of Mehemet Ali's troops from Greece after the destruction of the Egyptian-Turkish fleet at Navarino. Mehemet Ali, Pasha of Egypt, proposed in 1829 to bring back Tripoli, Tunis and Algeria to a state of real subjection to Constantinople, and to liquidate the questions of piracy and Christian slavery, as well as to give the French appropriate satisfaction for the Dey's insult. France was to finance the Egyptian expedition. Sir Robert Gordon, British Ambassador at Constantinople, induced the Sultan to refuse. Jean Serres has called attention to the interesting fact that the Kingdom of Sardinia (nucleus of the later unified Italy!) strenuously objected to any strengthening of the hold of others upon Tunis.

To give up the Algerian adventure without any recompense for the costly blockade would have invited ridicule in the French Chamber—already seething with discontent over political usurpations at home—which the unpopular Government hardly dared face. Nothing could be done with the Sultan of Turkey, and the Dey remained as stiff-necked as in the beginning. Accordingly, the French Government began to prepare an expedition, and the Foreign Ministry sent out a circular note dated March 12, 1830, explaining France's motives as the vindication of the national honor and the suppression of the general nuisances of piracy and Christian slavery. Promise was made that if the existing regime should be destroyed, the future of the Regency would be arranged in concert with the powers. The British Government merely commented upon the conditions, refraining from any open consent even to a punitive expedition which it believed would probably fail. In the delicate Near Eastern situation of 1830, a break with France was not to be risked over a trivial matter.

Algiers was considered impregnable, a long standing opinion which Lord Exmouth's naval expedition of 1816 had reinforced rather than weakened. Napoleon, who thought in terms of land attacks, had held a different opinion. In 1808, he had sent one Boutin, a Captain of Engineers, to Algiers as a spy to study the possibilities of an assault from the rear. Boutin's plans and maps, indicating a landing at Sidi Ferruch, down the coast, were followed almost to the letter in 1830. The expedition had the colossal luck of running into a week of perfect weather in which to take the sailing fleet across the Mediterranean and land the men and siege materials. Algiers, attacked from the land side, fell in a few days, the French taking possession July 5, 1830. Only 415 men had been killed. The Dey's treasure of forty-eight millions more than covered the expenses of assembling and handling the force, to date.

Hussein was deported, with his harem, his Janissaries, and enough of the administrative personnel that nobody left in Algeria knew who owned the land, how and from whom taxes had been collected, or much of anything else of practical value in carrying on the Government. Before that month of July, 1830, had run its course, a revolution had given France a new King and a new Government, on whose hands Algiers was a white elephant. At this point begins the second act in the drama, the unpremeditated conquest of Algeria as a whole. France had merely skimmed off what central government there was. She had to create another one before she could get the commercial and territorial concessions which would save her face abroad and help appease a parliament unlikely to forget the costly three-year blockade.

The July Revolution had swept eastward from France, unsettling national friendships. Czar Nicholas was as chilly toward the new July Monarchy as he had been warm to its predecessor. Poor Louis Philippe had ample reason to feel actually insulted, and to turn for consolation to the English, whose feelings about the change in France were precisely the opposite of those entertained in Russia. Down in Algiers, the generals fondly believed that they were within a few amiable arrangements of slipping into possession of the whole country. They did their best to render impossible an evacuation which would have been difficult in any case, and trained a battery of ink-pots upon public opinion and the Government in France. Mehemet Ali made more and more trouble in the Near East, and Great Britain was less and less in a position to sacrifice French coöperation. France's claims in Algeria were strengthened by the mere passage of time. By 1834, when the assumption of "possession" was officially made, it would have been hard for any European government to devise an alternative.

French opinion, inside and outside of the parliament, was anything but unanimous in support of the venture, even in the middle 'thirties. With few exceptions, the correspondence of the military leaders themselves reveals little confidence in the future of France as a colonizer. French colonization had received a rude shock in the eighteenth century, and another in Napoleonic times. Speculators, and even bona fide settlers, rushed to Algiers after the news of the victory. In the incredible administrative disorder following the disappearance of the Dey's government, these people got titles, good or bad, by fair means or foul, to a good deal of land. Whether and how to protect the claims and claimants was one of the hardest groups of problems. The ports were useless, expensive and even dangerous to hold without the hinterland which fed or starved them at will. French trade had been carried on mainly with the Beylik of Constantine in the East; but the Bey still regarded himself as a loyal subject of the Sultan of Turkey. The Dey had enjoyed almost no authority outside the central Beylik, and not too much there. France used intrigue at Tunis and open threats at Constantinople to prevent any direct contact between the Sultan and his loyal Bey at Constantine. A short-lived scheme for Algerian protectorates managed by relatives of the Bey of Tunis was abandoned because of the incompetency of these people in the very first stages. Negotiations with Ahmed, Bey of Constantine, having failed, the French claimed a sovereignty which the Dey had never possessed, technically or in practice, branded Ahmed Bey as rebellious to an authority which had never set foot in his capital, and summoned him to surrender. An expedition of 1835 against Constantine failed disastrously.

In the West, the young Emir Abd-el-Kader, whose training and prestige were religious at the outset, not military, had already made the French a vast deal of trouble. He had been practically put in authority on the Moroccan border by a treaty of 1834, had risen and administered a stinging defeat upon the French armies at the Macta in June, 1835, and had had his forces temporarily dispersed in the fighting which followed. By the famous treaty of Tafna two years later, General Bugeaud left Abd-el-Kader in control of the western two-thirds of Algeria, with the exception of the small coastal areas in French hands and vague general recognition of French sovereignty. This move has been called asinine, but the fact is that the French simply had to have all their troops for a new assault on Ahmed Bey at Constantine, which succeeded in the autumn of 1837 only after terrible hardships and sanguinary fighting. Within two years, Abd-el-Kader had armed and equipped a regular army of ten thousand men and arranged for a militia of fifty thousand. One of the most terrible wars in history went on from 1839 to 1847. The recorded French losses were around fifty thousand, and the number of Algerians exterminated is a matter of guesswork. In February, 1843, for example, some 1500 inhabitants of Medina-el-Kantara were chased out into a snowstorm to make room for a French column, and all the natives froze to death. Marshal Pelissier's asphyxiation of about 1000 natives of all ages and both sexes in a cave in the Dahra in 1845 raised such an outcry in the French press that a similar exploit by Marshal Saint-Arnaud was kept secret, and until recently the passage in one of his letters describing it was supposed to refer to the Pelissier case. That the Algerians also committed what were called atrocities even in those days is perfectly well established.

These cases of ferocity are of antiquarian interest for their own sake; but it is important that the situation they indicate made colonization artificially easy for the time being. Though colonists lost their lives in fairly general uprisings in the back country for a half century after the fall of Algiers, it may be stated that as a rule they were protected, sometimes at a cost of much embarrassment to immediate military aims. On the other hand, the number of those who perished from disease in this unfamiliar country is known to have been terrific, though never adequately recorded. Settlers from the North of France died like flies in the malarial plain back of Algiers. Typhoid long raged practically unchecked, and amœbic dysentery took its heavy toll of lives for decades before it could even be reliably diagnosed, let alone cured.

During the first four or five decades of the Algerian adventure, conditions in France were such that colonization tempted the northern rather than the Mediterranean elements. A Breton, Angevin or Lorrainer had no idea whatever of irrigation or biennial cultivation, as practiced in semi-arid lands. As a rule, he had a perfect contempt for native methods, and instead of trying to improve them by scientific study, he strove to impose a system of farming quite out of harmony with the basic environment. This was in large part the fault of the French Government, which wanted Algeria to be tropical (though all of it then held was in the North Temperate Zone), and had no passionate enthusiasm for improving grain fields, olive groves and vineyards to compete with French produce at home. The absurdities and oppressions arising from ignorance of the meaning of the Mohammedan Sacred Law as applied to land titles and various economic matters would make too long a story to include here. What finally saved the economic situation was the influx of Spanish settlers who had a knowledge of farming under similar conditions, plus a vine disease in France leading both to a shortage of wine and an emigration of skilled people, with their capital, to Algeria.

A glance at the old French colonial empire of the eighteenth century suggests the origin of the tenacious preference for tropical produce. It was not merely a matter of "group memory," or of paper precedents, but of a long adjustment of the economic system of France. Anyone tempted to believe that the motives back of what is sometimes called "economic imperialism" are new would do well to turn through such eighteenth century documents as the Béliardi papers. Of a total French trade with the Americas amounting to roughly fifty millions of our dollars on the eve of the Revolution, that with Saint-Domingue alone constituted four-fifths. Most of the remainder was also with colonies producing mainly tropical crops. Louisiana and Canada put together had never at any time sent France much more than a half million dollars' worth of goods a year. The East India trade, also tropical, ranked next to Saint-Domingue (or Haiti, as the country is now called) with roughly ten millions of dollars in exports and imports. West Africa, likewise tropical, was the remaining important colonial trade area, with roughly six millions, reduced to our dollars. France wanted coffee and sugar from Algeria, not grain and wine. It took something like thirty years for the elementary principles of geography to assert themselves fully over the whims of statesmen and the old habits and prejudices of business people in France.

Military methods have an inertia of their own. When the French tried to make war in the rough, roadless and oftentimes waterless back country of Algeria, they found their artillery of little use against the more mobile native forces. The Moorish rifle actually outranged the French musket. Marshal Bugeaud's horse-sense was wider awake in his professional field than in the less familiar domain of economics, law and social control. He copied his opponents' general scheme of fighting, and improved upon it by the better organization and technical material which European society afforded. It would be interesting to know what effect some decades of experience with this mobile type of warfare had in unfitting French ideas and preparations for a conflict in Europe, and hence in bringing about the defeat of 1870. Incidentally, American observer officers like General (then Lieutenant) Phil Kearny brought away an enthusiasm for French open fighting which must have added to the prejudices of Indian campaigners against tactics adapted to a settled country. Both sides had about the same mental handicaps in the American Civil War, but only the Germans had planned their combinations of velocity and weight for the terrain of the Franco-Prussian conflict.

Algeria furnishes a good illustration of the historian's troubles. It was once the distinguishing mark of history that its continuity was chronological. The details and the sequence of events already past were matters of fact, requiring only to be established and set down in the order of their occurrence. Anyone who did not care to defend the assumptions implied in this method had only to refrain from making them at once explicit and unpalatable. This Eden was emptied by reaching for the apple of logical continuity. What are we to do when events already past and beyond control do not display any real coherence? To demand logical explanation is often to ask why people of some eminence made apparently stupid or inappropriate applications of past experience which they evidently misunderstood from the records they had. Frequently all we have in the end is the rather patent fact that the means did not produce the desired ends under the circumstances, whatever any or all of these three may have been in detail if we could only reconstruct them. And Algeria is certainly not the only case in which the unforseen outcome eclipsed any or all of the conscious plans.

THE INSIDE OF GERMANY'S
WAR POLITICS

by

Charles A. Beard

VII

THE INSIDE OF GERMANY'S WAR POLITICS

EVERYBODY knows something about the terrible explosions produced in the historical camp by the publication of choice papers from the secret archives of Leningrad, Vienna, and Berlin. It upset the composure of statesmen who had participated in the drama described in the documents, shattered a hundred war myths, sent propagandists scurrying for bomb-proof shelters, and cleared the air for a closer understanding of international relations. Suddenly the historian of diplomacy was put fifty or a hundred years ahead of his predecessors, and it must be said that he made excellent use of his opportunities. Even remote country editors soon became dimly aware that the potted palms, viands, and table manners of diplomatic garden parties had not been exactly as described in their authentic "news" columns and that double-shotted leaders had often been worse than fiction— hopeless blunders.

But it is not commonly realized that the explosions of the World War illuminated the inner processes of politics in a great society, Germany—and thus universal politics—no less than the secret processes of diplomacy. The immense collections of foreign-office papers, upon which diplomatic historians have drawn, contain rich materials on the substance of domestic politics. By admitting us behind the scenes they make it clear who was pulling the strings. For example, what a picture of the Kaiser, William II, is afforded by his comments sowed along the borders of the papers submitted to his scrutiny! And this picture is no mere personal portrait; it is a representation of power. But rich as they were, the diplomatic papers were only the beginning of the revelations respecting the inner operations of German politics. They have now been supplemented by a huge collection of volumes, including stenographic minutes, prepared under the auspices of the Parliamentary Committee of Inquiry which investigated the causes of the German breakdown. Besides dealing with military and marine affairs, these volumes cover such topics as the working of the Reichstag during the War and the causes of the internal collapse.[1] To these two groups of official papers must be added personal memoirs, embroidering and enlarging them, and also the testimony taken at numerous state trials growing out of revolutionary or counter-revolutionary acts and charges of slander committed during or after the war.

For the American reader it is sufficient to suggest that the new German documents furnish for the study of politics materials about as significant as the records which a Senate Committee headed by the late Senator Lafollette would have unearthed from the archives of great corporations and conservative politicans in a five-year investigation with full power and no judicial interference. In other words, it is now possible to see through the façade of imperial and royal Germany and to observe the transactions that occurred behind the scenes in a great and revolutionary age—our very own time. Moreover, for the reader who has neither the leisure nor patience for the study of mountainous masses of documents there are two or three general and particular surveys which serve as guides and interpreters.[2]

[1] *Die Ursachen des Deutschen Zusammenbruchs im Jahre 1918.* Erste Abteilung: Der militärische und aussenpolitische Zusammenbruch. (3 vols.). Zweite Abteilung: Der innere Zusammenbruch (10 vols.). Deutsche Verlagsgesellschaft für Politik und Geschichte, Berlin.
[2] Especially Arthur Rosenberg, *Die Entstehung der deutschen Republik 1871-1918,* which is used as the basis of this analysis. Dr. Rosenberg was

I

The starting point of the new exploration is, of course, the state which Bismarck erected on the old orders of efficient power in Germany—the landed aristocracy, especially in Prussia, the army (officered mainly by men of this class), the bureaucracy, the dynasties, and the clerical authories, Catholic and Protestant. These well-rooted and rigid classes seemed to supply in 1871 the only materials out of which a constitutional system could be manufactured. The bourgeois had grown in numbers and wealth since 1848, but they had no adequate will-to-power, and Bismarck made little effort to fuse them with the landed classes in the scheme of politics. The only way they could function politically was through some kind of parliamentary government, and neither they nor Bismarck dared to risk that democratic experiment. Although a few merchants and industrialists, such as the Krupps, Stumms, and Schroeders, were elevated to the nobility, there was no such wholesale translation of cotton spinners, soap boilers, and brewers as occurred in England. It was not necessary to have a peerage to sit in the Prussian House of Lords, for that body included (besides hereditary and institutional members) a number of members nominated by the King from among rich citizens and celebrities. Unquestionably the Hohenzollern court at Berlin was more cordial to merchants, manufacturers, and men of science and art than was the Hapsburg court at Vienna, but its relations with the bourgeois were haphazard, accidental, inorganic. If Herr Ballin could rush in to see the Kaiser almost informally, the class which he repre-

---

a Referent des Untersuchungsausschusses des Reichstags für die Ursachen des deutschen Zusammenbruchs. He documents his book by references to the materials cited above. Also valuable are Veit Valentin, *Deutschlands Aussenpolitik 1890-1918;* H. P. Falcke, *Vor dem Eintritt Amerikas in den Weltkrieg;* Victor Naumann, *Dokumente und Argumente; The Memoirs of Prince Max of Baden.*

sented either had no will of its own or was beset by a great fear of social democracy. Particularly after a tariff *union sacrée* had been formed with the Prussian landed nobility and William II had given up "social politics," the industrialists had little reason to question the "best of all possible worlds."

Nevertheless the bourgeoisie was the most dynamic element in this order, with relation to both foreign and domestic affairs. As Dr. Rosenberg says: "The Prussian aristocracy had, on its own account, no ground at all for an imperialistic, warlike policy. For the landed gentleman of East Prussia carried on no trade in China and possessed no mines in Morocco. The deepest cause of difficulties in German foreign politics was rather the economic expansive energy of the German middleclass and the ill-tempers created by it among competitors, especially in England. If Germany had had a purely middleclass government, such as that of England or America, then the German bourgeoisie would have been forced to organize its own expansion in a systematic fashion. It would have then been compelled to bear the responsibility for its own economic interests. It would have considered what was attainable and what was not. It would not have split its energies and at the same time awakened enemies in all the corners of the earth." In other words, it possessed great economic power but left the representation of its interests to a monarch, an aristocracy, and a bureaucracy stiff with a sense of prestige and possessing none of the oleaginous arts of commerce and negotiation.

To put the case figuratively, from 1888 to 1914 the German state drifted like a giant ship, well-equipped and full-manned. On the bridge stood the Kaiser, splendidly uniformed, surrounded by army officers who, if a bit seasick, betrayed no signs of their discomfort. Next to the Kaiser stood the Chancellor, the personal choice of the

Kaiser—if any man subdued to the gossip and stew of a court may be said to have any powers of choice at all. The best cabins were occupied by rich bourgeois, who were pleased with the ship and quite content with slipping a word now and then to the navigating officer respecting directions. Down below in the boiler room were the Social Democrats, who as events proved, knew better than anybody else on board the probable outcome of the voyage but were powerless to do more than criticize the captain and passengers.

And who was really running the ship? The new documents admit of no exact answer, except that nobody was running it consistently. The army officers were of course loyal to the Kaiser and liked the fiction that he was running it as Bismarckian constitution provided; but if there was to be any fighting it was bound to be over goods from which the bourgeois would profit most. "Juristically speaking," the Kaiser was directing foreign affairs, but the bourgeois were supplying him with the problems—Venezuela (1902-03), Morocco, the Far East, the Bagdad Railway, &c. The Chancellor was the Kaiser's man, but what did that signify? Certainly he was not to take orders from the crew and passengers—at least if given in the form of resolutions. A round-robin he might consider but not a bill. The Chancellor's orders were to come from the Kaiser, if the Kaiser was not too tired, too pre-occupied, or too much inclined to say things that made trouble abroad. Cold-blooded calculation was needed in the new age of machines, business enterprise, and high finance, but the Kaiser was half-feudal, mystical, lyrical, and temperamental. When a storm cloud rose on the horizon he jumped around like a frightened schoolboy. Since nobody really knew where the ship was bound all storms were taken head-on, while the master of ceremonial prestige shouted: Augen gerade aus! Whereas in the United States, England, and France, the effective forces of politics went steadily on through all kinds of weather and party uproars, in Germany, the forces of government were divided against themselves. Neither the captain nor the passengers in the best cabins realized that the crew could be managed better if it thought that it was managing itself.

Yet from year to year there were signs of change on board the good ship Hohenzollern. It was evidently becoming more difficult for the nominal captain to keep up the appearances of directing affairs, especially as his early training had given him little capacity for dealing with new technological apparatus and his not unnatural reaction against the Anglicized teachings of his parents had driven him into a dislike for the "practical" mercantile spirit required by the age. When on calm days he discoursed on art, purity in letters, education, and archeology, signs of displeasure occurred among the first cabin passengers. From week to week more of them were to be seen reading the *Berliner Tageblatt* and *Simplizissimus*. The group gathered in the smoking room around Maximilian Harden increased, indicating a growing disrespect for the All Highest Captain and his system. That was more ominous, perhaps, than the widening unrest among the Social Democrats below.

To drop the figure, there were many signs between 1888 and 1914 that the system of divided and irresponsible government would have to go. One was the great popular disturbance made by the *Daily Telegraph* affair of 1908—the Kaiser's astounding performance in giving to the world amazing personal views on Anglo-German relations. Nothing could illustrate better the complete chaos in the German state system. Before William allowed the final draft of the article to go off to the *Daily Telegraph*, he submitted it to his Chancellor, Prince Buelow, with a request for an examination of the text and suggestions. In the press of affairs, Buelow sent it to the Foreign Office; the routineers in that office made a few pen corrections; and the paper was sent back to the Kaiser with an official approval. The "interview" was printed and made a storm. It is impossible to imagine how anyone could have read it in advance without foreseeing that it would make trouble.

But, as Dr. Rosenberg says, the whole affair was simply a classical example of the art by which Germany was governed under William II. "Now or never," he continues, "was the possibility of reform in the Bismarckian constitution. Foreign policy should have been placed in the hands of an imperial minister responsible to the Reichstag, and over him should have been established a collegiate imperial ministry responsible to the Reichstag. If Buelow and his bloc had proceeded in a determined fashion, anything could have been accomplished: the Kaiser was in a greater embarrassment than any of his predecessors since 1848. However, without the Conservatives no action was possible looking toward parliamentarization and the limitation of imperial power. The Conservatives would have had to pluck up courage and voluntarily transfer a part of their power to the bourgeoisie. A Conservative-Liberal imperial ministry and a Conservative-Liberal Prussian government would have necessarily arisen." But the Conservatives would give up nothing; they preferred the game of "tactics" to the serious business of organized political responsibility. So the opportunity went up in smoke.

In the winter of 1913-14 occurred a second incident which illustrated the art of government in the Wilhelminic era and indicated a movement in the make-weights of state; that was the Zabern affair. As a result of a trivial popular agitation in the little town of Zabern in Alsace, the colonel of a regiment stationed there ordered some soldiers to seize a few street demonstrators and clap them into the garrison cellar for the night. Besides being a clear violation of law, this action revealed the historic contempt which the military authorities had for the civilian population—a contempt by no means confined to Germany. The deed stood in a worse light because the Zabern district, though in Alsace, had long been represented in the Reichstag by a Conservative. As a result there broke out in the Reichstag a demonstration against the military caste and its works such as had never occurred before in the history of that body. The Chancellor, Bethmann-Hollweg and the war minister, von Falkenhayn, made a defense, the former in his half-hearted style (representing his position as a kind of fifth-wheel geared into nothing), and the latter with the customary military swagger and bluster. But the days of the barrack-room king were full of trouble.

At the election of the previous year the Socialists had cast more than one third of the total number of legal ballots. Taking all the opposition elements together, there was now a clear majority of the people aligned against the Bismarckian system. In the vote in the Reichstag on the resolution condemning the government for its position, respecting the Zabern affair, the new spirit was revealed: 293 members went on record in favor of the resolution, 54 against, and there were four abstentions. It was now made clear that the Catholic party had a left wing almost in touch with the Social Democracy—a radical wing which could not be ordered about at will by the Conservatives. The Kaiser, the Chancellor, and the army caste, had treated the Zabern dispute as a question of military prestige and had lost in the popular forum. But they got away with the shell of a victory. A military court, on a second hearing, cleared the Zabern colonel and his subordinates and all efforts to enact legislation restricting military power in civilian interest were defeated. There was a majority to protest in the Reichstag, but no majority with a will-to-power. Even before the World War broke out a few months later, the agitation over the Zabern affair had almost died away. Another opportunity to introduce responsible government had passed and the bourgeois had once more preferred a false security to the risk of responsibility.

II

Then came the war. A Reichstag that could not muster up enough courage to seize power in time of peace was not likely to attempt to control the army in war time. So things turned out. The Reichstag voted credits for the war, declared a civil truce, and went home. "The High Command," it was said, "has charge." Yes, but what was the High Command? It had always been a matter of pride among Prussians that the army did not interfere with daily politics and that politics was not allowed in the army. This is one of the pious ideals of military science. As a matter of fact the German High Command was the fruit of politics—court politics, army politics, historic schemes of promotions and pensions.[1] It is true, no political minister in the Reichstag had anything to say about selecting the chief of staff, but this did not mean that infallible military and engineering wisdom selected the one and only mind capable of solving the pressing problem of winning the war, should it come. It is sometimes assumed by innocent bystanders that if "politics is kept out of the army," triumphant intelligence automatically enters. This is a pure fiction and the history of military affairs in Germany from 1914 to 1918 illustrates superbly just what may be expected when "specialists" run things in their own way, subject to no popular criticism, free from democratic pressures and interference. War dominated by politics may be distressing (as Lincoln's troubles from 1861 to 1864 prove),

[1] Demotions were practically impossible.

but war without politics may be worse—that is, for the people who are trying to win a war. Moltke was chief of the German staff. Why? Court and army politics. Yet he was old, sick, crotchety, and really shrank from bloodshed—was, in fact, about the last man in the high military circle for such a task. Everywhere below him were old men, stiff, beribboned, and full of caste conceit in charge of a machine that was technically splendid, and trying to carry out a plan that had been drafted by a master mind. When Falkenhayn was substituted for Moltke, there was more vigor but no more intelligence at the head of the military organization.

Such as it was, the High Command directed German affairs from the summer of 1914 to the summer of 1916, as far as necessary to get men and munitions up to the fronts in sufficient quantities. It had its own system of censorship and often suppressed printed matter deemed innocent by the civilian authorities. Especially did it display anxiety about the discussion of war aims and peace terms, on account of the depressing effect upon the morale of the army. Whatever was required by "defense" and "security" was done by the High Command without "political" interference.

While the general staff was running the war, the other wheels of the German government turned loosely in mid-air. The Kaiser sank into the background. Nominal head of the army, he exerted no direct influence on the fighting itself; as not much glory was being wrested from fate, he won few laurels. Nominal head of the civil government, the Kaiser found little power left in that branch after the army got through with it. Germany was bending all her energies to winning the war, and the Kaiser was obviously not helping much; while his subjects were on short rations he had barrels of sugar safely stored away in his castle in Berlin.

His second in charge, Bethmann-Hollweg, the amiable Chancellor, continued in office, representing nothing in particular, irritating Conservatives by displaying liberalism with a view to keeping the Social Democrats in line, but not enough liberalism to win on the left the kind of support that meant strength for the civil government. The fourth wheel in the German system, the Reichstag, during these years, seemed about as futile as the Kaiser. Its chief function had hitherto been critical, and now it was estopped by the civil truce from practising this art. Furthermore the High Command kept it absolutely in the dark about the actual course of affairs on the various fronts; not until near the end did it know any more about the war than the German people; hence critical gestures, if made, would have merely punctured free air. The fifth wheel in the German system, the Marine Office, was likewise whirling around vainly; eager representatives of that department were showing how they could win the war if given a chance; but, as there was really no unity of energy anywhere outside of the traditional army, there was no will to decide.

While the High Command stuck at its job and the other pieces of government threshed around, dynamic forces were at work in German society, in spite of the civil truce. It soon appeared to the Social Democrats that under the sacred truce they were making all the concessions and sacrifices; nothing substantial, such as the reform of the Prussian suffrage system, seemed to be coming from the other side. Moreover the cost of living was rising, leaving in its wake embittered discontent. As a result there was a distinct popular movement to the left, even in the Center party. And strange to say, the Social Democrats now found friends among the peasants, particularly in Catholic Bavaria—once strong bulwarks of conservatism—because government control over food stuffs and prices deprived them of precious chances to make money and irritated them in addition.

While forces were being concentrated on the left, changes

of deep significance were taking place on the right. At last, the closed body of aristocratic army officers, representing the old traditions of the land, was being decimated—by war. Thousands of them had been killed at the fronts; thousands had moved upward to safer positions as the army expanded to meet war needs; and in consequence the lower front-charges passed into the possession of reserve officers and fighting lieutenants of humbler birth—young teachers, students, clerks, and other offspring of the middleclass— who could fraternize more readily with the rank and file. Perhaps it is not too much to say that Bismarck's system sank down forever in the crimson flood on the battlefield of the Marne!

With these changes foreboding a relocation of political power ran some discussion of war aims, notwithstanding the fears of the High Command. When the debate got started it was found to run along class lines, involving the fate of the Bismarckian system, not that of a mere cabinet, as would have been the case in England. In total ignorance of the actual course of the fighting, believing that the German armies were really winning, the landed aristocracy and the industrialists went in heavily for "a peace of victory" —more land for Prussians on the East and more coal and iron for capitalists on the West. And professors sprang up on every hand to show that it should be so. On the other side the Social Democrats and the laborers belonging to the left wing of the Center party—plain people who were fighting at the front and sweating in factories at home—held firmly to the opinion that they were sacrificing everything to defend their native land, not to win estates, coal, and colonies. They felt that the refusal to make a clear announcement about Belgium and continued insistence on imperialistic aims prolonged the war by frightening their foes, and that a smashing victory would fix the old dominant classes of Germany more firmly in the saddle than ever. It was highly probable that after a peace of untainted victory quite a number of independent Social Democrats would be shot.

By the summer of 1916—after the disastrous assault on Verdun—the movement to the left had gone so far that the middleclass, to say nothing of the upper layers, grew alarmed. A large body of dissident Socialists had broken away from the party discipline; the left wing of the Catholic Center had become "unreliable." According to Dr. Rosenberg, for a brief time political power lay in the street and whoever had the courage could have picked it up. Parliamentary government was again possible. But once more the opportunity passed. Under great pressure from the civilian population and the army, the Kaiser, on August 29th, let Falkenhayn go and installed in authority the two men who had obviously been "doing things," namely, Hindenburg and Ludendorff. Germany now had a master—Ludendorff, with his senior as a faithful second.

III

From August, 1916, until October, 1918, Ludendorff was dictator. His strength rested on no constitutional fiction. It did not depend on any popular confidence in the Kaiser. His dictatorship stood firmly on popular confidence in his capacity to deliver goods. Enjoying that support, he seized all power and risked it on the war. Though he continued to hold to the military fiction that there was no "politics" in war, Ludendorff was in fact reactionary to the core in social philosophy. He was savage in his attitude toward labor unrest and especially strikes, no matter what the cause. He gave countenance to the Pan-German party and believed that a peace of victory was necessary to save the classes for which he labored; Brest-Litovsk was a sign of his mentality. So shallow was his penetration into the spirit of his own times that he imagined it possible to play with monarchy in the historic style; to make the Kaiser Duke of Courland, to create a Lithuanian crown for the king of Saxony, and to provide "compensations" for other princes— as if Louis XIV were still ruling in France! Yet he did not have courage enough to restore the Tsar! In other words, Ludendorff's dictatorship widened the social cleavage in Germany. It represented one-sided power, without intelligence.

Its nature was illustrated by the history it made. It directed all military affairs without let or hindrance. It managed the Reichstag as if that chamber was a collection of school children engaged in a picnic. It inspired Stresemann's attack on Bethmann-Hollweg; made and unmade chancellors; allowed its man, Michaelis, to sneer at the Reichstag's peace resolution; permitted only those "democratic" demonstrations likely to be useful to its designs; forced the U-Boat issue, compelling the Center party to give in; by the Brest-Litovsk treaty, it flouted the Reichstag; and on one occasion it instructed the Crown Prince to take a hand in politics. With equal facility, the Ludendorff dictatorship managed the Chancellor's office. It ousted Bethmann-Hollweg, the Kaiser's personal friend; it chose and ousted his successors. When the Foreign Secretary, von Kühlmann, made in June, 1918, a speech displaying intelligence, which displeased the High Command, he was forced out of office on the orders of Ludendorff. Even the Kaiser's trusted friend, von Valentini, chief of the Civil Cabinet (bureau of appointments and promotions), had to step down and out when the High Command requested his dismissal. If the Kaiser seemed about to do something that did not suit them, Hindenburg and Ludendorff wrote firmly to him, offering him the alternatives of yielding to their wishes or accepting their resignation—a frightful thought.

Meanwhile the Kaiser and his office sank lower and lower into nothingness. Of this he was bitterly aware. Once he had expressed his personal convictions with a proud flourish on the margins of state papers; now his assurance is gone. Michaelis is acceptable to Ludendorff; the Kaiser bows to instructions although he admits that he does not know Michaelis. General Mackensen asks for instructions; the Kaiser approves the General's wishes, and adds that he does not oppose anything the Chief of the General Staff desires. An inspired article in a Berlin paper, obviously against Ludendorff, comes to his hand, and he writes "ja," "richtig," "sehr gut" on the margins near the passages strongly condemning the General. Opposite the passage calling for a statesman big enough to meet the situation and deploring the fact that conditions will not permit any statesman to become great, the Kaiser enters his verdict: "Right; either he displeases the Reichstag or Kreuznach [then the seat of the High Command] or both." Then in lament he exclaims: "By both sides the Kaiser is ignored." He desires a peace of moderations; he is compelled to give apparent sanction to the fanaticism of the Pan-Germans. The Hohenzollern monarchy has been swallowed up in Ludendorff's dictatorship.

For two years, Ludendorff ran Germany in his own way —until he lost on the battlefield. Then he tried to liquidate the bankruptcy in his own way. Convinced that President Wilson would not make a truce with a military dictator, he used his dictatorship to build a new political façade for the civil wing of his government. His idea was to get a truce, a breathing spell, and, if satisfactory peace terms were not forthcoming, to lead a popular uprising against the Entente —a levée en masse. Accordingly he forced upon the sur-

[123]

prised Chancellor and the dazed Reichstag a parliamentary system of government—a revolution from above that could not be stopped from above; what the bewildered middleclass never dared to take is now thrust into its hands for ulterior purposes. This done, Ludendorff forced the selection of Prince Max, of liberal aroma, as Chancellor to head the new show. When the Prince hesitated to take immediate orders and begged for time, he was roughly told by the Kaiser to stop his importunities and carry out the instructions of the High Command.

So far Ludendorff's scheme had worked to perfection. But at last it came to a dead stop: his new political machine would not fight, either because it would not or could not. Ludendorff ascribed its unwillingness to the incapacity and disloyalty of the political leaders he had thrust into power; they ascribed it to the revolution from below rapidly spreading from the marine base, Kiel, to Munich. The debate over this issue, naturally more political than historical, is not yet closed. But the facts remain: Ludendorff imposed parliamentary government on Germany in the hope of a "good truce" and then discovered that his "democratic government" would not support him in a last desperate effort to "save his country." Accordingly the thankless task of winding up his case in bankruptcy was given to the Social Democrats and politicians of the middleclass. Out of poetic justice they should have politely insisted that he finish the work in hand. But he was a warrior, not a statesmen—not a dictator at all costs—and his chief, the Kaiser, whom he had stripped of power, had fallen between two stools—Reichstag and the dictatorship—and now had no place to sit. Such is the outline of the domestic drama as it appears in the new historical documents.

AMERICAN CHRISTIANITY AND THE WORLD OF EVERYDAY

by

Harold U. Faulkner

VIII

AMERICAN CHRISTIANITY AND THE WORLD OF EVERYDAY

NOT since the Protestant Revolt has the Christian church been faced with problems more difficult of solution than those which have confronted it in the past half century. Emanating, as they have, from the industrial revolution of the eighteenth century and the cumulative scientific knowledge of the nineteenth, they have forced the church to revise its tactics to meet the new social and economic order, and, if possible, to bring its theology more in line with modern concepts of biology, psychology, geology, astrophysics and the other sciences. In America the task has been fraught with particular difficulties. In addition to the factory system, urbanization, the impoverishment of the proletariat and other early and customary effects of the industrial revolution, the church has been confronted with many special problems:—huge immigration and a racially heterogeneous population, great rural areas with a provincial outlook, and a rapidly moving frontier. To cope in any adequate way with these economic changes was in itself no small task, particularly at a time when the old theology was being sharply challenged by the new science, and it speaks volumes for the virility and adaptability of the Christian church that it has been able to survive the strain so well.[1] Much as has been done by recent scholarship in the field of church history, the story of the impact of industry and science upon the

[1] H. K. Carroll, *The Religious Forces of the United States,* (rev. ed., N. Y., 1912) lxix.

[127]

technique and theology of American christianity remains even yet an almost virgin field for the social and intellectual historian.

Any real awakening on the part of the American church to the fact that a new world had come into being waited upon the advent of a vigorous and aggressive labor movement in the decade of the 'eighties. It was then that the first definite overture to labor appears to have been made by the statesmanlike Cardinal Gibbons, whose appeal to Rome in behalf of the Knights of Labor brought a reversal of the condemnation which the Congregation of the Holy Office had directed against that organization.[1] While the wise move of the Catholic Cardinal brought his church into *rapport* with organized labor and was instrumental in saving to Catholicism a large number of the laboring class, the Protestant clergy saw their working class constituency steadily declining. "The Protestant churches," said Samuel L. Loomis to the Andover theological students in 1886, "as a rule, have no following among the workingmen. Everybody knows it. Go into any ordinary church on Sunday morning, and you see lawyers, physicians, merchants, and business men with their families:—you see teachers, salesmen, and clerks, and a certain proportion of educated mechanics: but the workingman and his household are not there." [2] Similar testimony is abundant,[3] and a generation later the situation had not notably changed. "The Protestant churches," asserted C. Bertram Thompson in 1909, "as a rule, are not made up of the common people, but rather of the employers," [4] while

[1] Allen S. Will, *Life of Cardinal Gibbons*, (N. Y., 1922) Vol. I, Chapters XVIII-XIX.

[2] Samuel Lane Loomis, *Modern Cities and their Religious Problems* (N. Y., 1887), 82.

[3] Josiah Strong, *The New Era* (N. Y., 1893), Chapter X; Washington Gladden, Applied Christianity (Boston, 1886), 149.

[4] C. Bertram Thompson, *The Churches and the Wage Earners* (N. Y., 1909), 8.

other students bemoaned the fact that immigrants, Christian and Jewish alike, caught in the whirl of the great industrial cities, were losing the faith of their fathers.[1]

The theory that the American Protestant church had become a bourgeois institution, was, of course, vigorously denied by prominent clergymen and laymen alike, and the failure of the working people to attend church was often attributed to the "comprehensive fact of total depravity." [2] The evidence, however, pointed to other causes. Washington Gladden in the middle 'eighties asserted that the chief reasons why the working people were "slowly and sullenly drawing away from the churches," [3] were "first, their inability to dress well enough to appear in a place as stylish and fashionable as the average church; secondly, their sense of the injustice that workingmen, as a class, are receiving at the hands of the capitalist employers, as a class." [4] Concerning the second of these causes, there is no difficulty in finding corroborating testimony. Wrote Samuel Gompers toward the end of the last century, "My associates have come to look upon the church and the ministry as the apologists and defenders of the wrong committed against the interests of the people, simply because the perpetrators are possessors of wealth. . . . The means and methods which my associates have, by experience, learned to be particularly successful in maintaining their rights and securing improved conditions —i.e., organization of the trade unions—have been generally frowned down upon with contempt, treated indifferently, or openly antagonized by the ministers and apparently staunch supporters of the church." [5] In the same vein, John

[1] H. B. Grose, *Aliens or Americans* (N. Y., 1906).
[2] Washington Gladden, *Applied Christianity*, 153.
[3] *Ibid.*, 153.
[4] *Ibid.*, 155.
[5] From a letter to H. Francis Perry quoted in H. Perry, "The Workingmen's Alienation from the Church," *American Journal of Sociology*, IV (March, 1899), 622-623.

B. Lennon, general secretary of the Journeymen Tailors'
Union of America, said: "Workmen stay away from the
church because their employers attend and control the
church, and in their daily life, in shop and factory, the workman receives but little of Christian treatment from the employers",[1] or, as it was more tersely put by a woman labor
leader of Haverhill, Massachusetts, "The churches are not
built by them, [the workers] nor for them, but with money
taken from them to be used against them."[2] And this complaint with many variations was constantly made.

To many of the abler leaders this situation was obviously
a challenge. Some would save labor for the church for the
sake of the church, others for the sake of suffering humanity. Reacting from the *laissez-faire* philosophy of Mill and
his associates, which for so long had dominated the intellectual class, a small but influential group of churchmen
interested themselves seriously in Christian Socialism. The
rise of Christian Socialism in America was coincident with a
revival of it in England in the 'eighties and its inspiration
was largely derived from both the Christian Socialists and
the Scientific Socialists of England. There was, however, an
American tradition which may have contributed. Radical
ministers had taken a lead in the anti-slavery movement,
and communistic religious groups had existed continuously
from the Pietist and Dunker settlements of colonial Penn-
sylvania to such nineteenth century ventures as the Hope-
dale, Massachusetts, community established by the Universalist clergyman, Adin Ballou and the Oneida, New York,
colony of the Rev. John Humphrey Noyes. It is likewise
more than probable that a careful searching of mid-nine-
teenth sermons would reveal an occasional leaning toward
Christian Socialism on the part of those not connected with

[1] *American Journal of Sociology*, IV (March, 1899), 622.
[2] *Ibid.*, 622; see also W. D. P. Bliss, "The Church in Social Service,"
Independent XL, 135.

the socialist communities. An interesting forerunner is also discovered in the Christian Labor Union of Boston (1872-1878), an organization containing several clergymen, the leading patron of which was T. Wharton Collens of New Orleans, an ex-judge and member of the Catholic Church.[1]

The movement for Christian Socialism may be said to have been definitely launched with the organization of the Society of Christian Socialists in Boston on February 18, 1889, the founder and guiding spirit of which was William Dwight Porter Bliss. Born in Constantinople, 1856, the son of an American missionary, Bliss served charges on both the Congregational and Episcopalian churches. Tremendously impressed, as were many of the leaders of his day, with the writings of Henry George, Bliss threw himself into the labor movement, became a Master Workman of the Knights of Labor and a delegate to the Union Labor Convention of 1887. It was Bliss who edited *The Dawn*, the organ of the society,[2] and who toured the country for years in an effort to organize the Christian Socialist movement.[3] Other prominent leaders included Mary A. Livermore, Edward Bellemay and Hamlin Garland.

Two years before the organization of the Society of Christian Socialists, Bliss had participated in the founding of the Church Association for the Advancement of the Interests of Labor (Episcopalian), commonly known as the "Cail." In 1891 an American branch of the English Episcopalian Society, the Christian Social Union (of which Bliss was later the traveling secretary) was also founded. Although neither society was strictly socialist, they attracted many socialists

[1] G. E. McNeill (ed.), *The Labor Movement: The Problem of Today* (Boston, 1887), 146.
[2] *The Dawn* was first published on May 15, 1889, and discontinued in 1896, by which time it had become a denominational organ. The Boston Public Library contains a file of this paper for the period May 15, 1889-April, 1892, and January, 1894-March, 1896.
[3] *Dictionary of American Biography*, II, 377-378.

within the Episcopalian church and so weakened the unde-nominational Socialist movement. They were also significant as the forerunners of several similar organizations. In 1889 a group of Baptist ministers in New York City began the brief publication of *For the Right,* a paper devoted to Chris-tian Socialism, and this same group in 1892 led in the or-ganization of the undenominational "Brotherhood of the Kingdom," a society devoted to the study and propaganda of the social teachings of Jesus. Many years later (1907) the Methodists followed with a similar society, the Methodist Federation for Social Service.

The educational foundations for the new interest in social christianity were laid not only by Christian Socialists but by many forward looking church leaders. Particularly should be mentioned two Congregational clergymen, Washington Gladden and Josiah Strong. As early as 1876 Gladden wrote a book on workingmen and their employers and his busy pen was active for the next three decades in calling the church to a new conception of its duty.[1] Josiah Strong, gen-eral secretary of the Evangelical Alliance 1886-1898 and then President of the League for Social Service,[2] even more, perhaps, than Gladden was identified with advocacy of the social gospel. His early volume *Our Country* (N. Y., 1886), was, in the opinion of Mathews, epoch making, for it not only was provocative of social sympathy but was a pioneer in the sociological approach to religion.[3] To the efforts of these men there came valuable assistance from Lyman Ab-bott, Congregational clergyman and for many years editor

[1] Among the works of Gladden especially devoted to this subject were *Workingmen and Their Employers* (1876), *Applied Christianity* (1887), *Tools and the Man* (1893), *Social Facts and Forces* (1897), *The Christian Pastor and the Workingman* (1898).

[2] Name changed in 1902 to the American Institute of Social Service.

[3] Shailer Mathews, "The Development of Social Christianity in America During the Past Twenty-Five Years," *Journal of Religion,* VII (July, 1927), 378.

of the *Christian Union* and the *Outlook,* and in academic circles from Albion W. Small, who as editor after 1895 of the *American Journal of Sociology* printed many articles on the sociological background of religion.

The clarion call once sounded, its notes quickly caught the attention of many of the younger clergy and sociologically inclined laymen. Richard Heber Newton, rector of All Soul's Church, New York, and one of the earliest American clergymen to introduce institutional features into church work, published a little volume *Social Studies* (N. Y., 1887) in which he assembled several articles on social problems, dating back to 1876. The young economist, Richard T. Ely, published in 1889 his *Social Aspects of Christianity,* Rev. George D. Herron, professor at Grinnell, wrote in the early 'nineties several powerful appeals,[1] and in 1901 Francis G. Peabody, in charge of the course in practical ethics at the Harvard Divinity School, a man who had been dealing with social problems in his lectures since 1883, published his *Jesus Christ and the Social Question* (N. Y., 1901). In 1908 Bliss found interest sufficiently widespread to edit an *Encyclopædia of Social Reform.* As the new century advanced the tiny vanguard of prophets was augmented by many of the ablest leaders in each of the denominations,—Father John A. Ryan, Bishop Francis J. McConnell, John Haynes Holmes, Shailer Mathews, Harry Ward, Charles Stelzle and a host of others. Above all the Baptist, Walter Rauschenbush, impressed his ideas upon the rising generation of theological students, and his books offered to many of the younger clergy a new source of inspiration.[2]

[1] *The Larger Christ* (1891), *The Call of the Cross* (1892), *The New Redemption* (1893), *The Christian Society* (1894), and *The Christian State* (1895).

[2] Walter Rauschenbush, *Christianity and the Social Crisis* (N. Y., 1907); *Christianizing the Social Order* (N. Y., 1912).

This growing interest in the social gospel soon had its effect upon the curriculum of the theological seminaries. No longer could they devote themselves exclusively to history, languages and exegesis, but were forced to introduce or broaden courses in practical theology, missions and sociology. Some inklings of a sociological interest in the theological seminaries are to be found as early as the 'seventies. Princeton announced in 1871 that it "proposed to add next year an Ethical Course, discussing Christian Ethics theoretically, historically and in their living connection with various branches of Social Science—"[1] Professor W. J. Tucker at Andover in 1879 took over the work in practical theology and made it virtually a course in sociology, and in the 'eighties Harvard, Hartford and Newton interested themselves in the sociological approach to ethics. In describing in 1891-2 the course in Christian Ethics at the Universalist Seminary at Tufts the catalogue noted that "The Seniors attend more especially to Practical Ethics, dealing with the leading contemporary problems, such as Education, Charities, State Aid, Temperance, Socialism, etc."[2] A new burst of interest took place in 1892 when the Divinity School of the University of Chicago appointed Charles R. Henderson professor of Ecclesiastical Sociology and the Chicago Theological Seminary made Graham Taylor professor of Christian Sociology. The lead taken by these mid-western institutions was followed within the next decade by all of the more progressive seminaries. Christian sociology in 1880 was a subject hardly known in American theological training; by 1910 the courses in that subject were among the most popular in the seminaries.

This great interest in Christian sociology and in the "social gospel" was not artificially aroused by a small group

[1] Catalogue of Princeton Theological Seminary (Princeton, 1871-2), 15.
[2] Tufts College *Catalogue* (1891-2), 92.

of conscientious leaders who took seriously what they called the "social message" of Christ. It was, in no small degree, a reflection of a period which for want of a better name might be styled the "era of disillusionment." The grinding economic battles of the 'eighties and 'nineties, the monetary question, the trust and railroad problems, the tariff controversy, and the agrarian discontent had all sobered the American people, and the opening years of the new century found a nation seriously ready to take stock of its civilization. Not even the exhilaration of an absurdly easy victory in a popular war dispelled the mood, and the reaction came with the era of "muckraking." Like other institutions in close touch with the popular drift, the church found itself responding to the new day. Even in the darkest period of *laissez-faire* the church had continued its philanthropic work, but with the coming of a new social consciousness, an added impetus and a new turn was given to it. It was, for instance, a group of Episcopalian laymen who founded the East Side House in New York (1890), the Methodists who founded the Northwestern settlement in Chicago (1891), Professor William J. Tucker of Andover Theological Seminary who was influential in the establishment of the Andover House (since 1895 the South End House),[1] and Rev. George Hodges, who organized the Kingsley House in Pittsburgh (1893).[2]

Fortunately for the social gospel a practical demonstration of what it could do was early given and remained an object lesson throughout this era of reform. When William S. Rainsford became pastor in 1883 of St. George's parish on the lower East Side of New York the membership had dwindled to about twenty families. Sixteen years later he

[1] Eleanor H. Woods, *Robert A. Woods, Champion of Democracy* (Boston, 1929).
[2] R. A. Woods and A. J. Kennedy, *The Settlement Horizon* (N. Y., 1922), Chap. IV.

had a membership of more than seven thousand people, of whom five thousand lived in tenements, seventeen hundred in boarding houses and apartments, while the majority of those living in private homes were domestic servants.[1] This was done by making the church not alone a place for spiritual refreshment, but a complete community center where a medical department and infirmary were maintained, and where social recreation and educational facilities were afforded.[2] Gladden, Strong and Rauschenbusch told the church what it should do, Rainsford showed it how.

It was likewise the aristocratic Episcopalian church, as we have seen, which early in the movement sponsored the organization of two societies aiming to break down the antipathy of labor toward the church,[3] and which in 1900 appointed a Standing Committee on Church and Labor.[4] In that year their example was followed by the national council of the Congregational Church when it appointed a labor committee,[5] later (1904) known as the Industrial Committee, to study such questions as organized labor, child labor, immigration and socialism, and at its national meeting in 1904 urged its churches "to take a deeper interest in the labor question and to get a more intelligent understanding of the aims of organized labor."[6] The Presbyterian Church, hoping to effect a *rapprochement* with labor, established in 1903 a Department of Church and Labor under the Board of Home Missions, and put at its head Charles Stelzle, a cler-

[1] L. A. Weigle, *American Idealism* (New Haven, 1928), 216. The work of several of the early institutional churches is described by Josiah Strong, *Religious Movements for Social Betterment* (N. Y., 1900), 15 ff.

[2] David Graham Phillips, "The Business Organization of a Church," *Harper's Monthly Magazine,* CVII (July, 1903), 208-13.

[3] Church Association for the Advancement of Labor (1889) and the American branch of the Christian Social Union (1901).

[4] *Encyclopædia of Social Reform,* 211-212.

[5] *Minutes of the National Council of the Congregational Churches, 1901* (Boston, 1901), 37.

[6] *Minutes of the National Council of the Congregational Churches, 1904* (Boston, 1904), 414-429.

gyman who had served an apprenticeship at the machinist's trade.[1]

The Methodist Episcopal Church (North) had also its prophets. Bishop John H. Vincent, a founder and leader of the Chautauqua movement, had requested the economist, Professor E. W. Bemis, to prepare a tract in 1890 on "The Relation of the Church to Social Questions," a little pamphlet which urged the minister "to preach his gospel everywhere as a means of reforming this world fully as much as of preparing for the next," and this pamphlet the good bishop presented to every minister whom he ordained. Various memorials urging a more definite social program were presented to successive General Conferences from 1892 on, and in 1907, as we have noted, the Methodist Federation for Social Service was organized by ministers and laymen of that church.[2] The matter finally came to a head in 1908 when the General Conference recognized the newly founded Federation, directed that three bishops be appointed to its Council and ordered the Committee on the State of the Church to prepare a statement on social questions. This statement, unanimously adopted, put the church on record as favoring protection of the worker against dangerous machinery, occupational diseases and other evils of the industrial system, as favoring the abolition of child labor, the "sweating system," the seven-day week, and as urging arbitration, a living wage, workingmen's compensation and "suitable provision" for old age. "The organization of labor," asserted the Conference, "is not only the right of laborers and conducive to their welfare, but is incidentally of great benefit to society at large." [3] An even more advanced

[1] Charles Stelzle, *A Son of the Bowery* (N. Y., 1926)), Chapters VII, VIII.
[2] Ward, Harry F., *A Year Book of the Church and Social Service in the United States* (N. Y., 1914), 43-47.
[3] *Journal of the Twenty-Fifth Delegated General Conference of the Methodist Episcopal Church, held in Baltimore, Maryland, May 6-June 1, 1908* (N. Y., 1908) 134-137, 545-549.

stand was taken in 1912 with Rev. Harry F. Ward in charge of the work as field secretary of the Federation.

With the leading denominations expressing themselves in this manner it is not surprising that the Federal Council of the Churches of Christ in America, finally organized in 1908, should from the start advocate a forward-looking social program. Such a stand was also to be expected both from the liberal leadership of the council and from the forerunners of the movement, notably such a body as the New York Federation of the Churches and Christian Organizations formed in 1896 to eliminate sectarian rivalry and coöperate for a common end. One of the earliest moves of the Federal Council was to adopt with some additions the Methodist statement of 1908.[1] With the pronouncement of the Federal Council practically all of the Protestant churches were now officially on record as advocates of a liberal social gospel. The only great denomination outside the Federation, the Catholic Church, had early been encouraged by the encyclical, *Rerum Novarum* (1891), to bestir itself in behalf of labor. It was not until the World War, however, that the American Catholics through the National Catholic War Councils (1917) and its successor, the National Catholic Welfare Council (1919), formulated a definite social program, but its plan, when finally enunciated, was both definite and far-reaching.[2]

Other evidences of the growing interest of organized religion in the wage earner were not wanting. In many cities ministerial associations appointed "fraternal delegates" to the City Central labor union, and in 1905 the American Federation of Labor at its Pittsburgh meeting recommended that its state and city bodies follow this example wherever

[1] *Federal Council of the Churches of Christ in America, Report of the First Meeting of the Federal Council, Philadelphia, 1908,* 239.
[2] *National Catholic War Council, Social Reconstruction* (Wash., 1919).

practical.[1] Various denominations urged their pastors to observe Labor Sunday on the Sabbath preceding Labor Day.[2] The kind of thing that Rainsford had done in the 'eighties was now the aim of many city churches, and the practicability of it was demonstrated anew by Stelzle in 1910 when he took over an old church about to close at the corner of Fourteenth Street and Second Avenue, New York, and speedily made it a humming center of community interest and social service.[3]

Nor were evidences lacking of a developing conscience in the church. At the height of the muckraking movement in 1905 Washington Gladden threw a bomb into the annual meeting of the Congregational Mission Board at Seattle when he introduced a resolution that the Board should "neither invite nor solicit donations to its funds from persons whose gains had been made by methods morally reprehensible or socially injurious.[4] This resolution was finally tabled, but the debate over the acceptance of "tainted money" which followed in the religious and secular press, caused much searching of hearts. "A year ago," said Mr. Dooley in 1906 regarding John D. Rockefeller, "anybody wud take his money. Now if he wanted to give it even to Chancellor Day he'd have to meet him in a barn at midnight." [5]

Impassioned pleas of social-minded clergyman, *pronunciamentos* of official bodies and the work of institutional churches, however, did not make a sociologically minded church. The South, destined before many years to assume leadership in the fight to preserve the old theology, had not yet experienced the full force of the industrial revolution

[1] *Report of the Proceedings of the Twenty-Fifth Annual Convention of the American Federation of Labor,* 155; Stelzle, *A Son of the Bowery,* 89.
[2] Stelzle, 89.
[3] *Ibid.,* Chap. XI.
[4] Washington Gladden, *Recollections* (Boston, 1909), Chap. XXVI.
[5] F. P. Dunne, "Mr. Dooley on the Power of the Press," *American Magazine,* LXII (Oct., 1906), 611.

and was little interested in the social gospel. Christian Socialism had found many adherents in the middle West during the throes of Populism, but with returning agricultural prosperity, interest in the new religion was found chiefly in the larger centers. In the manufacturing East the churches were dominated by the well-to-do, whose bourgeois philosophy might incline them toward philanthropy but instinctively turned them from the social teachings of Jesus. Bliss, who had given his life to the new gospel, wrote bitterly in 1906 that in New York, a "city almost crying out for reform," "we have not one denomination . . . to which economic or social reform can look with any hope." [1] Four years later John Haynes Holmes asserted that "in the great battle of industrial democracy, the distinctive battle of our time, the church is the champion not of the downtrodden many, but of the dominant and selfish few," and offered as the chief reasons, excessive denominationalism, too much interest in "religion for export," concentration on the world to come rather than the evils of this world, the theory that the church had nothing to do with political or industrial questions, and the tyranny of the pew. "The typical church of today, especially in the city," he said, "is a class institution, and the men and women responsible for the peculiar political and industrial evils, are the very ones who compose that class which is today inside the church." [2] Harsh as this criticism of the church sounds, it was not without cause. Any serious challenge of the existing order found the church on the side of the *status quo*. The *Bibliotheca Sacra*, for instance, had some interest in the problems of the unfortunate or persecuted, but it also found room for a vicious and lying

[1] W. D. P. Bliss, "The Churches in Social Service," *Independent*, LX (Feb. 8, 1906), 314.

[2] John Haynes Holmes, "The Indifference of the Church to Child Labor Reform," *Proceedings of the Sixth Annual Conference on Child Labor* (N. Y., 1910), 31.

attack upon Debs at the time of the Pullman strike.[1] When "Golden Rule" Jones and his successor, Brand Whitlock, attempted to introduce some literal Christianity into the administration of a twentieth-century city, they found their chief opposition from the churches.[2] Labor's early distrust of the church persisted, and the influence of the church in healing labor disputes or effecting better relations between labor and capital appears to have been slight.[3]

The failure of the social gospel to make greater progress was due to many causes. It rose and declined with the whole liberal movement. The wave of reform which blazed out in the journalism of the "muckrakers" reached its climax in the Progressive campaign of 1912. Soon after came the World War, during which time the churches found some compensation for violating the principles of the Prince of Peace by special war work, but any reform movement was bound to languish except where war needs forced an artificial speed. With peace came the black reaction, when mere identification with a humane movement meant an honored place upon the black list of some so-called "patriotic society" and almost any effort for human betterment was denounced as emanating from Moscow. Certain reforms, of course, had already been accomplished, as in the matter of labor legislation, and with the return of prosperity after the depression of 1920, the need for a thorough revamping of the social order was, perhaps, not so evident. Furthermore, the church had become identified with one or two specific reforms, particularly prohibition, and its interest in the world of everyday was largely taken up with the attainment and perpetuation of legislative prohibition.[4] The readi-

[1] Swift Holbrook, "The American Republic and the Debs Insurrection," *Bibliotheca Sacra*, LII, 224 ff.
[2] Brand Whitlock, *Forty Years of It* (N. Y., 1914).
[3] Thompson, *op. cit.*, 112.
[4] P. H. Odegard, *Pressure Politics* (N. Y., 1928) describes the Anti-Saloon League as "The Church in Action," Chap. I.

ness with which the American church surrendered itself to the warmakers, to the hatred of wartime, and to the post-war reaction is a disheartening story indeed, and it left the church badly discredited among humanitarians. How the church could reconcile the Sermon on the Mount with its wartime belligerency and still maintain its self respect can be explained only by a belief in miracles.[1] Even in the war-time reaction, however, certain leaders again showed themselves far ahead of the rank and file. The Inter-Church World Movement, organized to use the coöperative spirit of the war days for the greater glory of God throughout the world, was headed by men who insisted upon an investigation of the steel strike of 1919,[2] but their activity in this respect is believed to have caused a withdrawal of financial support and an untimely end to the movement.

The church had likewise hardly recovered from the vitiating experience of the World War before its social energies were again undermined by a revival of the time-worn struggle between liberal theology and "fundamentalism." By 1900 the battle for a more liberal theology seemed all but won. The Biblical story of creation so gorgeously retold by Milton had been badly battered by the cumulative researches of Darwin and his successors. The application of scientific methods to the study of the scriptures and of religion had resulted in the "higher criticism" and in a truer perspective of Christianity. The new psychology even questioned the possibility of "freedom of the will," and numerous other phases of dogma were under fire. Recognizing the implications of the newer science, the more liberal of the clergy did what they could to reconcile science and religion and turned

[1] Granville Hicks, "The Parsons and the War," *American Mercury*, Feb., 1927.
[2] *Report on the Steel Strike of 1919 by the Commission of Inquiry, The Interchurch World Movement With the Technical Assistance of the Bureau of Industrial Research, N. Y.* (N. Y., 1920).

their attention from theology to ethics. The older school retired in sullen discomfiture, defeated but not convinced. Their opportunity, however, was not long in coming. In the conservative reaction following the World War, a reaction world-wide in its influence, but particularly strong in the United States, the old theology blossomed anew. As the exponents of the new and the old lined up in their religious convocations to do battle for their cause, the problems of human brotherhood naturally attracted little attention in the prevailing atmosphere of suspicion and recrimination. In those denominations where fundamentalists and modernists struggle for control, the social gospel has little to expect, and it seems likely to languish until a new interest in reform sweeps the nation. The church, lagging in the rear of human progress, will, if true to tradition, wait for some outside impetus to again give it its cue.

BAYLE'S PROFANATION OF SACRED HISTORY

by

Howard Robinson

IX

BAYLE'S PROFANATION OF
SACRED HISTORY

THE *Dictionnaire Historique et Critique* of Pierre Bayle has long been regarded as one of the most important influences in modern thought. The "rationalistic" century was just about to open when it was first issued from a Rotterdam press in 1697. Since Pierre Bayle had already made sharp attacks on many superstitions, on intolerance in church and state, and on careless thinking in general, the *Dictionary* came as the climax to a life time of extraordinary literary activity. It also ushered in the critical and destructive influences for which the eighteenth century is well known. Emile Faguet has not inaptly named it "the Bible of the eighteenth century."

Bayle originally intended, by collecting errors in dictionaries and histories, to form a work that would be a "touchstone of books," "an insurance office of the republic of letters." When the *Dictionary* appeared, it proved to be that, and more. The work is essentially a general biographical dictionary, ranging from Adam down to the date of its publication. A brief main article stated the important facts, to which Bayle appended lengthy notes where he gave free vent to his critical judgment, discussed motives of conduct, treated matters of religion, morality, philosophy, and history. The great vogue of the work was partly the result of the author's efforts to make it piquant. Many a note not only enlightened the reader but lightened the *Dictionary*. Some thought Bayle altogether too flippant in discussing such persons as Helen of Troy, St. Augustine, and "little" Albert the Great. His scepticism seemed to be wielded with a malign satisfaction as he discussed the checkered history of Christianity and the philosophical crudities of the Christian epic. The method proved so successful that the *Dictionary* did much to mould the thought of the eighteenth century. Voltaire, who was deeply indebted to Bayle, called it the "bibliothèque des nations," and the author the "avocat-général des philosophes."

Possibly the greatest innovation was Bayle's frank examination of Biblical history. It seemed rank "atheism"—to use the term in the loose way common at the time—to regard sacred history in the same way as its profane complement. This boldness was a distinct contribution to modern historical criticism. It took much more courage to examine dispassionately the life of King David than to sweep into the land of fable King Pharamond, Priam's mythical grandson, and the presumed founder of the Gaulish monarchy. It is to this aspect of Bayle's historical scepticism—his disregard for the sacredness of sacred history—that it seems worth while to call attention. Here he was attacking the greatest obstacle that yet remained in the way of the historical critic.

The immemorial division of history into sacred and profane yet remained without a serious, open challenge. The few encyclopædias previous to Bayle's *Dictionary* showed little perception of the problem. Knowledge was yet being summarized from a theological viewpoint. Some advance had been made, it is true, earlier in the century, with the tendency to use the modern languages in place of Latin, and an alphabetical arrangement instead of a topical grouping. But the older bisection of history remained. Juigné's *Dictionnaire Théologique, Historique, etc.* (1644) accepted Biblical history at its face value; David, for example, was "one of the most perfect men who ever held a scepter, so full of all virtue that he had witness from God that he was a man after His own heart." Moréri's *Grand Dictionnaire Historique* (1674) was the most noteworthy of the time. The author, a devout Catholic, admitted that it might not be perfect, "for even the sun has its spots." His *Dictionary* was decidedly uncritical, the subtitle fittingly describing it as a *"mélange curieux de l'histoire sacrée et profane."* [1]

Nor were the writers on historical method any bolder. Bodin's famous *Methodus and Facilem Historiarum Cognitionem* (1566) regarded history not as a unity but a trinity— history was divided into the human, the natural, and the divine. The last was "sui natura plane immutabilem." The critic was "scelus" who would try to "go beyond the sacred fountains of the Hebrews." Subsequent writers on historic method before Bayle but reiterate this accepted truth. [2]

Bishop Bossuet's *Discours sur l'Histoire Universelle,* which appeared in 1681, was a brilliant sketch of the workings of Providence. The great ecclesiastic was conscious of the need of "adjusting the course of profane history with that of sacred history;" in case of difficulty, however, preference would certainly be given to Holy Scripture, "even if one did not know it was dictated by the Holy Spirit." In-

[1] *Moréri* had gone through seven French editions before Bayle set out to correct it. It was put into the English in 1694, "the first of the sort that ever was extant in English," according to the Preface. Such works as *Chambers* (1728), the *Britannica* (1768) and the *Encyclopédie* of Diderot (1751) were yet to appear. Biblical encyclopædias were as uncritical as *Moréri,* such as H. R. Simon's folio *Dictionnaire de la Bible* of 1693. Richard Simon's *Histoire Critique du Vieux Testament* (1678) was a pioneer in the textual criticism of the Bible, yet Simon did not doubt the plenary inspiration of Scripture.

[2] To La Poplinière, Moses was "the first, the most worthy, and the most universal historian among men." (*L'Histoire des Histoires,* 1599, p. 139.) The other "methods" of the time furnished no jarring note. The writer has examined the anonymous *La Science de l'Histoire* (1665), Le-Moyne's *De l'Histoire* (1670), Saint-Réal's *L'Usage de l'Histoire* (1671), Rapin's *Instructions pour l'Histoire* (1677), and Thomassin's *Méthode d'étudier . . . les Historiens profanes par rapport . . . aux Ecritures* (1693).

[149]

deed, Bossuet was not so much the historian as the apologist using history for his purpose. "What an evidence of truth," he wrote, "to see that, in the times when profane histories have related to us only fables, or at best confused and half-forgotten facts, Scripture, which is unquestionably the oldest book in the world, leads us by so many precise events to their principle, which is God."[1]

Even in the sceptical school of thought there was no open objection to the time-honored division of history into sacred and profane. La Mothe le Vayer, the chief link between Montaigne and Bayle, was an historical Pyrrhonist. But he never applied his criticism to Scripture. At times one feels that he is about to do it, or would like to, but the courage is lacking. His scepticism expressly accepted "divine history, which has its foundations in our respect for the Old and New Testaments, . . . on which one cannot, without impiety, form the slightest doubt, since the Holy Spirit has revealed and dictated it." Yet La Mothe le Vayer's questionings were so insistent that he confessed in one of his last works that "only faith in the true religion can prevent us from giving way to the temptations that the enemies of our repose and of our salvation suggest to us."[2]

Bayle was tempted in all points like La Mothe le Vayer— and gave way to the temptation. An examination of the *Dictionary's* treatment of biblical characters will show the depths to which Bayle "fell."

According to the Preface, Bayle intended to give an account of most of the persons mentioned in the Bible. He actually confined himself, however, to some of the principal characters of the Old Testament, in order to give more space to "moderns." There are long articles on Adam, Eve,

[1] French edition of 1682, pp. 26, 46-7, 179.
[2] The first quotation is from *Du Peu de Certitude qu'il y a dans l'Histoire* (1668), p. 78; the last, from *Les Soliloques Sceptiques* (ed. of 1875, p. 11), first published in 1670.

Cain, Abel, Lamech, Noah, and Ham. The Abrahamic stories fascinated Bayle, with the result that articles appear on Abraham, Sarah, Hagar, and Abimelech. King David received uncommon publicity, as we shall find. The New Testament was almost completely avoided.

Bayle's approach was one of seeming respect. If there is no certain interpretation of a circumstance, Bayle virtuously suggests that the best way out is "to implore the direction of the Holy Spirit." But he adds, "I do not see how this can compose differences, for each will boast he has implored the direction of the Holy Spirit." This, in turn, leads him to censure severely the "distillers of the sacred letters," who "use the word of God as a nose of wax, to the great scandal of good and pious souls, and to the great satisfaction of profane men and free thinkers." He objects to two standards of testing narratives, "two weights and two measures," as he put it, asserting in his article on David, for example, that the "Holy Scripture relates the facts only historically, and, therefore, every one is at liberty to pass a judgment upon them." In the same article he affects surprise that Saul should not have recognized David at the time of the duel with Goliath: "If such a narrative as this should be found in Thucydides or Livy, all the critics would unanimously conclude that someone had made foolish additions. But no suspicion ought to be entertained of the Bible. Nevertheless, some have been so bold as to pretend, etc." [1]

The members of the first family did not escape. Bayle collected all the absurd rabbinical legends about Adam and Eve, and added others that did not "seem contrary to the analogy of faith or probability." He did this, not because he believed them, but in order to ridicule the credulities regarding the "first family." He gravely discusses the question as

[1] The Beuchot edition of the *Dictionnaire* (16 vols., 8vo, 1820) is the most accessible. Reference is made to it. See, for the quotations in this paragraph, vi, 328, Note A; xiii, 71, B; v, 409; v, 404, D.

to whether Adam knew as much as Aristotle, and whether he was bisexual, "as some have asserted." He inquires as to whether Abel's dispute with Cain was over a woman. There is a lengthy inquiry as to why God sent out Cain with a mark on him, "lest any finding him should smite him." Since there were no other people on the earth at the time save the family of which Cain was a member, Bayle maliciously suggests that Cain's troubled conscience "must have made him forget what his father, doubtless, had often told him about the origin of mankind." [1]

Bayle finds that the "account of Abraham's family is attended with numberless difficulties. Not the least, were the moral standards of the father and source of the faithful." A part of the main article on Sarah will illustrate Bayle's approach.

> We ought not to forget that she (Sarah) was very beautiful, and that her beauty and the complaisance she had for her husband—not to call herself his wife but his sister—exposed her to the danger of two rapes, whereby her chastity had suffered shipwreck, had not God intervened. A singular providence saved her in this danger. . . . One cannot easily clear Abraham and Sarah in this matter, nor about the business of Hagar.

In a long note on the last sentence quoted, Abraham's conduct is tested and found wanting: "The suppression of a truth is a real lie, if it is intended to give the hearer a false impression. . . . Abraham and Sarah were guilty of this." [2]

The treatment of Abraham's shortcomings is mild in comparison with the picture drawn of David. It was bad enough to pick flaws in Abraham, but to sully David's character was positive impiety. David was the "man after God's own heart," a prophet, and the acknowledged author of the Psalms, the accepted hymnal of the Christian church.[3] Yet

[1] I, 198; iv, 301, and Genesis iv, 15.
[2] I, 90, C; xiii, 100; xiii, 107, D.
[3] See I Sam. xiii, 14 and Acts xiii, 22. The significance of Bayle's emphasis may be realized if one recalls the first verse of the New Testa-

he was handled as freely as if he were Caligula, Louis XI, or Henry VIII. After a lively summary of the biblical narrative, the main article on David continues in more pointed fashion:

David's piety was so conspicuous in his Psalms and in many of his actions that one cannot sufficiently admire him. There is another thing no less admirable in his conduct, that he was so skilful in accommodating his piety to the loose maxims of the art of governing. It is generally believed that his adultery with Bathsheba, the murder of Uriah, and the numbering of the people are the only faults with which he is to be reproached. This is a great mistake, for there was much else in his life deserving of censure. He is a sun of holiness in the church, where his writings scatter a fruitful glow of consolation and piety that one cannot sufficiently extol. But the sun had its spots. Even in his dying words we find the obliquities of politics. . . . Let us conclude by saying that the history of King David should reassure many crowned heads, alarmed as they may be by those who insist that it is impossible for a king to be saved. (v, 409).

Many of the "spots" were elaborated in the notes. In one he makes a study of David's buccaneering activities, when he occupied a Philistine town lent him by the king of Gath.

To speak plainly, this conduct was very bad; in order to conceal one fault (sacking a Philistine town), he committed a greater (making the king believe he had attacked the Hebrews). . . . If to-day a person of any nation behaved himself as did David, he would be called very dishonorable names. . . . What opinion, I say, could we have of a prince of the blood of France, who, disgraced at court, went about raising contributions in the countries where he camped, and put to the sword all that refused to pay his taxes? (v, 410).

Bayle, of course, would not have thought of testing David by seventeenth-century standards had not David been protected by biblical inspiration. "The profound respect one should have for this great king and prophet should not prevent our disapproval of his faults. Otherwise, we shall give

ment: "The book of the generation of Jesus Christ, the son of David, the son of Abraham."

the profane reason to reproach us, and to say that an action, to be just, only needs to be done by persons we reverence." The longest and most outrageous note enlarges on "many other things in his life that deserve censure." David's polygamy leads to the sneer: "We cannot say, with regard to the pleasures of love, that he took much pains to mortify nature." David's cunning at the time of Absalom's revolt is called "unworthy of a prophet, a saint, and a righteous man." His wars are also condemned, "for Holy Scripture represents him pretty frequently as the aggressor." The death of Adonijah, and the slaughter of the people of Ammon were the result of a policy "in some respects like that of the Ottomans." [1]

Such a frank outburst of moral disgust with the "man after God's own heart" had not been known. The article on David was so forthright that it raised the morals of Old Testament heroes and the sacredness of sacred history into the realm of controversy.

The local Huguenot consistory—Bayle was still a member of the Reformed church—felt impelled to action. The daring author was brought before the consistory, and was lectured for having drawn a "frightful picture of David" and for having treated many of his actions "in an unworthy and scandalous manner." Bayle promised to leave no "stumbling-block" in the article on David when the second edition of the *Dictionary* appeared. The ecclesiastical body even gave him directions for the revision:

He shall entirely reform the article, David, . . . and in doing so shall conform to what Scripture says of this great prophet. He ought even to write a vindication of him, and to show that, far from judging the actions of this prince by the common and ordinary course of earthly kings, he shall show that David was authorized to exterminate the Canaanites; that we ought to be silent where Scripture is silent; that its silence, far from giving a pretext against David, is rather equivalent to an approba-

[1] V, 412, 415, 418.

tion; and, finally, he shall take care to establish solidly the prophetical and canonical authority of David's writings. (xvi, 288-9).

Though Bayle agreed to whitewash David, the job was very carelessly done in the second edition of the *Dictionary* (1702). In the main article he omitted much of the long quotation given above. But the phrase, "the sun had its spots," was retained, and a new note added after this fashion:

His amours with Uriah's wife and the killing of Uriah by his orders are two very great crimes. But he was so troubled for them, and atoned by so admirable a repentance, that this incident contributes not a little to the edification of faithful souls. One learns from it the fragility of saints, and how to lament our sins. . . . I suppress certain things in this edition because some persons, who are very much more knowing than I in such matters, have assured me that all these clouds are easily dispersed. . . . They may convince us of David's innocence in a conduct, which in general appears bad, and would be so to-day. (v, 405-6).

Four of the most objectionable notes were omitted. At the end of one that was retained, Bayle omitted the sentence, "What scandal is here given to pious souls to see so much infamy in the family of this king!" But Bayle forgot to "blue-pencil" the "infamies" that preceded this judgment!

The consistory, indeed, might better have kept quiet. Not only was Bayle remiss in his corrections, but the demand for the original article was so great that it was reprinted as a separate pamphlet. All the later editions of the *Dictionary*—there were eleven in French besides English and German translations—include both articles. The reader was allowed to choose the one he preferred.

The attack on, and defense of, the *Dictionary* in the first half of the eighteenth century, is one of the most interesting chapters in the history of rationalism. The Parisian censor, the Abbé Renaudot, refused to allow its appearance from a French press despite the desire of the book trade. Among the reasons he gave were "the licentious and impertinent reflections on the history of Abraham. . . . What he has written on David is still worse." And he added: "We are astonished to see such things tolerated in a country where they profess to believe in the Bible." Renaudot's strictures were published in Rotterdam by one of Bayle's bitterest enemies, the Huguenot pastor, Jurieu. The latter also attacked Bayle directly, accusing him of "pushing Christianity to its ruin" and of mistreating "the greatest saint in the Old Testament." To Jurieu the *Dictionary* was the most pernicious work that had appeared for a hundred years.[1]

Jurieu saw clearly the dangerous influence the *Dictionary* was to exert. It became a veritable arsenal for rationalism both in England and in France. Not the least of its influences was the effect it had on the approach to sacred history. From this point of view the article on David proves to have been of uncommon importance.

The *Dictionary* was first translated into English in 1710. Not long after Bernard Mandeville published his *Fable of the Bees or Private Vices Publick Benefits*, with the result that Baylian scepticism was blamed for this surprising paradox. Yet so great was the demand of the English reading public that a second edition of the *Dictionary* appeared during the years 1734-38. One result of the revived interest in Bayle was a renewed defense of David against the attacks of a writer who was accused, curiously enough, of attacking morals as well as religion. In 1740, an Irish clergyman, Patrick Delany by name, published a three-volume *Historical Account of the Life and Reign of David*, "in which Mr. Bayle's criticisms upon the conduct and character of

---

[1] See *Le Jugement de l'Abbé Renaudot* (1697). For Jurieu's attack on the *Dictionary*, see *Le Philosophe de Rotterdam accusé, atteint et convaincu* (1706, pp. 5, 97, 134). Jurieu was largely responsible for the dismissal of Bayle from his teaching position in 1693.

that prince are fully considered." Delany proved so ardent a defender of David that he apologized for those crimes of which the Hebrew king himself repented!

But Delany is hardly representative. In the meantime, Viscount Bolingbroke had written his *Letters on the Study and Use of History*, in which the Baylian point of view is expressed in no uncertain fashion. The third letter dealt at length with ancient history both sacred and profane. After a sharp discussion of profane history, Bolingbroke turns to the Bible as "all that remains to give us light on the first ages." "But even these books," he wrote, "must be reputed insufficient to the purpose by every candid and impartial man, who considers either their authorities as histories or the matter they contain." He found the Jewish Scriptures "broken and confused, full of additions, made we neither know when nor by whom." He would limit their authenticity to those parts that concerned law, doctrine, and prophecy. The contents were examined in the Baylian manner. Bolingbroke makes much of the rabbinical lore, such as the story, for example, that Abel's death was caused by a dispute over a woman. Reference is made, also, to the arguments that "Bayle and others have employed" by which the "authenticity and sense of the Bible have become disputable." [1]

Though Bolingbroke wrote his *Letters* while the second English edition of *Bayle* was appearing, they were not published until after his death. Their appearance was the signal for a renewed defense of Scripture. Bishop Clayton published a *Vindication*, and Abraham Le Moine rose to the *Defence of the Sacred History*. The well-known John Leland stepped into the lists with some *Reflections*, and a writer who was unwilling to reveal his name launched *Critical Remarks* on these "posthumous abortions of his Lord-

[1] The first edition (1752), I, pp. 83, 94, 113, 122, 181.

ship's brain." And these are but a selection of the replies that the "late Lord Bolingbroke" aroused.

The blameworthiness of Bayle was brought out even more clearly by a controversy that arose just after the death of George II. On November 9, 1760, Samuel Chandler preached a sermon in the Old Jewry on the "occasion of the death of his late Majesty." The text was the epitaph of the "sacred historian" about David: "And he died in a good old age, being full of days, riches, and honor." Chandler lauded David as having the "peculiar protection and favour of Divine Providence," declared that David's private virtues were "many and distinguishing," and asserted that he is always spoken of "in the sacred writings in terms of high respect." The preacher was led to make the comparison between the two kings by the happy coincidence that George's reign lasted just as long as David's—thirty-three years.

A Deist, who knew his *Bayle,* thought this too good a chance to let slip. Accordingly, in 1761, there appeared a pamphlet on *The History of the Man after God's Own Heart.* The author—probably Peter Annet—declared that George II had been compared to a monarch in no way resembling him. The pamphleteer rose to the defense of George II and the honor of the British nation, though the condemnation of the "sacred character" of David was his real motive. Delany's "pious palliations" were brushed aside. After drawing a shocking picture of tribal banditry, Annet concluded: "There, Christians, are the outlines of the life of a Jew, whom you are not ashamed to continue extolling as the man after God's own heart!" The pamphlet made it clear that the chief source was "Monsieur Bayle."

Chandler replied with a *Review* of the pamphlet, in which its author was accused of being "little more than a retailer of Mr. Bayle, and a retailer without Mr. Bayle's decency and good manners." Others, too, came to the assistance of the hard-beset Hebrew ruler. Porteus Beilby preached a university sermon in 1761 on the *Character of David* in which he rightly judged Annet's attack to be directed, not only against, David, but against the "authority of the sacred books." He held that the famous phrase describing David did not refer to private virtues but to public conduct, to David's abhorrence of idolatry. In the next year Dr. Thomas Patten attempted to "vindicate King David." "As far as men can judge," he wrote, "it doth not appear that any king's character would be insulted by a comparison of it with that of King David."

The original pamphleteer continued the battle of the books by a *Letter to the Reverend Dr. Samuel Chandler;* he insisted anew that to examine the life of David was to examine a "piece of history." Chandler retorted with a *Critical History of the Life of David.* Though he argued that David is the "man after God's own heart" because of his public service, he did his best to make the King a moral man. Chandler's efforts to palliate the "affair" with Bathsheba certainly rise to the level of the heroic; the wife of Uriah is blamed rather ungraciously as "too easily yielding to the king's inclination, and thereby rendering it almost impossible for him to suppress it." [1]

In France, the Baylian viewpoint was reaffirmed again and again. The philosopher of Rotterdam could have had no more potent "retailer" of his ideas than Voltaire. Though they differed much in temperament, the dependence of Voltaire on Bayle is recorded on almost every page of the former's voluminous prose works. Bayle is woven inextricably

[1] Published in 2 vols., 1766; see I, 325-330; II, 245. There were a number of other answers. Some saw the difficulty of defending David; Edward Harwood, a biblical critic, deplored the attempt. William Warburton in his *Divine Legation of Moses Demonstrated* even held Chandler's sermon to have been ill advised.

into Voltaire's thinking, so much so that Sainte-Beuve, for example, held the one to be the great precursor of the other. Emile Faguet has strikingly put it in saying that Voltaire was really a "bilious Bayle."

The "master of doubt for the whole eighteenth century" had much to do with shaping Voltaire's philosophy of history. In the *Siècle de Louis XIV*, Bayle is given honorable mention as a writer who was persecuted "because of his famous article on David." That Voltaire knew the famous article well is shown by his references again and again to Davidic morality. In the *Dictionnaire Philosophique*, there is an elaborate article on the "Nero of the Hebrews," in which the story is told with Baylian boldness. It concluded: "When and by whom were these marvels written? I know not, but I am sure they were not written by a Polybius or a Tacitus." In the article on History in the same work, Voltaire reaffirms his conviction that Bayle had "good reason to believe that all the facts reported in the Jewish books were not holy actions."[1]

Voltaire professed to accept the division of history into sacred and profane, and to respect the sacred portion. In the article on "History," which he contributed to Diderot's *Encyclopédie*, Voltaire held sacred history to be a "series of divine and miraculous operations by which it pleased God to lead the Jewish nation in former times, and to test our faith." But elsewhere his satire is usually neither delicate nor concealed. His well-known *La Philosophie de l'Histoire* airs the newer point of view very clearly. He assures his readers, for example, that in treating biblical history, "we do not touch in any way sacred things." Of Abraham he wrote: "I do not touch at all that which is divine in this history," adding, "We believe these prodigies and all others without any

[1] For the references in this paragraph, see the Moland edition (1877-1885), xiv, 38; xvii, 319; xix, 396. Bayle's treatment of David is also defended in the article on philosophy. Voltaire's hatred for Jurieu was intense.

examination"—after he had made a distressingly full examination in the spirit of Pierre Bayle.[1]

Voltaire's disregard for sacred history was fortified by the English controversies which have been passed in review. He wrote an *Examen Important de l'Écriture Sainte*, and attributed it to Lord Bolingbroke. His *La Bible enfin Expliquée* made considerable use of Annet's pamphlet, which had been translated into French in the 'sixties. Indeed, this pamphlet seems to have stimulated Voltaire to write his drama of *Saül*, or *Saül et David*, as it was entitled in some editions. Voltaire even pretended that the drama was translated from the English of M. Huet, who, according to Voltaire, had previously written in 1728 (!) the little work on *The Man after God's Own Heart*. The preface to *Saül* would have us believe that Huet was led to write the pamphlet by hearing a preacher compare David to George II, "who had never assassinated anybody, nor burned his French prisoners in brick-kilns." The play, which is more concerned with David than with Saul, is a bitter and savage picture of the "Jewish kinglet's" amours and immoralities.

By 1760 the reservations of Bodin and Bossuet in regard to sacred history are no longer uttered with sincerity by historians, if uttered at all. Profane history has essentially absorbed the "Jewish books," as Voltaire liked to call them. In this advance from Bodin and Bossuet to Bolingbroke and Voltaire, the principal explanation seems to be Bayle. As we have said, Faguet called the *Dictionary* the "Bible of the eighteenth century." If so, it was a bible inspired by a profane spirit that had ceased to regard such figures as Abraham and David with the respect due to the "saints" of the Old Testament. Voltaire wrote with much truth that "Bayle has rendered service to mankind by saying that God, who, doubtless, dictated all of Jewish history, has not canonized

---

[1] See xi, 29, 48.

all the crimes reported in that history." [1] Bayle's frank examination of the moral shortcomings of Abraham and David gave a great impetus to the consideration of all history from a single, critical point of view. Historically speaking, David's private vices had become public benefits.

[1] See xx, 198.

THE ESQUISSE OF CONDORCET

by

J. Salwyn Schapiro

X

THE ESQUISSE OF CONDORCET

T H E R E was an eighteenth-century mind as there had been a Medieval mind. A new attitude toward life began with the scientific revolution in the sixteenth and seventeenth centuries, which became clear, definite, and militant in the eighteenth. It completely repudiated the Medieval heritage of Christianity, whether Catholic or Protestant; of scholasticism, whether theological or metaphysical; and of authority, whether religious or secular. The eighteenth-century man was the first truly modern man if the test of modernism be a rational attitude toward all problems, private and public. The vast change in the conception of the universe and man's relations to it, inaugurated by the great scientists from Copernicus to Newton, had little popular influence in its day. These scientists were isolated thinkers who did little to spread their ideas; they were only too happy when let alone by the authorities. Furthermore, the Protestant Revolution had the effect of distracting attention from the revolutionary thoughts of the scientists to the acrid theology of the Protestant reformers. And not until the eighteenth century, when the religious strife was somewhat stilled, did the scientific revolution assume its momentous importance.

The popularization of the new views and the new attitude was the work chiefly of the French philosophes. They were a new intellectual species, the first *intelligentsia,* and they made uncompromising war against the intellectual basis of the then existing system. Condorcet gives a vivid description of the methods of the philosophes. Less concerned with discovering truth than with spreading it, they used "in turn all the arms with which erudition, philosophy, wit, literary style could aid reason. They employed all methods from the humorous to the pathetic, from learned tomes to novel or pamphlet; covering the truth with a veil to hide it from those of feeble eyes, but which permitted others the pleasure of piercing it; shrewdly praising prejudices in order better to give them a mortal blow; never threatening any of them either singly or in the mass; sometimes quieting the enemies of reason by pretending to favor only partial toleration in religion and only partial liberty in politics; applauding despotism when it fought religious absurdities and applauding religion when it fought despotism; attacking both in their fundamental principles and yet appearing only to attack revolting or ridiculous abuses; in other words, striking at the roots of these baleful trees and seeming merely to prune a few stray branches; sometimes teaching the friends of liberty that superstition, which covered tyranny with an impenetrable shield, should be first attacked, the first chain to be broken; sometimes, on the contrary, denouncing superstition to the despots as their real enemy and frightening them with pictures of their hypocritical conspiracies and their bloody turbulence but always proclaiming the independence of reason and the freedom of thought as the salvation of mankind; fighting with indefatigable energy against the crimes of fanaticism and of tyranny; fighting all that was oppressive, cruel, or barbarous in religion, in government, in manners, and in laws; commanding, in the name of nature, soldiers, magistrates, and priests to respect human life; reproaching them severely when their policies or their indifference wasted human life in war or in punishment; finally taking for their battle cry, "Reason, Tolerance, Humanity." [1]

[1] Esquisse, *Œuvres* (ed., 1847-49) VI, p. 12.

If the philosophes had one characteristic in common, from the moderate and cautious Turgot to the militant atheist, Baron d'Holbach, it was the exaltation of reason and the repudiation of all authority based on revelation or tradition. The philosophe was as hostile to metaphysics as he was to theology. If the latter was a snare, the former was a delusion. Against both he raised the banner of common sense which, for the first time, was elevated to the rank of a philosophy.

When one thinks of the philosophes, the names Voltaire, Rousseau, and Diderot immediately spring to mind. In truth, these figures are too famous to be typical. Lytton Strachey, by treating comparatively minor figures in his *Eminent Victorians*, made a more acute study of the Victorian mind than if he had treated Gladstone, Mill, Darwin, and Thackeray. Most typical of all the philosophes is Condorcet, who is barely a name outside of France. His writings form an almost perfect synthesis of French thought in the eighteenth century in all its strength and weakness. "He who knows Condorcet well has an almost complete idea of what one would call the state of mind around 1780," is the view of a hostile but competent critic of Condorcet.[1] His comparative oblivion may be explained by the fact that in political science he was overshadowed by Rousseau, in economics by Turgot, and in anti-clericalism by Voltaire. However, Condorcet was a pioneer of the most modern of modern ideas, feminism, popular education, and constitutional law; and he was the chief protagonist, though not the originator, of the idea of Progress.

Of all the famous philosophes Condorcet was the only one who lived during the French Revolution, in which he was continuously active from 1789 to 1793. His career during that period is an exceedingly interesting study of the be-

[1] F. Brunetière, *Histoire de la litérature* III, p. 583.

havior of a revolutionary intellectual when confronted by the realities of social warfare. In his attempts to make abstract ideas of political science fit the concrete political events of 1793 Condorcet was proscribed by the Terror along with the Girondins, though he was not a member of that group. It is an amazing fact that the most important and best known work of Condorcet is a slim volume, really a pamphlet, written at the end of his life while in hiding from the Terrorists. This is the famous *Esquisse d'un Tableau Historique des progrès de l'esprit humain* published after his death in 1795,[1] composed mainly from memory and reflection with little aid from books and notes. It is a philosophic review of the history of mankind from primitive times to the French Revolution. Like Socrates under similar circumstances, Condorcet was never more his calm, rational, altruistic self than when discussing the philosophy of history under the shadow of the guillotine. The *leitmotif* of the Esquisse is the idea of Progress, or the indefinite perfectability of mankind, an idea which penetrates all of Condorcet's writings and inspires all his views. As Bury has pointed out in his *Idea of Progress* it is essentially a modern notion, and was one of the creative ideas of the eighteenth century. It was first suggested by Turgot in his *Second Discours en Sorbonne*, delivered in 1750. Kant, in his *Idee zu einer Geschichte in weltbürgerlicher Absicht* (1784), speculated on progress from the ethical viewpoint. But the Esquisse, for the first time, fully and completely develops the idea of Progress and makes it the determining factor in all history. Unlike the other philosophes Condorcet did not regard history as *un ramas de crimes, de folies, et de malheurs* which mankind would do well to disregard. "He recognized," says Bury, "the interpretation of history as the key to human development, and this principle controlled subsequent speculations on Progress

[1] *Œuvres* (ed., 1847-49), VI.

[168]

in France." [1] In his Introduction to the Esquisse Condorcet maintains that history has two uses: (1) to establish the fact of progress, and (2) to discover its laws in order to determine the future development of mankind. The progress of mankind is explained as being "subject to the same general laws that are observed in the development of the faculties in each individual because it is the result of that development, at a given time, of many individuals united in society. But the situation disclosed at each instant depends on what preceded it, and in turn it influences future development." [2] History should, therefore, present the changes that have taken place and the influence of each event upon its successor. In this way it would establish the fact of progress, or the indefinite perfectibility of man, which "has no limit other than the duration of the globe in which nature has placed us." Progress may be more or less rapid but it will never retrograde "as long as the earth occupies the same place in the universe and as long as the universal laws neither destroy our globe nor produce such changes in it that man's faculties will no longer be able to function." [3] The great obstacles to progress are *préjugés*. In each epoch of history certain prejudices arise that continue to have an influence long after they have been discredited because men cling to the prejudices of their childhood, of their nation, and of their century. Most of our prejudices are, therefore, not really ours at all but a heritage of our ancestors, and history should expose their origin and influence in order to prevent the evils that come from them. [4] Progress, however, has determined enemies whom the historian must overcome. These are the conservative philosophers who oppose new truths, the masses who retard the spread of truths already

[1] J. B. Bury, *The Idea of Progress*, p. 215.
[2] Esquisse, *Œuvres* VI, p. 12.
[3] *Ibid.*, VI, p. 12.
[4] *Ibid.*, VI, p. 23.

known, and the powerful vested interests who profit by the existing system.

History has another, and an even more important aim, according to Condorcet, and that is to discover the laws of human behavior in order to foretell the future. "If there exists a science of foretelling the future progress of mankind, of directing it, and of accelerating it, the first foundation of that science must be the history of progress already achieved." [1] But man's history was not an isolated phenomenon because man was no longer regarded as a special creation, apart from the rest of the universe; he was part of nature and subject to its laws. The philosophes made man's moral problems the object of secular inquiry, and, as a consequence, "the moral sciences are divorced from theology and attach themselves, as if by a prolongation of them, to the physical sciences." [2] The assimilation of man to nature was a cardinal doctrine of Condorcet whose belief in human progress was a reflection of his belief in the undeviating character of natural law. "The only ground for the belief in the natural sciences is that universal laws, known or unknown, which regulate the phenomena of the universe are necessary and constant; and why is this principle any the less true for the development of the intellectual and moral faculties of man than for the other operations of nature?" [3] If natural phenomena, whose laws are known, can be predicted, why should it be regarded "as chimerical to trace a fairly plausible picture of the future of mankind based upon a knowledge of history." [4] Condorcet criticizes the historians for occupying themselves too much with great men, *qui forment. véritablement l'espèce humaine,* instead of studying laws, institutions, and ideas. The historian should be a social philosopher who would do for humanity what the scientist

[1] *Œuvres,* VI, p. 22.
[2] H. A. Taine, *The Ancient Régime* (transl. by J. Durand), p. 177.
[3] *Œuvres,* VI, p. 236.   [4] *Ibid.,* VI, p. 236.

does for nature. This view of history, enunciated at the end of the eighteenth century, would be considered quite "advanced" at the beginning of the twentieth.

The Esquisse is barely even a sketch. All history from primitive man to the French Revolution is divided into nine brief chapters, called Epochs. Some of the Epochs Condorcet later elaborated in another volume, the *Fragment*.[1] In the first and second Epochs Condorcet describes the primitive and the pastoral stages in man's history. From the very first, humanity encounters an inveterate and uncompromising enemy, religion. In fact, the entire book depicts history as the scene of a struggle between the god of light, Progress, and the god of darkness, Religion, each striving for man's soul. As a devout disciple of Voltaire, Condorcet outdid even his master in his hatred of revealed religion, especially of Christianity. In those early times, he declares, the low state of man's faculties explains "the credulity of the first dupes as well as the vulgar cleverness of the first impostors." [2] And in time the art was perfected "of deceiving men in order to despoil them and of dominating their opinions by chimerical hopes and fears." [3] The third Epoch is devoted to the agricultural stage. Human relations now became more complex, due to the division of labor and to the rise of commerce and industry. The prevailing social system was feudalism, the existence of which Condorcet does not believe was "an evil peculiar to our part of the world, but one that could be found almost everywhere during similar periods of civilization." [4]

The first people to appear in the Esquisse are the Greeks to whom is devoted the fourth and most of the fifth Epochs. On the history of the Jews, to which Bossuet devotes so much space in his *Discourse on Universal History*, Condor-

[1] *Œuvres*, VI.
[2] *Ibid.*, VI, p. 30.
[3] *Ibid.*, VI, p. 35.
[4] *Ibid.*, VI, p. 47.

cet does not say a single word. In all probability he, like Voltaire, regarded Judea as the primal source of the intellectual demoralization of Europe. Much of the chapter is a eulogy of the philosophers especially of Socrates. Wonderful and unique, Greek civilization nevertheless perished, chiefly because the Greeks did not develop a good system of communication. The fifth Epoch describes the advance of science, especially of mathematics in which Condorcet had distinguished himself early in his career. Greek decadence became evident during the Alexandrian period, when the judgment of a book "depended on its age or on the difficulty of understanding or finding it." It was during this decadent period that the idea, "so false and so evil," became prevalent of the degeneracy of mankind and the superiority of ancient over modern times.[1]

One of the astonishing things about the Esquisse, for which it has been sharply criticized, is that it gives so little space to Rome, merely a few paragraphs in the fifth Epoch. Condorcet seems to imply that, from the cultural point of view, Rome is unimportant, and that Latin culture is merely a variation of Greek decadence. Curiously enough, Rome is important, in Condorcet's view, in relation to Christianity. He describes with bitter sarcasm the spread of Christianity in the Empire. "Twenty sects, Egyptian and Jewish, united to attack the religion of the Empire. But they fought one another with equal fury and ended in all being demolished by the religion of Jesus. From their *débris* was formed a history, a dogma, ceremonies, a morality which drew little by little the mob of visionaries." The spirit of the new faith was "in harmony with the period of decadence and misfortune," and oppressed humanity welcomed a religion in which all were equal in slavery. Contempt for human knowledge was one of the leading characteristics of Christianity,

[1] *Œuvres*, VI, p. 107.

therefore, its triumph signalized "the complete breakdown of science and philosophy." [1]

The sixth and seventh Epochs deal with the Middle Ages which are painted in colors of the darkest hue. A "disastrous epoch" was the early Middle Ages when the people groaned under the triple tyranny of king, warrior, and priest. "Barely did a glimmer of the light of talent or of human greatness and goodness pierce its profound darkness. Theological moonshine and superstitious impostures were then the only characteristics of human genius, and religious intolerance the only morality." [2] Yet this uncompromising enemy of all revealed religion gives an enthusiastic account of Mohammedanism and a favorable view of its founder. Of all religions, he writes, Mohammedanism is "the most simple in its dogmas, the least absurd in its practices, and the most tolerant in its principles." The Arabs had *l'élévation et de la douceur*. They loved and cultivated the arts and sciences. Mohammed had the talents of a statesman, poet, and warrior which he employed *avec addresse, mais avec grandeur*.[3] In the most recent sketch of universal history, *The Outline of History*, Mr. H. G. Wells, expresses similar views of Christianity and Mohammedanism. Is it because Christianity was near and Mohammedanism far away? And "every ship has a romance on board except the one in which you are sailing." Or is it because both Condorcet and Wells knew more of Christianity than of Mohammedanism, at least of the seamy side of these two faiths?

At best, according to the Esquisse, the Middle Ages contributed not something positively good, but something relatively bad from which better things arose. These were (1) scholasticism whose subtleties, used as a means of embarrassing and ensnaring an opponent, sharpened the wits of its practitioners and were the beginning of philosophic

---

[1] *Œuvres*, VI, pp. 101-3. [2] *Ibid.*, VI, p. 109.   [3] *Ibid.*, VI, pp. 121-24.

analysis; (2) serfdom which made the common man a member of a lower class, not an article of merchandise as he had been under slavery; and (3) gunpowder "which seemed, at first, to threaten the destruction of the human race" but which, by revolutionizing the art of warfare, destroyed the superiority of the nobles over the common people.[1]

The eighth and ninth Epochs are treated at great length. The eighth treats roughly the period of the Renaissance and the Protestant Revolution. Condorcet is of the opinion that the greatest invention of modern times was printing, and the greatest discovery was America. The Esquisse contains an enthusiastic eulogy of printing, the importance of which Condorcet cannot exaggerate. It was the most redoubtable enemy of kings and priests who, luckily for mankind, did not suspect its powers, otherwise they would have suppressed it. In vain do tyrants try to shackle freedom of writing; as long as there exists a corner of the world in which printing is unshackled, it "could still spread enlightenment pure and free." Moreover, there are many methods of circumventing the inquisitors.[2] The discovery of America made possible the study of humanity in all lands and in all stages of civilization. A clearer idea could now be had of the influence of nature and of institutions upon mankind. Unfortunately, however, the discovery of America resulted in reviving the ancient institution of slavery.

Condorcet was the first to realize the vast importance, in the history of mankind, of the scientific revolution of the sixteenth and seventeenth centuries to which he devotes considerable space. He pays glowing tributes to Copernicus, Galileo, Bacon, and Descartes through whose labors, tradition and authority "gave way to universal natural law and human reason." The growth of modern languages was another distinctive contribution of the period. Latin, as the language

[1] *Œuvres,* VI, pp. 134-35.   [2] *Ibid.,* VI, p. 142.

of the educated, was an "eternal obstacle to true equality" inasmuch as it perpetuated errors and prejudices by dividing mankind into learned and ignorant.

These great steps of progress occurred during the period of the Protestant Revolution when "the monster of fanaticism irritated by his wounds, seemed to redouble his ferocity." [1] Condorcet has little enthusiasm for Protestantism except as an exposure of Catholicism. Free thinking people, he declares, found restraints in both Protestant and Catholic countries. Protestantism did, however, give freedom of thought to Christians, if not to men, and it had fewer absurdities than Catholicism. "The chain was not broken, but it was less heavy and more extended." [2]

The ninth Epoch treats of the period from Descartes to the French Revolution. It is the age when Newton established the true system of the universe, when Locke analyzed human nature, and when Turgot and Rousseau analyzed human society. Enlightenment spread in all countries of western Europe, and governments followed enlightened opinion, though at a distance. Religious intolerance abated its fury, and customs and manners became milder. To Condorcet the eighteenth was the greatest of centuries. Until then, man's life and thoughts were dominated by prejudices, and all history was the Dark Ages, pierced now and then by a fitful gleam of enlightenment as in Greece. "Living in this happy age," he exclaims rhapsodically, "and being witnesses of the last efforts of ignorance and of error we have seen reason emerge victorious from this struggle, so long and so difficult, and we can at last cry out: Truth has conquered and mankind is saved!" [3]

Condorcet devotes considerable space to the leading idea of the Age of Reason, the rights of man. He praises Rousseau, whom he personally disliked, as the one who "merits

[1] *Œuvres*, VI, p. 158.   [2] *Ibid.*, VI, p. 153.   [3] *Ibid.*, I, p. 390.

the glory of putting the rights of man among those truths which one can no longer forget nor oppose."[1] Toward the end of the eighteenth century, he points out, enlightenment was so widespread that its influence was no longer slow and intangible as formerly. It directly and powerfully influenced the masses, and the outcome was the American and French Revolutions. Condorcet makes an important distinction between these two movements. The American Revolution, he says, had the sympathy of all the nations, chiefly because it had no feudal system to overthrow. But the French Revolution was social and economic in character, and in destroying the feudal system at home it challenged that in the rest of Europe. Therefore, it was opposed by all except *la voix de quelques sages, et le vœu timide des peuples opprimés.*[2]

The last chapter of the Esquisse deals not with the past but with the future. It is the most original chapter of all, and has been the subject of widespread comment, far more so than the book itself. Condorcet lays down the general principles of social development and gives an outline of future society. But what he foretells does not arise from his imagination but from the laws of progress derived from a study of history. Condorcet is an altruist, not a utopian, and in his work "the historic approach makes a *scientific junction* with the utopist."[3] The Esquisse was written during the most vivid period of the French Revolution when the enlightenment of the eighteenth century was being rapidly translated into new institutions and laws. Progress at last became visible, and Condorcet could well have thought that the future was no longer a dream but a reality.

Unlike the past, the future, according to Condorcet, will be based upon (1) the equality of the nations, (2) equality of individuals within a nation, and (3) perfection of man-

[1] *Œuvres,* VI, p. 178.   [2] *Ibid.,* VI, p. 201.
[3] See V. Branford, "The Founders of Sociology" in *American Journal of Sociology,* Vol. X (1904).

kind. Are the differences in civilization, noticeable in the various races, due to nature or to defects in their social systems? History, says Condorcet, which alone can answer that question, gives the strongest reasons for believing that "nature has put no limits on our hopes" and has condemned no race to remain permanently backward. The principles of the French Revolution are accepted by the enlightened everywhere. In the New World the tendencies of the colonists are markedly in favor of establishing independent nations. In Asia and Africa the tyranny of the Europeans will be resented by the natives, who will free themselves by using their European masters "either as useful tools or as generous liberators." Hitherto, the colonies had served for the enrichment of the monopolistic trading companies; but in future they will become "the homes of industrious people who will come to these happy climes to seek the prosperity denied to them in the land of their birth."

As a result of the equality of nations war will be regarded "as the greatest of evils and as the greatest of crimes." A permanent league of nations is the only means of maintaining universal peace and the independence and freedom of the nations. What is necessary are not projects of perpetual peace, "which have occupied the leisure and consoled the souls of some philosophers," but new institutions and a universal language which will bind nations together and so hasten the progress of fraternity.[1]

The inequality of individuals is due to differences in wealth, in inheritance, and in education. These differences have natural causes, and therefore it would be absurd, and even dangerous, to try to abolish them. But they can be greatly diminished by a just system of government and society so that only the natural inequalities will remain. Inequality in wealth can be diminished by laws favoring the

[1] *Œuvres*, VI, p. 265.

distribution, not the concentration of wealth, through establishing freedom of commerce and of industry. The poor suffer because of their lack of capital, therefore ways should be found to popularize credit. Too much depends on the father of a family who generally has only his labor; a system of social insurance should be devised, especially old age pensions and allowances for widows and orphans. There is another great inequality, that between the sexes. Condorcet was a pioneer advocate of the rights of women, and his writings on that subject [1] anticipated both Mary Wollstonecraft and John Stuart Mill. The most important factor in future progress, he writes, will be the "complete destruction of those prejudices which establish between the sexes an inequality of rights that is bad even for the favored sex. In vain does one try to justify it by differences in physical organization, in force of intelligence, in moral sensibility. This inequality has no origin other than force, and in vain does one endeavor to excuse it by sophistry." [2]

Inequalities in education can be diminished by a universal system of education. In this field, too, Condorcet was a pioneer. His famous report to the Legislative Assembly, [3] in 1792, recommended the establishment of a national system of education, of all grades, open to all, free, and secular. Equality of education would correct, and not exaggerate as now, the bad results of inequalities of ability. According to Condorcet great inequalities of fortune would be impossible when universal education awakened dormant abilities in many. Even in the most enlightened countries "not one-fiftieth of those whom nature has endowed with talent receive the instruction necessary to develop it." [4]

[1] See *Lettres d'un bourgeois de New-Haven, Œuvres,* Vol. IX, and *Sur l'Admission des Femmes au droit de Cité,* Vol. X.
[2] *Ibid.,* VI, p. 264.
[3] See *Sur l'Instruction Publique, Œuvres,* VII.
[4] *Ibid.,* VI, p. 254.

Population will increase as a result of these beneficent reforms. But will population increase beyond its subsistence, and therefore cause humanity once more to retrograde? This calamity will be avoided by the progress of science which, in time, may be able to convert the elements into food. And new machines will multiply the force and abilities of men by increasing their products and by diminishing the time and labor necessary to produce them. Less land will produce more food. If these methods do not solve the problem of subsistence, people should practice birth control. If ridiculous prejudices did not give morality "an austerity that corrupts and degrades instead of purifying or elevating it, men would know that their obligations to those who are not yet born do not consist merely in bringing them into the world but also in assuring them well-being. The purpose of these obligations is the welfare of humanity, of the existing society, and of the family, not the puerile idea of encumbering the earth with useless and unhappy beings." [1]

Finally, comes a prophesy which has been ridiculed by the critics of the Esquisse as the most chimerical part of the most fatuous of books. It is the perfectibility of the human organism. Condorcet believes that the duration of human life has no assignable limit, and that the span of life may be increased indefinitely by perfecting the human body. It can be done "by preventive medicine, proper diet and housing, a manner of living which will develop bodily strength through moderate exercise, and, finally, by the abolition of the two most active causes of human degradation, poverty and riches." [2] Preventive medicine will abolish contagious and hereditary diseases, and also those due to

---

[1] *Œuvres*, VI, pp. 257-58.

[2] *Ibid.*, VI, p. 273. Condorcet's idea of prolonging human life appeared absurd to Malthus. "It may be fairly doubted whether there has been really the smallest perceptible advance in the natural duration of human life since we first had any authentic history of man."—T. R. Malthus, *Principle of Population* (ed., 1872), p. 267.

[179]

climate, to food, and to the nature of employment. And the abolition of all disease is not a vain hope. Doubtless "men will not become immortal" but a time will come "when death will be nothing more than the effect either of an extraordinary accident or of the slow destruction of the vital forces."

The Esquisse appeared soon after Condorcet's death in prison, and was distributed by order of the Convention, which was now stirred to compassion for the *philosophe infortuné*. Its influence was not felt much at first, but later it became, in the opinion of a historian of the idea of Progress, "a point of departure for the social philosophy of the nineteenth century."[1] In France the first thinker to realize the significance of the Esquisse was Saint-Simon. "It was Condorcet," he says, "who first conceived the idea of writing a history of the past and future of general intelligence. His project was sublime, but his execution, worthless." Saint-Simon condemns the Esquisse on three counts. The first is that it gives an impression that man possessed language from the very beginning, whereas language came only after a long process of development. The second is that it presents religion as an obstacle to human welfare. History teaches, writes Saint-Simon, that "men of genius civilized mankind" by means of religions which can never be anything else than "philosophic systems materialized." Religious institutions, like others, have their periods of infancy, maturity, and decadence. The third is that the idea of the indefinite perfectibility of mankind is erroneous. The capacity of the human mind does not increase; it merely replaces what it loses. The ancients were even superior to the moderns in literature and in the science of war, though the moderns are superior to them in scientific achievements.[2]

A far greater admirer of the Esquisse than Saint-Simon

[1] J. Delvaille, *Essai sur l'histoire de l'idée du progrès* (1910), p. 670.
[2] See Correspondence avec M. de Redern, Saint-Simon, *Œuvres* (1868), XV, pp. 113-18.

was Auguste Comte who enthusiastically proclaimed Condorcet his "spiritual father." "After Montesquieu," he writes, "the most important advance in the fundamental conception of sociology was made by the unfortunate Condorcet in his memorable work, the Esquisse . . . for the first time the scientific idea, truly primordiale, of the social progress of mankind was at last clearly and definitely pronounced."[1] The "immortal few pages" of the Introduction and the last chapter on the future of mankind are, in his opinion, the bases of all subsequent development of sociology. These parts of the Esquisse, for the first time, clearly show that civilization is the "outcome of a progressive development, all the steps of which are closely related to one another through the workings of natural laws that could be revealed by a philosophic study of history and that determine for each epoch, in a manner entirely positive, the high degree of civilization that society experiences either as a whole or in its parts." But Comte severely criticizes the body of the Esquisse as being contrary to the aim and purpose announced in the Introduction. The division of the Epochs shows on interrelation and no connection, and, as a consequence, the Esquisse becomes "a long and tiresome declamation." Condorcet's treatment of the Middle Ages as a conspiracy against mankind was the "insensate result of eighteenth century philosophy." It presents a general contradiction between "the immense perfection attained by humanity at the end of the eighteenth century and the retrograde influences that he constantly attributes to the entire past, to all its doctrines, to all its institutions, to all its effective forces." There is, then, a hiatus between the theologic and autocratic past and the free-thinking democratic present; therefore history becomes "a perpetual miracle,

[1] In a recently published letter, Comte writes that he considers Condorcet far superior to Montesquieu. See *The Journal of Modern History*, June, 1929.

and the progressive march of civilization becomes an effect without a cause." Although Condorcet had the concept of social progress he did not, according to Comte, discover its true laws, and, for this reason, his vision of the future is defective.[1]

As a work of history, the Esquisse cannot be taken seriously. Even in the pre-Rankian period there was a Gibbon, a Hume, and even a Voltaire, but Condorcet shows only the most meagre knowledge of historical sources and historical methods. He has no idea at all of the value of documents, even false ones, as permanent expressions of changing historic conditions. While it is perfectly true that a document does not tell the whole story, it does express the tendencies of the existing society, even if not always the sincere views of its authors. Condorcet ridicules the search for documents and precedents. A proposition was not adopted because it was true, he says, but because "it was written in such a book or was believed in such a country where it was practiced since such a century." [2] The philosophe was always stronger than the historian in him, and he consequently saw as little connection between the Old Régime and the French Revolution, as between the eighteenth century and its predecessors. The extreme anti-traditionalism of the philosophes profoundly influenced the ideology of the French Revolution. In a sense the French Revolution was "unhistorical," for it avoided historical justification as deliberately as the English and American Revolutions had sought it.

Furthermore, the Esquisse is disfigured, as Flint says, by a "passionate and prejudiced spirit of sectarian fanaticism." [3] To Condorcet, a man of '93, monarchy and church stand

---

[1] For Comte's criticism of the Esquisse see *Cours de Philosophie positive* (1835-52), IV, pp. 252-63, and *Système de politique positive. Appendice générale* (1854), p. 109 ff.

[2] *Œuvres*, VI, p. 136.

[3] R. Flint, *Historical Philosophy in France* (1893), p. 329.

condemned at all times in all places, and their influence should be completely eradicated from all human life and thought. The propagandist spirit of the encyclopedist was not equal to the task of a scientific attitude toward historic institutions. It was too much concerned with the weight of the dead past on the living present to view them calmly as a heritage instead of a burden. In his essay on Condorcet Sainte-Beuve stigmatizes the Esquisse as "the last and most fastidious dream of pure reason infatuated with itself; it is the encyclopedist ideal in all its opaque beauty." [1]

Although Condorcet had an idea of progress he had no idea of evolution. Progress begins with enlightenment but evolution doesn't begin at all; and the Esquisse is not a study of the evolution of civilization but a succession of epochs, taken haphazardly and held together only by the author's passionate love of humanity. In discussing social and economic matters he does not explain how they are related to the ideas of the time. How, then, do new ideas originate and how do they influence mankind? Condorcet's answer shows him to be a perfect idealogue. They originate, he believes, in the minds of the *éclairés*, the great scientists and philosophers, and spread through propaganda, unless hindered by *préjugés*. The store of knowledge contributed by great thinkers becomes a social heritage; the larger it grows the greater is the intellectual ability of mankind. Behind the entire process is universal nature that comprehends all, from the fall of a sparrow to the birth of a new social order. Condorcet's views are an excellent illustration of the substitution of absolutes so characteristic of eighteenth century thought. For God, the philosophes substituted nature; for divine will, natural law; for revelation, creative ideas; for conversion, enlightenment; and for preaching, propaganda. They were utterly unaware of the influence of

[1] *Causeries du Lundi* (1882), III, pp. 345-46.

social and economic forces on man's ideas because their eyes were glued to the thin veneer of reason that covers the vasty deep of human irrationality.

Despite all its faults of omission and commission the Esquisse is a landmark in the history of History. It suggests methods of approach to the subject that are distinctively novel and enlightening. It is anti-antiquarian. Condorcet looks at the past with the eyes of the present, and consequently he has a consciously critical attitude. He makes no vain efforts to transport himself into the past in order to find a Golden Age in the "good old times." His Golden Age is in the future, to which the path of history inevitably leads. For almost the first time historical writing becomes tinged with optimism instead of pessimism.

The Esquisse is a "liberal" history. Condorcet denounces the historians of his day as being unsympathetic with human rights. "Nearly all of them," he writes, "seem to favor the party which, under the pretext of establishing a more stable, a more wise, and a more peaceful government, really aimed to concentrate authority in the hands of the rich. These historians have given the names 'factions' and 'rebels' to those who have defended the equality and the independence of the people whose influence they sought to augment." [1] The Esquisse, on the contrary, consistently favors those forces that make for progress and enlightenment, though not at all in a narrow, partisan sense. As a consequence emphasis is laid on those events that led to *changes* for the better.

Another characteristic of the Esquisse is its true cosmopolitan spirit; neither racial nor national sympathies or antipathies obtrude whatsoever. The Greeks, the Italians, the French, the English come into the story only when they have something to contribute to civilization, and their contribution is judged in the most objective manner possible. It is

[1] *Œuvres,* VI, p. 358.

a remarkable tribute to Condorcet that, although he lived at a time when France was at the very pinnacle of her intellectual influence, not a single patriotic word escapes his pen.

Finally, and most important of all, the Esquisse is a pioneer work in what is now called intellectual history. It is primarily a history of ideas and of their influence in the march of progress. Condorcet's assumption is that the human mind alone is the creative element in human life, and that it alone is capable of determining the fate of mankind. This intellectual determinism visualizes progress as the conscious and deliberate effort of man to better himself and the conditions under which he lives. Those who are interested in history as "the mind in the making" may also claim Condorcet as their spiritual father.

THE PHILOSOPHER TURNED PATRIOT

by

Carlton J. H. Hayes

XI

THE PHILOSOPHER TURNED PATRIOT

Some Reflections on the Curious
Spiritual Adventurings of Henry St.
John, Lord Viscount Bolingbroke

"Neither Montaigne in writing his essays, nor Descartes in building new worlds, nor Burnet in framing an antediluvian Earth, no, nor Newton in discovering and establishing the true laws of nature on experiment and a sublimer geometry, felt more intellectual joys, than he feels who is a real patriot, who bends all the force of his understanding, and directs all his thoughts and actions to the good of his country." —BOLINGBROKE (1736).

I

A GREAT deal of solemn drivel has been written about Henry St. John, perhaps because he wrote a great deal of more or less solemn drivel himself; more likely, however, because he was something of a chameleon and mystified contemporaries as well as posterity by the ease with which he displayed himself as profligate, politician, philosopher— and patriot. His profligacy, open and unashamed, pained the prim conscience of Victorian England, but excited no vehement protest in the age of Queen Anne, the first two Georges, and Lord Chesterfield. Oliver Goldsmith [1] was more amused than scandalized by the tale of St. John's running drunk and naked through the Park; and Harry's perfect licentiousness with the ladies was as conventional in his period as Georgian furniture. What gentleman of the early eighteenth century would cast the stone at a big, handsome, dashing fellow who pursued Bacchus with gusto and

---

[1] *Life of Henry Lord Bolingbroke,* in *The Works of Bolingbroke* (8 volumes, London, 1809), vol. I, p. vi. Later citations of Bolingbroke's *Works* are to this edition.

[189]

Venus with virility and both with eloquence and elegance? Manners were morals in those spacious days, in England as in France.

The profligate turned politician, as any gentleman in those days must. When he was twenty-three he took the seat in the House of Commons which his family bought him; and his epicurean suppers with the Tories and his ciceronian speeches in the House qualified him, three years later, for the post of Secretary of War in the cabinet and the conduct of England's military operations in the War of the Spanish Succession. Thenceforth, to the end of his life, the profligate was politician; the politician was profligate. But the politician, as time went on, showed a fatal tendency to bet on the wrong horse. In 1714 he bet on Queen Anne and Lady Masham, but Queen Anne suddenly died. In 1715 he bet on the Pretender and Louis XIV, but Louis XIV expired. In 1727 he bet on George I and the ugly Duchess of Kendal, but George I promptly quitted life. Three such fatalities, all in a row, must have been providential; or so, at any rate, they have been explained by Whiggish historians like Walpole and Macaulay and accepted by Victorian Englishmen of pure life and sound principles. What these merely disliked (or envied) in Beaconsfield, who succeeded, they reprobated with moral indignation in Bolingbroke, who failed.

The politician turned philosopher. Indeed, he was always a bit philosophic, and circumstances made him more so. Anybody whose soul, under the influence of wine, is accustomed at night to expand and to voice lofty sentiments and on the "morning after" to experience some slight depression, is prepared for philosophy; and anybody has need of it who would manage with seemliness both mistresses and wives. Solomon wrote proverbs; St. John, epistles. But while Solomon was handicapped all his life by being a statesman, a man of action, St. John was condemned for almost forty years to the reflections of a politician out of office; and there can hardly be a more inveterate philosopher than the chronic ex-solon.

Being a cultured gentleman of the eighteenth century, St. John's general philosophy was that of natural rights and natural law, reason and "enlightenment," humanitarianism and natural religion and Deism (he called it Theism). He admired classical antiquity, detested the Middle Ages, and lauded the modern times of Bacon and Newton. It was known that he was on peculiarly intimate terms with Dean Swift and Mr. Pope and that he repeatedly conversed with a fascinating Frenchman who was undergoing transformation from a pandering M. Arouet into a philosophic M. de Voltaire; it was even suspected that he encouraged Mr. Pope to indite the dubiously orthodox *Essay on Man*. But the full enormity of his contribution to philosophy was recognized only after his death, when his literary executor, David Mallet (the "cur" [1]), published *in extenso* the manuscripts that had been piling up during the many years from 1717 to 1751. Then it became apparent that Bolingbroke had outdone Pope and rivaled Voltaire in depreciation of the supernatural, the miraculous, the metaphysical, and in denunciation of the Bible and all ecclesiastical authority; that he had been "the first Englishman" to attempt a blasting of the "Rock of Ages." Great was the excitement. It reached the ears of the redoubtable Dr. Johnson.

On the 6th of March [1754, wrote Boswell] came out Lord Bolingbroke's works, published by Mr. David Mallet. The wild and pernicious ravings, under the name of "Philosophy," which were thus ushered into the world, gave great offence to all well-principled men. Johnson, hearing of their tendency, which nobody disputed, was roused with a just indignation, and pronounced this memorable sentence upon the noble author and his editor. "Sir, he was a scoundrel and a coward: a scoundrel,

[1] J. C. Collins, *Bolingbroke, a Historical Study* (New York, 1886).

for charging a blunderbuss against religion and morality; a coward, because he had no resolution to fire it off himself, but left half-a-crown to a beggarly Scotchman to draw the trigger after his death." [1]

The judgment of Samuel has seldom been questioned in English castle or in English cottage. To the godly, it has long been perfectly obvious that Bolingbroke's failure as a politician and success as a profligate were alike the retribution which Divine Providence visited upon the blaspheming philosopher.

For most moderns, however, whether godly or ungodly, Bolingbroke possessed one outstanding virtue. He was a patriot and a nationalist. At the very time when he was "stripped of the rights of a British subject," he remembered with pride that he was "a Briton still." [2] He assailed "the shameless crew who write against their country" [3] as mercilessly as Johnson attacked him for writing against his God. No wonder that admirers of Burke and Pitt, Nelson and Wellington, Disraeli and Salisbury, should believe that the patriot redeemed the philosopher and even the profligate. The Christian sinner played John the Baptist to modern English nationalism; and devotees of the New Dispensation have accordingly composed hagiographies of him, as those of the Old have preached sermons against him. This fact goes far to explain the inanity of much of the secondary literature on Bolingbroke.

It has been said, of course, that Bolingbroke was only a sham patriot; that he exploited patriotism in order to regain political preferment; and that he was particularly in Johnson's mind when the learned Doctor pronounced patriotism to be "the last refuge of a scoundrel." [4] But what passed in Johnson's mind, despite Boswell, is not always certain; and

[1] James Boswell, *Life of Johnson* (Birrell's ed.), vol. I, p. 218.
[2] *The Idea of a Patriot King, Works,* IV, 231.
[3] *Remarks on the History of England, Works,* II, 236.
[4] James Boswell, *Life of Johnson* (Birrell's ed.), III, 195.

any sterling patriot is prone to detect some dross in others. That Bolingbroke sought to exploit patriotism is probably true. Why not? What patriot does not? There is this to be remembered, however, that his patriotism was continuous and consistent, that he entertained its cardinal principles for a longer time than he engaged in office-seeking (which was indeed a long time), and that he closely related them to his general philosophy. St. John, it has been remarked, was always something of a philosopher. Likewise, he was always something of a patriot.

II

The philosopher turned patriot naturally. "The service of our country is . . . a real duty. He who admits the proofs of any moral duty, drawn from the constitution of human nature . . . , must admit them in favour of this duty, or be reduced to the most absurd inconsistency." [1]

The philosopher's God of Nature and Reason was remote and well-nigh unknowable; He certainly indulged in none of the easy familiarities of Christian or Pagan deities. But Bolingbroke was on fairly good terms with Him and was sure that He was the First Cause of a sequence of natural phenomena which ultimately imposed upon Englishmen the reasoned duty of national patriotism. It was He who had ordained that human beings should be relatively insignificant, distinctly depraved, and quite devoted to self-love, and that consequently they should be impelled "to enter into societies, to depart from their natural liberty, and to subject themselves to government." [2] At the same time He had promulgated two laws: one, "the universal law of reason,"

[1] *On the Spirit of Patriotism, Works,* IV, 199.

[2] *A Dissertation upon Parties, Works,* III, 160. *Cf. The Idea of a Patriot King, Works,* IV, 191-192, 301. In his *Fragments or Minutes of Essays,* he says: "There is a sort of genealogy of law, in which Nature begets natural law, natural law sociability, sociability union of societies by consent, and this union by consent the obligation of civil laws" (*Works,* VII, 376).

"the same to all, and obligatory alike on all"; the other, "the particular law or constitution of laws by which every distinct community has chosen to be governed." Through "reason," both these laws have been "revealed" to men; and "we can no more doubt of the obligations of both . . . than of the existence of the Lawgiver. As supreme Lord over all His works, His general Providence regards immediately the great commonwealth of mankind, but then, as supreme Lord likewise, His authority gives a sanction to the particular bodies of law which are made under it. . . . It follows, therefore, that he who breaks the laws of his country resists the ordinance of God, that is, the law of his nature." [1]

It was the philosopher's God, moreover, who had created nationalities on Earth. Though He may have united the inhabitants of another planet "in one great society, speaking the same language, and living under the same government," He constituted mankind "very differently," so that "we are by nature incapable" of surmounting national differences, of establishing a uniform language, "of uniting under one form of government, or of submitting to one rule of life." [2] Similarly, there is always some predestined difference in national interests, "a difference that arises from the situation of countries, from the character of people, from the nature of government, and even from that of climate and soil." [3] Such difference, coupled with human depravity, explains why one nationality is "inspired" to "invade and spoil" others and "to disturb the peace of the great commonwealth of mankind." [4] Militarist nationalism may be a sorry thing, but in

[1] *The Idea of a Patriot King, Works*, IV, 238-239.
[2] *Fragments or Minutes of Essays, Works*, VII, 413. On another page of the same work he says: "We love ourselves, we love our families, we love the particular societies to which we belong, and our benevolence extends at last to the whole race of mankind. Like so many different vortices, the centre of them all is self-love, and that which is the most distant from it is the weakest" (VII, 378).
[3] *The Idea of a Patriot King, Works*, IV, 305.
[4] *Ibid.*, IV, 301.

last analysis it must be ascribed to the providence of the God of Nature and Reason.

This God is indifferent to the form of government; He has instituted "neither monarchy, nor aristocracy, nor democracy, nor mixed government"; [1] He has ordained only that every national polity, whatever be its form, shall be "founded in the common rights and interests of mankind" [2] and that its citizens shall obey it. Current notions concerning the divine right of kings "have no foundation in fact or reason;" [3] though two distinctions must here be made. First, "the office of kings"—and presumably that of senators or presidents—"is of right divine and their persons are to be reputed sacred; as men, they have no such right, no such sacredness belonging to them." [4] Second, any governor, particularly a king, enjoys "a divine right to govern well, and conformably to the constitution; a divine right to govern ill is an absurdity, to assert it is blasphemy." [5]

Like most political theorists of his day, Bolingbroke put society and government on a contractual basis. He agreed with Hobbes in finding the need of it in human depravity, but with Locke and Rousseau in making it dependent upon its assurance of "the greatest good" to "the people." [6] For God intended "that government should be good." And the "legal reverence" which He has decreed that men shall owe to a king or any other government is "national, not personal." [7]

Bolingbroke himself esteemed monarchy "above any other form of government, and hereditary monarchy above elective." [8] This preference he rationalized in several ways. He

[1] *The Idea of a Patriot King, Works,* IV, 239.   [2] *Ibid.,* IV, 233.
[3] *Ibid.,* IV, 234.   [4] *Ibid.,* IV, 240.
[5] *Ibid.,* IV, 239.
[6] *Ibid.,* IV, 261. Cf. *Authority in Matters of Religion, Works,* VI, 484.
[7] *Ibid.,* IV, 240-241.
[8] *Ibid.,* IV, 237.

insisted that monarchy can be "more easily and more use-fully" tempered with aristocracy or democracy, than either of these with monarchy.[1] He claimed that "national calami-ties" often attend elections.[2] He revealed that "God is a monarch, yet not an arbitrary but a limited monarch," [3] and God, if not exactly hereditary, was certainly not elective. As to the extent of the limitations on the monarch, they "ought to be carried as far as it is necessary to secure the liberties of a people." [4] By "liberties" were not meant all the individual liberties which French revolutionaries subsequently enunci-ated, but rather the traditional liberties of Englishmen which a Tory aristocrat needed not to specify. Above all, the "spirit of liberty will be always and wholly concerned about na-tional interests." [5]

To promote true national interests, any form of govern-ment should contain an aristocratic element, for the "Author of nature has thought fit to mingle" in every nationality "a few, and but a few, of those on whom He is graciously pleased to bestow a larger proportion of the ethereal spirit than is given in the ordinary course of His providence to the sons of men. These are they who engross almost the whole reason of the species: who are born to instruct, to guide, and to preserve." The "herd of mankind" have only to obey.[6]

In such wise Bolingbroke quarried from his Deistic phi-losophy the building blocks for a new edifice of nationalism, which should supplant the old fanes of ecclesiasticism. Skep-tical about the old, he was credulous about the new. Whilst denying that "traditional Christianity" was derived from a

[1] *The Idea of a Patriot King, Works,* IV, 243-244, 270. *Cf. A Dissertation upon Parties, Works,* III, 217-251.
[2] *Ibid.,* IV, 241-242, 270. In *A Dissertation upon Parties,* he adds that "absolute power is tyranny, but absolute democracy is tyranny and anarchy both" (*Works,* III, 216).
[3] *Ibid.,* IV, 245.
[4] *Ibid.,* IV, 246.
[5] *Remarks on the History of England, Works,* II, 135.
[6] *On the Spirit of Patriotism, Works,* IV, 187-189.

supernatural God, he affirmed that nationality came straight from the God of nature. Authority, which he denounced as tyrannical in the Christian Church, he acclaimed as reasonable and divine in the National State. Perhaps to a greater degree than humbler and less dogmatic folk, he felt himself obliged to replace old Gods with new. At any rate he fashioned from his own spiritual experiences a sacred ark of the national covenant.

The formal religion of most eighteenth-century philosophers was somewhat chilly. Their God was very remote, very impersonal, very scientific, and veritably enslaved by ineluctable laws of decorum and orderliness. They did not usually spell Him with capital letters. They could not be excited about Him or hold revival meetings in His honor. They discussed His attributes—His bigness and His helplessness—with solemnity and in finely balanced sentences that pleased the mind and mildly titillated the sentiments. But other outlets they had to have for emotional enthusiasm and heart-felt worship; other cults they had to seek for personal devotion. Some turned to humanitarianism and Freemasonry. Bolingbroke turned to patriotism.

III

Bolingbroke laid foundations for generic nationalism in the hard concrete of his philosophic theology. But the specific nationalism which he proceeded to rear on those foundations was reënforced and rendered attractive by the ardor of his personal consecration to Britannia.

His *Remarks on the History of England,* his *Dissertation upon Parties,* his *Letter on the Spirit of Patriotism,* and his *Idea of a Patriot King* were alike directed to the exaltation of the national British State and its glorious constitution. He expressed unbounded admiration for the constitution as a "system of government suited to the genius of our nation, and even to our situation." [1] "A British spirit and the spirit of the British constitution are one and the same," [2] and "they who talk of liberty in Britain on any other principles than those of the British constitution, talk impertinently at best." [3] Under the constitution could properly function a patriot king, a national church, and an enlightened landed nobility. In accordance with it the national State could follow a domestic policy with the good of the people uppermost in mind, and a foreign policy wholly and exclusively British.

The lodestone of the constitution, according to Bolingbroke, should be the king, provided he be a real patriot. For it is his task to unite his people in defense of British liberty, that is, of the British constitution, and thereby to create that national union without which no national interests, domestic or foreign, can be safeguarded. Only a king who is, "in the true meaning of the word, a patriot, can govern Britain with ease, security, honour, dignity," [4] and to do so is "a duty that he owes to God by one law and to his people by another." [5] A patriot king must believe that "the ultimate end of all governments is the good of the people, for whose sake they were made, and without whose consent they could not have been made." [6] Wherefore he must maintain liberty and the constitution, twin pillars of British freedom. But this requires the active coöperation of the "spirit and character of the people" [7] and the revival of that "true old English spirit, which prevailed in the days of our fathers, and which must always be national, since it has no direction but to the national interest." [8]

To follow national interests, it is necessary, furthermore, "to lead men, from acting with a party spirit, to act with a

[1] A Dissertation upon Parties, Works, III, 201.
[2] Ibid., III, 30.   [3] Ibid., III, 202.
[4] The Idea of a Patriot King, Works, IV, 247.
[5] Ibid., IV, 259.   [6] Ibid., IV, 260.   [7] Ibid., IV, 266.
[8] Remarks on the History of England, Works, II, 114.

national spirit." [1] "Party is a political evil, and faction is the worst of all parties. The true image of a free people, governed by a patriot king, is that of a patriarchal family, where the head and all the members are united by one common interest, and animated by one common spirit: and where, if any are perverse enough to have another, they will be soon borne down by the superiority of those who have the same." [2] The consequences of such "national union" will be "glory and happiness." [3]

Bolingbroke waxed especially eloquent about English monarchs of the past who had approximated to his ideal of the patriot king—Alfred, Edward I, Edward III, Henry V, and, above all, Elizabeth. [4] Indeed, Elizabeth was his ideal. She "united the great body of the people . . . and inflamed them with one national spirit, and thus armed, she maintained tranquillity at home and carried succour to her friends and terror to her enemies abroad." [5] She "considered the interest of no kingdom, no state, nor people, no not even the general interest of the reformation, as zealous a protestant as she was, nor the preservation of a balance of power in Europe, as great a heroine as she was, in any other light than relatively to the interest of England." [6] It was a result of her wise policy, for instance, that England and Scotland "are now one nation under one government," having "one common interest, the same friends, the same foes, the same principles of security, and of danger." [7]

[1] *The Idea of a Patriot King, Works,* IV, 285. The *Dissertation upon Parties,* as well as much of the *Idea of a Patriot King,* is devoted to an exposition of the evils of government by faction or party, and to a plea for the formation of a truly national party; and the *Remarks on the History of England* point the same moral.
[2] *Ibid.,* IV, 280-281. *Cf. ibid.,* IV, 290-302.
[3] *Ibid.,* IV, 303.
[4] *Collection of Political Tracts* (London, 1748), pp. 266-267. *Cf. Remarks on the History of England, passim.*
[5] *A Dissertation upon Parties, Works,* III, 82.
[6] *Remarks on the History of England, Works,* II, 279.
[7] *Ibid.,* II, 297.

For the strengthening of the national State, there were, in Bolingbroke's mind, two special desiderata. One was religion. "There must be a religion; this religion must be national; and this national religion must be maintained in reputation and reverence."[1] The national religion, of course, should be Deistic; it might well be the "genuine Christianity" of "the Gospels." But it must not be "traditional Christianity" or involve anything superstitious or theological, or lay claims to any independence of the national State. Rather, it should be largely formal and strictly subordinate to the civil power. Every patriot should adhere to it; and the State, though recognizing freedom of conscience and tolerating private religions, should make membership in the national religion a test for public office[2] and should "direct the publick and private influence of the clergy in a strict conformity to the letter and spirit of the [British] constitution, the servants of which in a much truer sense they are, than what they affect sometimes to call themselves, the ambassadors of God to other men."[3]

Outstanding patriots should be the saints of the national religion;[4] and all its ceremonials should doubtless be attended by that "decorum," that "decency," that "grace," that "propriety of manners" which St. John dearly loved.[5] The Church of England, as it was in his day, might conveniently embody his religion of nationalism: it was decent

[1] *Authority in Matters of Religion, Works,* VII, 274. The protestant reformation had been "to the honour of religion surely" (*ibid.,* VII, 236), but it would also have been "to the honour of Christianity" if at the same time silence had been imposed on several dissenting doctrines (*ibid.,* VII, 245).

[2] *Ibid.,* VII, 274-275.   [3] *Ibid.,* VI, 480.

[4] "They deserve to have their festivals kept, instead of that pack of anachorites and enthusiasts, with whose names the kalendar is crowded and disgraced."—*On the Spirit of Patriotism, Works,* IV, 188. "Britain hath been the temple, as it were, of liberty. . . . Here she hath her saints, her confessors, and a whole army of martyrs, and the gates of Hell have not hitherto prevailed against her."—*A Dissertation upon Parties, Works,* III, 194.

[5] *The Idea of a Patriot King, Works,* IV, 321-325.

and decorous; it was perhaps not too Christian; and it was national. With singleness of purpose, therefore, the patriot in his young manhood strenuously championed in Parliament the Conformity and Schism Bills of 1702 and 1714 against Dissenters and in favor of the Established Church,[1] while in his riper years he pleaded, in behalf of national religion, that "all other religions must be kept too low to become the rivals of it." [2]

The other special desideratum for the national State is "coöperation of the landed and moneyed interests." Though the former are the pilots of the political vessel and the latter but passengers in it, landed men have not only "a right to expect that the passengers should contribute their proportion to save the vessel," but also a duty to aid the moneyed interests by promoting trade and commerce.[3] For trade is a national tradition of Great Britain. It had developed before the reign of Queen Elizabeth, "but the great encouragements were given, the great extensions and improvements were made, by that glorious princess. . . . It was she who gave that rapid motion to our whole mercantile system." [4] It should ever be the principal business of the national government "to give ease and encouragement to manufactory at home, to assist and protect trade abroad, to improve and keep in heart the national colonies, like so many farms of the mother country." [5]

With commerce, Bolingbroke associated not only national

---

[1] The "Bill for Preventing Occasional Conformity," introduced by St. John and two other Tory members on Nov. 4, 1702, became law in 1711: it provided that anyone who had qualified for public office by taking the sacrament in the Church of England and should afterwards be convicted of worshipping with Dissenters should forfeit his office and be fined. The Schism Act of 1714, drafted by Bolingbroke himself, prohibited Dissenters from maintaining schools or teaching in them. *Cf.* A. Boyer, *An Impartial History of the Occasional Conformity and Schism Bills* (London, 1717).

[2] *Authority in Matters of Religion, Works,* VII, 274.

[3] *Some Reflections on the State of the Nation, Works,* IV, 388.

[4] *The Idea of a Patriot King, Works,* IV, 308.

[5] *Ibid.,* IV, 309.

wealth but national might and prestige. Such was essentially the politician's defence of his part in the negotiation of the Treaty of Utrecht, and it was the theme to which the philosopher—and patriot—repeatedly adverted. "As trade and commerce enrich, so they fortify, our country. The sea is our barrier, ships are our fortresses, and the mariners, that trade and commerce alone can furnish, are the garrisons to defend them." [1] "By a continual attention to improve . . . her maritime strength," Britain "may be the arbitrator of differences, the guardian of liberty, and the preserver of the balance [of power]." Occasionally Britons "must be soldiers, and for offence as well as defence. . . . Like other amphibious animals, we must come occasionally on shore: but the water is more properly our element." [2]

Sound national policy requires, according to Bolingbroke, an avoidance of entangling alliances or military engagements with European Powers and at the same time a readiness to profit in wealth and prestige from their conflicts.[3] This consideration of the British patriot nicely bolstered the faith of the eighteenth-century philosopher that "a national spirit cannot be other than a defensive, and therefore, unprovoked, a harmless, inoffensive spirit." [4] As philosopher, too, he never expressed dislike of aliens or contempt for foreign nations.

As politician, however, he opposed a Bill which the Whigs enacted in 1709 for the unrestricted immigration and naturalization of "poor foreign protestants." "Let me entreat you," he wrote to the British electors the following year, "never to elect those who love any foreigner whatsoever better than a Briton; who are for stocking the kingdom with

[1] *The Idea of a Patriot King, Works,* IV, 305.
[2] *Ibid.,* IV, 311-312. *Cf. Remarks on the History of England, Works,* II, 289-294.
[3] *Ibid.,* IV, 310-311.
[4] *Remarks on the History of England, Works,* II, 120.

imported beggars, when their own poor are ready to starve." [1] And when the philosopher turned utter patriot, he could chant a pæan to "the fleets covering the ocean, bringing home wealth by the returns of industry, carrying assistance or terrour abroad by the direction of wisdom, and asserting triumphantly the right and the honour of Great Britain, as far as waters roll and as winds can waft them." [2] Near his end he contributed three stanzas to the immortal nationalist anthem of *Rule Britannia,* including the following:

> "Should war, should faction shake thy isle,
> And sink to poverty and shame;
> Heaven still shall on Britannia smile,
> Restore her wealth, and raise her name.
> Rule Britannia, rule the waves:
> Britons never will be slaves." [3]

Before Bolingbroke lifted his patriotic soul in poetry, he had already adumbrated a philosophy of history, which he deemed "new" and which was basically "national." In his eyes, history was no mere scientific quest for truth. He would rather "make as many anachronisms as a Jewish chronologer," than sacrifice half his life "to collect all the learned lumber that fills the head of an antiquary." [4] The kind of history which makes us neither better men nor better citizens is at best but "a creditable kind of ignorance." History is "philosophy teaching by examples." It should be written and studied for "improvement in private and publick virtue." [5] It should, of course, tend to "keep our minds free from a ridiculous partiality in favour of our own country, and a vicious prejudice against others; yet the same study

---

[1] *The Examiner,* No. 10, Oct. 5, 1710, p. 61.
[2] *The Idea of a Patriot King, Works,* IV, 333.
[3] *Works of David Mallet* (London, 1759), vol. III, p. 69. *Cf.* Thomas Davies, *Memoirs of the Life of David Garrick* (London, 1780), vol. II, p. 39.
[4] *On the Study and Use of History, Works,* III, 320.
[5] *Ibid.,* III, 323, 349.

will create in us a preference of affection to our own country." [1]

Much of the history which Bolingbroke wrote was undoubtedly intended to justify his politics or his philosophy, but it served primarily to justify his patriotism. He utilized many "examples" in frontal attacks on theologians or for sharpshooting at Whigs, but a greater number he employed to adorn his constant teaching that, if we "desire to be esteemed good men," we must unite to heal "national divisions," "to change the narrow spirit of party into a diffusive spirit of publick benevolence," and to procure "the peace, the strength, and the glory" of our country. [2]

"Patriotism," Bolingbroke finds, "has in all ages and among all nations been acknowledged a glorious virtue; and the more generous the genius of a people is, the more exalted honours do they pay to those fathers . . . who have made the welfare of their country their great and early care." [3] Besides, a life dedicated to patriotic service admits the full enjoyment of other pleasures: Cato loved wine and Cæsar loved women. [4] But whatever may be the pleasures of such loves (and Bolingbroke should have known), they are incomparably less than that which attends the love of country. The patriotic statesman, Bolingbroke discloses, enjoys a "pleasure like to that which is attributed to the Supreme Being on a survey of His works." [5]

IV

"I turn my eyes from the generation that is going off, to the generation that is coming on the stage." [6] So wrote Henry St. John, Viscount Bolingbroke, with greater truth

---

[1] *On the Study and Use of History, Works,* III, 333-334.
[2] *A Dissertation upon Parties, Works,* III, 40.
[3] *The Craftsman,* No. 54, p. 59.
[4] *On the Spirit of Patriotism, Works,* IV, 202.
[5] *Ibid.,* IV, 203.   [6] *Ibid.,* IV, 209.

[204]

than even he could guess. Could he now come to life and survey the men and movements of the two centuries which have elapsed since he penned those lines, he would doubtless reap the full reward of the philosopher turned patriot. He might be momentarily depressed by the discovery that theologians are still with us and that "traditional Christianity" still flourishes, but eventually, as he contemplated what of modern nationalism he had wrought or foreshadowed, he must share in the ineffable joy of his Supreme Being. Apotheosis must be his.

He would look with fatherly eyes upon George III, the "Patriot King," and upon the King's Friends, and upon the whole later nation that has sung *Rule Britannia* in heart-felt devotion to Victoria, her son, and her grandson. He would particularly patronize Chatham and the younger Pitt, Wellington, and Nelson, Castlereagh and Canning, Disraeli and Salisbury, Cecil Rhodes and Rudyard Kipling, Lord Randolph Churchill and Winston too. He would glory in the abiding English Toryism of patriotism and empire.

He would discern some merits in the utilitarianism of Jeremy Bentham and John Stuart Mill: its principle of hedonism, its watchword of "the greatest good of the greatest number," and its ultimate support of national good works. He would even recognize some value in modern liberalism: its emphasis upon the secular nature of the State, its devotion to trade and commerce, its advocacy of peace and retrenchment and the right of national self-determination.

He would exult in the praises of the British Constitution by Blackstone and Burke and Beaconsfield. He would sympathize with the French Revolutionaries so long as they conceived of a "Jacobin nationalism" within the framework of institutions akin to those of England, but thereafter he would be shocked by their "excesses" and would applaud the "traditional nationalism" which Burke expounded in Great Britain and Bonald in France.

He might perceive a connection between nationalism and nineteenth-century romanticism. But romanticism, in its strangely medieval stained-glass attitudes, and with its curious interest in folk-ways, he could not comprehend and would not endorse. On the other hand, he would understand positivism and would probably approve of its use by Charles Maurras for the "integral nationalism" of French neo-royalism.

In the garden of Fascist Italy, Bolingbroke might perhaps discover the perfect growing specimen of the species of shrub which he had tried to cultivate in a hot-house long ago. True, the gardener now was a patriot duke rather than a patriot king, but the title was immaterial. Here, at any rate, was a people actuated entirely and solely by the spirit of national patriotism, without particular parties or factions, rallying to one national party, intent upon the pursuit of national interests, vigorous in defense of national honor.

"Those who live to see such happy days and to act in so glorious a scene, will perhaps call to mind, with some tenderness of sentiment, when he is no more, a man, who contributed his mite to carry on so good a work."[1] That man, who too modestly described himself, is our philosopher turned patriot. It is high time that nationalists should, "with some tenderness of sentiment," erect a monument, imposing but chaste, to the memory of Henry St. John, Viscount Bolingbroke.

[1] *The Idea of a Patriot King, Works,* IV, 333-334.

THE PLACE OF HISTORY AMONG THE SCIENCES

by

Preserved Smith

XII

THE PLACE OF HISTORY AMONG
THE SCIENCES

THOUGH truth is not only stranger but more interesting than fiction, the main purpose of the veracious historical narrative is not to furnish entertainment. Though it may be true that "histories make men wise," the main purpose of the true historian is not to furnish lessons in moral and political prudence. The true aim of history is like that of the other sciences, to investigate and explain the facts of a particular field of reference. That it has often been written with the purpose of furnishing entertainment or moral instruction does not differentiate it from the other sciences. Astronomy is often presented to the public in such a way as to arouse astonishment at the size of the universe and at the multitude of the stars—it is then "popular science," which is not really science at all, but fiction founded on fact. It has often been treated with the purpose of giving moral lessons—it is then astrology. Only when it is studied with no purpose but to understand the phenomena of the heavens is it science.

But is history a science at all? The question has been debated with much acumen and not a little passion. By those who argue in the negative it is urged that natural science is general, history particular; that the natural sciences, in that they are systems of concepts, speak entirely of universals, and that history speaks entirely of individual facts; that the phenomena studied by science are eternally the same, and those expounded by history are always unique. But this objection breaks down in the face of the consideration that scientific phenomena are universal only when treated in the large; they are unique and varied when treated in the particular. Every star in the heavens differs from every other star; every leaf on every tree has its own individual stamp; every bee in the hive is a distinct personality; and as for the atoms and molecules, that seem so uniform when treated statistically by the billion, there is good reason to suspect that if we knew them each personally they would show as much individual character as do our aunts and cousins.

Moreover, many of the natural sciences are really natural histories in the full sense of the term. Astronomy is a history of the stars and of the solar system; geology the history of the earth, palæontology and biology the history of evolving life forms. Not one of the phenomena treated by these sciences is stable; all are changing from age to age and even from day to day.

But surely, it is urged, the observed facts or demonstrated truths of natural science are more or less colligated by being brought under general laws, whereas the phenomena of human society are incapable of such treatment. This argument errs doubly in overestimating the validity of natural laws and in underestimating the regularity of social phenomena. The leading chemists and physicists are now becoming convinced that scientific laws, which were once held to be so absolute, are in reality but expressions of averages which approximate accuracy only when they concern large numbers. Every atom, every electron, apparently, has its own private preferences and its own incalculable, if not anomalous, action. Two gases mix just as two crowds mix when each unit in both is allowed to move as it chooses; the movement of the unit is incalculable but the general result of the movement in given conditions can be predicted with high accuracy.

And the action of men can be predicted in the mass according to the same rule of average. Nearly the same percentage of murders and of suicides and of marriages occurs year after year in the same population; while the rate of crime, of marriage, and of all other social phenomena varies under seasonal and economic conditions according to ascertainable laws. In fact, the action of men is exactly like the action of atoms or of bees, unpredictable in the individual but nearly constant in the mass. That the laws of social change differ from the laws of biological or of astronomical change is natural.

Another argument of those who deny the title of science to history is that historiography is really an art. Science understands but art creates. Now, from this standpoint, the phenomena of social change in the past are both too varied, too imperfectly known, and too deeply colored with human interest, ever to allow that thorough and impartial study necessary to form a cool scientific judgment. We may *feel* history, it is said, but we cannot explain it. And this is the province of the art: to resurrect the past, to make it vivid to our imagination, to select from the multifarious phenomena those which will appeal to our aesthetic sense of the fitness of things. This tendency has given rise to the expressionistic history of the Germans, who boldly claim that the true function of history is to give sense to the senseless material, and who argue that, while science is knowledge, history is poetry. But this idea, carried to its logical conclusion, is suicidal. It amounts to saying that, provided the narrative is interesting and self-consistent, it makes no difference whether it is true. But, if one can study human society in the past at all, one can arrive at some conclusions about it.

The fact that history is one of a group of kindred studies bent on describing and explaining human society lends powerful support to the view that it is a science. If politics, economics, social psychology, and sociology are sciences, history, which exploits the same field and which works by largely analogous methods, must be their sister. The sociologist or economist studies the static aspects of society; the historian, the dynamic. The one is concerned chiefly with a specious present; the other with the records of a past. History is therefore related to sociology as palæontology is related to botany, or palæobotany to the botany of living plants. Its purpose is to investigate and describe the facts of social evolution, and to explain that evolution in its connection with the relevant physical and psychical factors.

By "explaining" the phenomena of history we mean putting the observed facts in their proper relationships, especially in that causal relationship which, in spite of what philosophers have said against the possibility of such a thing, has usually been accepted by the human mind as the most illuminating means of grasping reality. To claim, as some do, that history is a purely descriptive science, concerned only with fact finding, and that it should leave to sociology or philosophy the formulation of generalizations, is an error fatal to all true understanding even of the facts described. For, masses of fact can be grasped only when gathered into bundles under the collective action of some generalization. To describe facts promiscuously, without arrangement or order, is merely to produce the effect of a buzzing, strident confusion in the most pluralistic of worlds.

What, then, are the causal relationships most helpful in understanding the real processes of social evolution? They are those which lead us to see beneath the surface events of politics and the accidental action of personality the great cosmic forces governing and shaping the development of social forms. The older chroniclers saw in political actions, in wars and revolutions and party politics the essence of the historical process, and in the personality of the actors the mainsprings of the social drive. The history of the world was held to have been shaped by fifteen decisive battles, or by twenty decisive love-affairs, or by some other events equally dependent on the personal factor. But deeper study has shown that what was once worshiped as a first cause is but a secondary effect of the operation of underlying forces. The illusion of the importance of the personal factor in history is in part due to the natural interest of man in his fellows. Could the bees write history, their annals would doubtless consist chiefly of individual portraits. They would extol the beauty of Queen Melissa XXIII, and reprove the hot temper of Queen Melissa XXIV; they would immortalize the virtues of Queen Dido who led the swarm to found their particular hive, and they would sing the prowess of the charming drone Tristram who sought a love-death in the embrace of his mistress.

To an observer as free from human as we are from apiarian passions the life of humanity would seem as regular as the life of the bee seems to us. Beneath the political surface lie several depths of social currents which can be sounded by various scientific methods. Next below the political comes the economic layer. The political revolution is due to the growth or decay of various classes, and this in turn is due to the operation of economic factors. Beneath the economic is a layer of material conditions, geographical, climatic, and technical, on which the course of economic evolution largely depends. More profound than these influences is that of psychology, which determines the use made, by various groups, of material conditions, and which in turn is determined by anthropological, or racial, factors.

Deepest of all the layers to which we can profitably penetrate lies the biological. As man is an animal, his whole life is a perpetual struggle for existence and a perpetual adaptation to environment. But history differs from biology in that man has a unique method of adapting himself to his environment, or rather his environment to himself, due to his intelligence. Other animals modify their environment to create conditions favorable to their survival, but they do it by instinct, changing their methods so slowly that no progress can be observed in thousands or even in millions of years. They do change their technique, to be sure, as they change their bodily forms. The nest of the bird, the honey-comb of the bee, the dam of the beaver, have all evolved from simpler forms, but they have evolved by a series of infinitesimal and accidental improvements, not by any conscious invention. But man's nature is art; his instinct is intelligence. He changes his environment to meet an observed need, and he hands on his improved method to his posterity, to be in turn further perfected by them. On this simple but momentous fact hangs the whole vast complex of historical evolution. In the case of any particular group or nation a change of life may follow contact, friendly or hostile, with another group. But the only creative and original factors in the evolution of the world as a whole and of world culture are the inventions or discoveries by which man has found a new way to change the conditions of his life.

It is true that the most momentous changes following the introduction of a new technical process or the acquisition of fresh knowledge of nature, have not usually been those forseen by the inventors. The invention of clothes, probably for ornament, changed the course of sexual selection and removed some of the limitations of climatic conditions. The invention of printing, by cheapening knowledge, caused one democratic revolution after another. The invention of the steam engine, as an aid to pumping water out of mines, within a century doubled the population of the world and multiplied its wealth in an even higher proportion. So it is with all inventions; their originators could not foresee their ultimate effects. Discoverers are magicians able to summon spirits from the vasty deep, but unable to conjure them back again to their former habitations, or to control their activity on earth. The race is like a child who has half-accidentally started an automobile, but is unable to stop or to guide it.

As habit is the chief regulator of the life of the individual, so custom is the flywheel of society. The end for which customs and for which society itself were evolved is the preservation and expansion of the group. Custom, therefore, and conformity to the patterns of conduct set by the herd have a high survival value, and are enforced not only by the herd instinct but by tremendous institutions of social control. But, though all the unconscious and most of the conscious passions of the group are bent to make perpetual the existing customs and arrangements, the faculty of men for invention and imitation so changes conditions that customs themselves change, and the most powerful institutions give way to a new order of things.

"Invention" must be understood in the widest sense as any improvement in technique, or any discovery in science, or even as any artistic creation of a decidedly innovating kind. It operates in various ways. In the first place it kindles the imagination of men, changing the prevailing world picture or world view, on which so much in religion and ethics depends. When America is discovered the quest for the kingdom of El Dorado supplants the quest for the kingdom of the Holy Sepulchre. When the Copernican astronomy is accepted, the cosmogony of Dante gives way to the cosmogony of Newton.

Secondly, to some extent new lines of action on the part of geniuses produce imitation on the part of the masses. The initiator sets the pattern which the common people adopt—

and the rivalry of the various patterns is the history of the world. But the chief importance of direct influence of this kind is that it sets the run of attention on which the particular line of future invention shall depend. The competition of the various patterns is strictly limited by social conditions; those which are advantageous to the survival of the group in the long run win; those which are harmful perish.

The most important of all the methods by which inventions influence the life of the race is in their power to increase man's mastery of nature. A discovery produces an art; an art produces a comfort or cheapens a necessity; a cheapened staple adds family to family of the population. A new system of production of wealth shifts power from one class to another; improvement in military science gives to one race the dominance over another. And, from the new situation thus created a new type of social life emerges, with fresh needs and novel demands in the intellectual and spiritual, as in the material, sphere.

Whence come the inventions so decisive in history? To say that the birth of geniuses is pure accident is but a partial truth. In a sense, the genius in history is like the mutation or variation in biology. In the one case as in the other science has not fathomed the ultimate causes which insure the production of remarkable individuals. But the true scientific problem is to explain the survival of a given variation in the animal world, or of a given innovation in society. The tendency of the race to produce remarkable individuals must be assumed as a variable; the only problem that can be answered is the use made of such men, and the extent and nature of their influence.

Sociologists and others have, moreover, made it plain that the inventions made at a given time and in a certain society depend more than anything else on the state of culture then and there prevalent. Nothing is more obvious than that every advance in mathematics, for example, is entirely dependent on the state of that science. In general, also, the problems are set, the stream of attention is directed, by the social needs of a special environment. So that it often, in fact usually, happens that several minds simultaneously arrive at nearly the same conclusion, and there is therefore difficulty in deciding to whom is due the priority in making an invention. To ask which comes first, the invention or the social demand, is like the question about the chicken and the egg. Each new invention creates a slightly new situation; each new situation makes new demands. Finally, the greatest inventions are not complete in themselves, but are usually but small improvements accumulated through years and sometimes through ages. The modern locomotive is not a single creation, but is a protracted evolution, the product of a long process of experiment and of successive improvements.

If, then, we could describe every new discovery by which the milieu in which man has lived has been altered, if we could trace every revolution in politics to its source in social shifts or economic changes, and these in turn to their springs in applied science, if we could show that religious belief and philosophical speculation and artistic creation were determined by the social mould and that this in turn was shaped by the state of man's knowledge and by his methods of adapting his environment to his needs, should we have a perfect history? Theoretically, yes; but yet the mind has its misgivings. Try as they may to jump out of their skins, men cannot write about other men as they write about bees and about atoms; and could they do so they would miss one of the great interests of study. To lay stress on the personal is to make history unscientific; to omit it altogether is to make our study inhuman. The one fails to satisfy the intellect; the other to interest the emotions, which have their reasons the reason knows not of. Like so many philosophical dilemmas, this one to which the historian is reduced presents two equally sharp and uncomfortable horns. "Ion," said Socrates to the poet, "would you prefer to be considered dishonest or inspired?" a similar question would reduce the modern historiographer to an extremely awkward predicament in answering.

HENRI de SAINT-SIMON

by

Leland Hamilton Jenks

XIII

HENRI DE SAINT-SIMON

ONE of the wicked speculators of whom Robespierre sought to purge the Republic was a certain Citoyen Simon, born Comte de Rouvroy, better known as Henri de Saint-Simon.[1] During the months that Simon lay confined on suspicion in the Luxembourg, his ancestor Charlemagne appeared to him one night, as he wrote his nephew Victor— then serving Napoleon in Spain—in 1810. "From the beginning of the world," Charlemagne addressed him, "no family has enjoyed the honor of producing both a hero and a philosopher of the first class; this honor was reserved for my house. My son, your success as philosopher will equal that which I obtained as soldier and as statesman." The Thermidorian reaction opened the doors of the Luxembourg soon after and enabled M. de Saint-Simon to reap a considerable fortune before he dedicated himself in 1797 exclusively "to study the march of the human spirit, and afterward to work for the perfecting of civilization."

The *grand seigneur sans-culotte*—in Michelet's phrase— was then a well-known person in Paris. A fine figure of a man, with open face and laughing manner and remarkable eyes above his penetrating nose, he was all absorbed with business and women, always with zest, prodigiously curious,

[1] The incompleteness of the records of Saint-Simon's life give it much of its superficially fragmentary appearance. The memoir of Hubbard, N. G. A., *Saint-Simon, sa vie et ses travaux* (Paris, 1857), based upon data supplied by Olinde Rodrigues, has been drawn upon largely for the historical notice prefixed to the *Œuvres de Saint-Simon et d'Enfantin* (47 vols., Paris, 1865 ff.), I: 1-133. Saint-Simon left several autobiographical fragments, which are accessible in the *Œuvres*, Vol. I (Paris, 1868).

incessantly observing. His personal charm won him inseparable companions of all classes, partners who made him partial recompense for their double-dealing, servants who were to provide him subsistence when the quest of science had ruined him in pocket and in health, students of science of whom he was at once patron and disciple. His latter contacts enabled Saint-Simon to rationalize the catholicity of his tastes, the unconventional lack of discrimination in his conduct. To make important discoveries in philosophy, he explained in an autobiographical fragment (1809), it was necessary

"1. To lead the most original and active life possible during all the years of one's prime;

"2. To become thoroughly acquainted with all theories and all practices;

"3. To frequent all classes of society, placing one's self personally in the greatest number of different social positions, and even creating relationships which have never existed;

"4. Finally, to employ old age in summing up one's observations upon the effects which have followed these actions for others and for one's self, and to found principles upon these résumés."

Life as a consummate laboratory experiment, in short, was the unifying conception which gave meaning to the mature Saint-Simon for his varied career.

It was an experiment that may be thought by some to have failed. For Saint-Simon has not achieved the renown, which he sought, of a Bacon, a Descartes, a Newton. And little short of that would reward his soaring ambition. Consideration, credit, glory—these were the compelling goals that in reality polarized his life. The story may be apocryphal that in his teens Saint-Simon instructed his valet to rouse him at dawn and say, *"Levez-vous, monsieur le comte, vous avez de grandes choses à faire."* But it typifies the youth who at thirteen escaped prison where he had been confined for refusing communion; who was in America fighting for independence at nineteen; who achieved a colonelcy at twenty-two and lost one inheritance, after he had tried to interest the Viceroy of Mexico in a project for a canal through Panama; and who worked at plans for a joint expedition to India with the Dutch and upon a project for building a canal from Madrid to the Mediterranean, before the coming of the Revolution destroyed his maternal inheritance and left him at twenty-nine to build his fortunes anew and eagerly as an egalitarian. In retrospect Saint-Simon declared that he sought money only as a means. Indeed he claimed only 144,000 livres from his partner when he retired from active business. Nevertheless to buy up all the *biens nationaux* of a *département*, to establish a commission house, to organize a wine business, to deal on a large scale in Paris building property and to project a colossal bank, were "great things" enough to attract comment in the days of the Directory. It seemed more hardy to the soldier and promoter of thirty-seven to embark on a career of forwarding science.

Certainly it was no new idea with Saint-Simon, even as he cherished compensatory dreams in prison. He had been schooled by D'Alembert; and he wrote his father from Yorktown of his impatience "to do a scientific work useful to humanity." Now he began by attending lectures at the École Polytechnique for several years and later at the École de Médecine. He mingled with professors and students, helped them freely from his funds, made his house a center where good wine and good cheer promoted lively discussion. Conversation was as profitable to him as books. In order to maintain a more pretentious salon, he married, in 1801. But the small talk of the heavy thinkers was disillusioning. His funds simultaneously ran low. Mme. de Staël, intellectual and enormously rich, was left a widow.

Shedding bitter tears at parting from a woman of whom he continued to be very fond, Saint-Simon divorced his wife (who later as Mme. de Bawr achieved minor literary fame) and sought out Necker's daughter. "The first man of the world could not have as spouse but the first woman." The son of such a union could not fail to climb the philosophic heights even should the father fail. Mme. de Staël did not recognize her opportunity, however. And Saint-Simon was left to a lonely, impoverished struggle to find meaning for the knowledge he had acquired and to obtain recognition for doing so.

Was it in reaction from his own headstrong, libertarian career, or from the social disorder of the First Republic, that Saint-Simon sought zealously to establish order, relationship, unity in the world of ideas? It was the chaos and anarchy of the universe as left by the critical science of the preceding century that chiefly impressed him. In his first writing, published anonymously, the *Lettres d'un habitant de Genève* (1803),[1] Saint-Simon announced somewhat apocalyptically that all phenomena, physical and moral, were subject to one universal law, and that that law was the principle of universal gravitation. God had appeared to Saint-Simon in a dream, he pretended,[2] and had not only revealed this great truth but had prophesied the replacement of Rome by a scientific hierarchy as His Church, dedicated to the cult of

[1] There is no complete edition of Saint-Simon's writings. The most accessible collection is the *Œuvres de Saint-Simon* (11 vols., Paris, 1868-76), published by the executors of the will of Enfantin. Some writings not here included were reprinted by Lemonnier in his *Œuvres choisies* (Bruxelles, 1859). Original editions of Saint-Simon are very scarce, and it is believed that the Bibliothèque de l'Arsenal is the only place where they are all to be found.

[2] Saint-Simon wrote steadily with tongue in cheek. In the same work he declared religion to be "a human invention . . . the only sort of a political institution which tends to the general organization of humanity." A little later (1808) he wrote that "Socrates invented God." Moses also did so. On other occasions it is possible to find Saint-Simon declaring that he "believes in God" (1810 and 1825). It seems that his divinity, however, was the law of human progress.

Newton. A *Conseil de Newton,* composed of twenty-one elected men of science and of art, was to be endowed with enormous funds, invested with consideration, and empowered to direct the social activities of mankind toward the advancement of science.[1] The verification of the law of gravitation was to be the starting-point for its program of studies.

Most of Saint-Simon's fundamental attitudes emerged, well-developed, in this most romantic of his writings. There was a "humanity" for whose steadily increasing well-being individuals and society existed. The good, the deification, of humanity was to be sought in the *progrès des lumières*—the advancement of knowledge. The scientist was therefore the great spiritual leader of society. It was essential to his independence (and hence to his fruitfulness) that there be a distinct separation of the spiritual from the temporal power, that ample social consideration and means be accorded scientists and artists. "And all men shall work; they shall look upon themselves as laborers in a workshop whose task it is to approximate human intelligence" to a postulated absolute.

For ten years Saint-Simon worked at the philosophy of science and scientific method, elaborating his conception of what he called alternatively *physicisme* and *philosophie positive.* He sought to develop his idea in such shape that it would receive recognition from the scholarly world, and would bring collaborators in what he felt himself would be beyond the powers of a single individual. He worked at times in great distress. "For three weeks I have eaten dry bread and have drunk water," he wrote in 1813, enclosing a manuscript copy of his *Travail sur la Gravitation Universelle* to one whose patronage he solicited; "I have worked without

[1] A year later, in writing to a friend, Saint-Simon described a *Parlement de perfection,* that was to enjoy supreme spiritual power, direct a system of public education, and have the functions of certification and removal of all public functionaries. There were to be fifteen *industriels* in this body as well as thirty *savants* and five *artistes.* It was this conception, rather than that of the cult of Newton, which Saint-Simon later developed.

[225]

fire and have sold everything down to my last shirt to defray the expense of copies necessary to make my work known." The eminent members of the Institut left their pages uncut. Like the Bureau of Longitudes, to which Saint-Simon had earlier appealed, they seemed "but scientific anarchists," denying "the existence, the supremacy of general theory." Nor could Napoleon's attention be secured, no matter how suave the dedicatory prefaces, no matter how tempting the subtitle, *Moyens de faire reconnaître aux Anglais l'Indépendance des Pavillons*. Life had been for the *ci-devant* count, as he declared, "a series of failures." Pursuing what all regarded as a chimæra, he seems at this time most like the hero of Balzac's tragi-comedy, *La Recherche de l'Absolu*.

Meanwhile Saint-Simon's attention had been shifting from the universe to society, or, as he put it, from astronomy to physiology. The great work of the nineteenth century, he wrote a friend in 1804, would be that "the science of social organization will become a positive science." As the astrologers had been banished from astronomy and the alchemists from the study of chemistry, though they had rendered useful service in preparing the way for those sciences, so the moralists were to be expelled from physiology before a comprehensive positive philosophy would be possible. And the quest of universal gravitation had not deterred Saint-Simon from filling the limited editions of his writings with long sequences of ideas upon the "history of the past and future of the human species," which seemed to him the method by which "social physiology" could be formulated.

A severe illness interrupted Saint-Simon's work in 1813 and combined with the desperate stand of Napoleon against the Sixth Coalition to fix his mind more exclusively upon the immediate "amelioration of the lot of humanity" and the "discovery of remedies for the ills that afflict at this time all humanity, especially European society." His *Mémoire sur la*

Science de l'Homme (1813), a "prodigious" manuscript, not published until 1858, formulated with great hardihood considerations looking toward a cultural anthropology. And it acquired for him his first pupil-collaborator, Augustin Thierry, whom Saint-Simon—perpetual undergraduate—encountered at the École Normale. Science must do something, it seemed then, if only in the interest of its own tranquillity, to regenerate the actual world. "You alone can bring calm to Europe," Saint-Simon pleaded to the savants; "you alone can reorganize European society; time presses, blood flows, hasten to pronounce yourselves; circumstances are so imperative that principles must be applied by simple inspection; this time practice must march before theory."

While scientists maintained such calm as was possible in the face of the prospective overthrow of the man to whom they owed their dignities, Saint-Simon and his pupil labored at a book, *De la Réorganisation de la Société Européenne* (1814). For the first time in his intellectual career, the Comte de Saint-Simon made some stir. Not for want of boldness. The proposals for a union of France and England as the first step toward the organization of a common politico-economic system for all Europe, accorded ill with the prevailing egoistic national currents which Saint-Simon decried. The advantages for industry and commerce of a common banking and currency system may be thought to have found their first concretion in the International Bank just mooted in the Young plan. And the idea of a grand parliament of peoples, judge of disputes between governments, director of peaceful enterprises of public utility for all Europe, promoting a common system of public instruction, inculcating a common moral code, and exerting a common effort toward the Europeanizing of the world, is only now putting forth roots for its partial institutional realization. It was characteristic that Saint-Simon imposed productive

[227]

work as a qualification for members of his European parliament. He would admit merchants, scientists, magistrates and administrators, some of each group to be proprietors of land, some to be non-proprietors. The electorate was to be based upon professional groups, by countries, rather than upon smaller territorial areas. These important matters settled, Saint-Simon did not trouble greatly about forms. He stipulated hereditary monarchy and, at this time, an hereditary peerage composed of men of great fortunes recruited frequently from the ranks of those who had performed services of great importance for European society. Saint-Simon concluded his book with the eloquent phrase which summed up his own philosophy and has been in some measure the keynote of social aspiration since his day:

"The golden age of the human race is not behind us, it is before; it is in the perfection of the social order; our fathers have not seen it, our children will some day arrive; it is for us to make the way to it for them."

For a year Saint-Simon busied himself with political writing, developing his pacifist idea, seizing the return from Elba, the victory of the Allies, and the peril to purchasers of the national domains from the returning *émigrés* as topics discussion of which might redound to his credit. In none of these did he broach the vein of ideas whose development was to be his most distinctive contribution to modern thought. He became impressed in 1816, however, with the heavy burdens of indemnity which France must bear. Only by work could the wealth be acquired to meet these obligations. The object of France must then be industry. And the idea flashed into Saint-Simon's mind that in the social and political exaltation of the *industriel* was the clue to social reorganization. When he hoisted the epigraph, *"Tout par l'industrie, tout pour elle,"* as his banner, he felt renewed conviction that he had found a work of social consequence which would bring him that "living, speaking glory" which he avowed was the goal of all his efforts. The prospectus of *L'Industrie, ou Discussions politiques, morales et philoso-phiques, dans l'intérêt de tous les hommes livrés à des travaux utiles et indépendants* (1817) fairly represents the spirit of the work which absorbed Saint-Simon's energies from the autumn of 1816:

"The eighteenth century did nothing but destroy; we are not going to continue its work: what we undertake is, on the other hand, to lay the foundation for new construction . . . it is to see that politics, morals and philosophy, instead of stopping forever at idle and impractical con-templations, shall be brought at last to their true occupation, which is to establish social welfare; it is, in a word, to see that liberty may be no longer an abstraction, nor society a romance.

"Society rests in its entirety upon industry. Industry is the sole guar-anty of its existence, the only source of wealth and of prosperity. A state of things most favorable to industry is for that very reason the one most favorable to society. There is in a nut-shell the starting point and the goal of all our efforts."

This was not quite literally true. But the promise helped to make Saint-Simon no longer a lone worker or in desperate straits. A distinguished list of bankers responded to his ap-peal for funds. Numerous disciples collaborated in preparing the publications which now in almost monthly instalments appeared over the name of "Henri Saint-Simon." A succes-sion of secretaries followed Thierry, who was promoted to be *fils adoptif* before he undertook his historical labors in-dependently. Among others, a young mathematics teacher named Auguste Comte joined the Saint-Simonian establish-ment and remained on the terms of greatest intimacy as Saint-Simon's assistant, pupil and collaborator for six years.

It must be made clear that when Saint-Simon spoke of *industrie* and coined the terms *industriels* and *système in-dustriel,* he was not specially aware of phenomena which have been brought about by the introduction of machinery.

[229]

Technological advance in France had been delayed by the revolutionary and Napoleonic régimes. France was still essentially an agricultural country. Thirty years after Waterloo, seventy-five per cent of the population were still rural. Yet machinery was being introduced in Saint-Simon's day and industrial concentration was under way. Steam power was rare before 1830. Commercial banking had developed only in the largest centers and with limited application. *Industriel* applied, therefore, not merely to manufacturers, but to all persons engaged in productive work. Over against them in true interest, Saint-Simon now classed the *oisifs*, the *rentiers*, the governing and possessing classes, who lived upon revenue without making positive contribution of social usefulness. Scientists, artists, artisans and men who worked with the hoe were *industriels* as surely as the master of a forge or the owner of a shipping concern.

Thus Saint-Simon developed the view of society as "the ensemble and union of men devoted to useful tasks." France had "become a great manufacture, and the French nation a great workshop." Politics was "the science of production." And the object of the political association of Frenchmen was "to prosper by pacific works of a positive utility."

The prevailing institutions of France, Saint-Simon recognized, did not conform to this analysis of underlying realities. There was instead a "government of producers by nonproducers"; an arrangement by which "the great culprits, the robbers general, are charged with the punishing of petty offenses against society." Government was in fact an expensive survival which, while it had once served to protect industry from banditry and invasion, was now largely a wasteful and injurious burden, interested in promoting policies which would make it as expensive as possible. Both wealth and consideration went to those who were least useful to society. It was from this great disharmony between the real interests and forces of the community and the dominating institutions that arose the conditions of chronic revolution which had prevailed for thirty years. And confronted by revolution and instability, Saint-Simon yearned as always for order, organization, unity. The existing situation was one of social disease, he felt; and as a social physician he diagnosed the complaint.

Briefly, the body politic was in a condition of crisis caused by a "transition from the feudal and theological system to the industrial and scientific system." The critical philosophy of the eighteenth century had broken the hold of theological conceptions in the intellectual realm. The Revolution had destroyed the feudal system. But the old order had been replaced on the one hand by metaphysicians, mistaking words for things (liberals like Benjamin Constant, authoritarians like Bonald and de Maistre), and on the other by legists and the bastard mixture of feudal and industrial institutions called constitutionalism.

Saint-Simon enforced and clarified his interpretation by an elaborate appeal to history, voiced in a series of fugitive publications which are a puzzle for bibliographers.[1] He had always viewed history as consisting in the steady march of civilization toward the greater happiness of mankind. He now saw more than the steady advancement of human knowledge, which had prompted his quest for the principle of universal gravitation, more than the continuous movement of thought from fetishism, through polytheism and theism toward the scientific view of the universe. This movement of ideas, he still felt, was primary. Corresponding changes in social valuation—in *morale*—were indispensable prerequisites to changes in institutions. He now read also in

[1] *Le Politique* (1819), *L'Organisateur* (1820), *Du système industriel* (1821-22) and *Catéchisme des industriels* (1823-24) were the titles under which Saint-Simon assembled the most considerable of these sequences.

history a steady development of institutions, premised upon a long struggle between the military classes on the one hand and the industrial classes on the other.

Slavery had been the lot of the *industriels,* so ran his summaries of civilization, in ancient times. The revolution in ideas heralded by Socrates and continued to the triumph of Christianity had implemented the transmutation of slavery into serfdom. There had arisen in the Middle Ages under the leadership of the Church an organic, harmonious society, in which social institutions corresponded to the state of knowledge. That the Middle Ages were not static, Saint-Simon was ready to urge. For it was their principal glory that they cradled the movements which promoted a progressive alteration of the intellectual and material aspects of society.[1] Contact with the Arabs led to the continuous development in Europe of scientific observation. The emancipation of the communes correlatively marked an early step forward for the industrial classes. And there had ensued a steady encroachment of the *industriels* upon the military, governing classes, partly resulting from the changing military technique which rendered governments more dependent upon materials which manufacturers could supply, partly due to the increasing wealth and self-esteem of the *industriels.* The foundation was laid for the growth of solidarity of interest between various branches of industrial life by the rise of banking practices in the days of Louis XIV. The political position of the *industriels* had been furthered by the English and French Revolutions. And their steady upward trend in social consequence would continue, Saint-Simon inferred, until all power would rest in their hands, until the time when the nation would

[1] So far as I am aware, Saint-Simon deserves credit for having first grasped thus completely the significance of what James Harvey Robinson has called the "continuity of history."

"regard savants, artists and artisans as the most useful men and consequently as those who should receive the greatest consideration . . . when the functions of governors will be reduced to that of college proctors."

Then and then only, there would be possible a new organic constitution of society, based upon positive law instead of upon theology or metaphysics. And mankind would move forward unhampered to enjoy "all the individual and collective happiness to which human nature can pretend."

Meanwhile what could Saint-Simon do, besides discerning and describing this great phenomenon which was under way? Was it incumbent upon this philosopher in quest of great things, this promoter with heart beating high for the good of humanity and his own glory, to await inactively the inevitable consummation? What was "most worthy the wisdom of man, to creep toward his goal, or to run?" Unless the knowledge of the inevitable changes led to scientific prevision, to the careful preparation of public opinion, to the planning of the steps by which it could most conveniently take place, Saint-Simon was confident that the social transition would proceed as former changes had done, through conflict and disorder, injurious to the peaceful interests of industry, and likely to delay still further the eventual well-being. It was to move persons of consequence, bankers, great manufacturers, the reigning Bourbon, the Holy Alliance, to take a directing part in the industrial transformation, that Saint-Simon bent his principal energies. He won spasmodic subscriptions, sporadic sympathy, one prosecution, and a *Chant des industriels* from the pen of Rouget de Lisle.

Saint-Simon's greatest difficulty was to furnish those with whom he argued with a clear conception of the *système industriel*. What would the industrial state be like, aside from the great consideration which was to be reserved for the producing classes?

The great concern of the coming order, Saint-Simon

claimed, would be to administer, not to govern. The principal task of its leaders would be to invent, examine and execute great projects of general social usefulness. The functions thus indicated would be in the hands of those professionally qualified to exercise them. The task of inventing ideas for realization he assigned as a work of the imagination to a board of engineers and artists. Examination, inquiry as to the social value of these ideas, was assigned to a board of scientists, which also was to direct public instruction and inculcate a scientific catechism. Final approval, the arrangement of the budget of national expenditures, and the execution of projects was for a board composed of the leaders of each branch of material industry, headed by the banking group. The last-named body would have the highest temporal authority in the new order.

The existing functions of government were to have but a subordinate place in the *système industriel*. No doubt an army of some sort would be needed, but not a professional one. The industrious people must be protected from disturbance. The functions of police were, however, incidental to the main business of society. Saint-Simon argued vigorously on behalf of a system of industrial arbitration for the adjustment of civil difficulties by way of conciliation. National hatreds were feudal survivals which would pass as *industriels* of all nations realized the solidarity of their interests. The king would be the first *industriel*, as he had been the first soldier. As for democracy, there could be no justification in a positive science of politics for the exercise of functions by persons who had not been specially trained for the purpose.

There were many questions, which have filled the discussions of socialism since Saint-Simon's day, which he left almost unnoticed. He was inclined to minimize the possibility of conflict between different groups of producers. That workmen and their employers were at loggerheads in England, he could not fail but see. But he thought that French masters could be so enlightened as to perceive the identity of interests of all producers, and would make common cause with instead of against the industrious masses. For in the new order to which he pointed the way, Saint-Simon believed that the great *entrepreneurs* of the industrial system would earn much greater wealth as well as enjoy consideration.[1]

But the march of civilization was nothing for Saint-Simon if it did not mean the advancement of humanity. And with the changes which he began to visualize concretely in 1820, just as the *Ultras* triumphed in the elections, Saint-Simon began to stress other values in the new order besides peace and prosperity. He specified that the first charge upon the budget of the *système industriel* should be the provision of work for those who had no other means of subsistence. Compulsory education of the entire population in the elements of the positive sciences, physical and moral, was presently another first charge upon the national budget. And by 1825, Saint-Simon was adding provision for pleasures and amusements for all, appropriate for the development of the intelligence.

Such philanthropy, Saint-Simon would argue, was not quixotic. That the basis of moral science was the principle, "Love one another; do good one to the other," seemed to him increasingly a matter of positive demonstration. Not that individuals as such were motivated except by notions of self-interest. But with the complication of the industrial processes of society, the distinct interests of individuals in-

[1] It remained for the Saint-Simonian follower, Bazard, in his *Doctrine de Saint-Simon: Exposition* (1829) to develop the abolition of inheritances as an important feature of the system. Bazard portrayed the system as a gigantic investment bank. Saint-Simon's writings that I have been able to examine, contain no hint of this.

creasingly approximated the common interest of the mass. While the social transition meant that individuals would be less dependent upon other individuals, they would be increasingly dependent upon cooperation with larger groups. Consideration and other rewards would attend the accomplishment of great things for humanity, in this other society in which Saint-Simon was constrained to feel that he did not yet live.

There were times when, as in March, 1822, Saint-Simon could write his daughter that he expected "great and heroic results" within a couple of months. A year later, resources temporarily exhausted, he was convinced that a longer campaign than he had expected would be required to prepare the way for the social transformation. Only the faithful Juliana remained, and his dog Turk. Commending Juliana to the banker Ternaux, Saint-Simon worked away at his manuscript until the appointed hour, then put six bullets in his head. As he recovered from this painful experiment, which he observed with scientific zeal, he encountered a young Jewish banker, Olinde Rodrigues, whose devotion was less circumscribed than that of the myriad other men whose friendship Saint-Simon had previously made and rewarded, but who could not keep pace with his imperious impatience.

Saint-Simon now perceived more keenly than before, although not for the first time, that there was need for a transformation of the sentiments of the intellectual and industrial classes. Most of all was it necessary to struggle against the spiritual basis upon which the rising authoritarian reaction in France was based, and to oppose to it something more positive than the echoes of the Voltairean critique which haunted the political liberals. This need Saint-Simon sought to meet in his last work, *Nouveau Christianisme* (1825). The book was a slashing attack upon Catholicism and Protestantism for their failure to realize the primitive Christian ethic. That both theological systems had been useful, he admitted, in conformity with his belief in continued progress. Now there must come a religious reconstruction, with a clergy schooled in positive science and preaching nothing in conflict therewith, and with a consistent ethic based upon the principle, *"Tous les hommes doivent se conduire à l'égard les uns des autres comme des frères."* Saint-Simon appealed to the monarchs of the Holy Alliance to institute the new religion:

> "Hearken to the voice of God, who speaks to you through me; . . . united in the name of Christianity, fulfil the duties it imposes on the powerful; remember that it commands them to use all their powers to increase as rapidly as may be the social welfare of the poor."

Rare bursts of hortatory eloquence such as this have caused some students of Saint-Simon's career to regard him primarily as a great social mystic, as a "positivist Messiah," and have helped to enforce the popular label of him as a "utopian socialist." [1] Indeed he wore at times the garb of a prophet, for the world as he experienced it was something that with all his indefatigable zeal he could not adequately report. No doubt Saint-Simon experienced crises of mystical emotion; he must repeatedly have been hungry. And the

[1] Cf. Brunet, G., *Le mysticisme social de Saint-Simon* (Paris, 1925); Dumas, G., *Psychologie des deux Messies positivistes: Saint-Simon et Auguste Comte* (Paris, 1905). The term *précurseur du socialisme,* rendered current by Weill in his capital study, *Saint-Simon et son œuvre* (Paris, 1894) defines accurately his position with reference to the socialist movement. The grossest misconceptions of Saint-Simon have been set forth by the most respectable authorities. Faguet in *Politiques et Moralistes du dix-neuvième siècle* (1903) calls him a "feudal philanthropist." Bury, J. B., *The Idea of Progress* (London, 1920), charges that Saint-Simon's one idea was the law of alternation of organic and critical stages, a conception which was in fact only an implication with Saint-Simon, drawn upon as the basis of the idea-systems both of Comte and of the Saint-Simonian school. Janet, *Saint-Simon et le Saint-Simonisme* (Paris, 1878) is the fairest summary of his work.

progrès des lumières, which Saint-Simon so much admired, causes later generations to be keenly aware of the short-comings of his information. It is not the vagueness of his considerations, however, so much as their radical clarity that must impress the student who, like Sainte-Beuve, views Saint-Simon in the milieu of his contemporary political romantics. He must find in him an unrivalled capacity for generating ideas, coupled with inadequate talent for their development by means of analysis, methodical verification or rationalization. Saint-Simon's mind literally teemed with new conceptions of social relationships, nearly all of them practicable, however unique, and many of them of distinct merit. His was not, however, the art of verbal liaison. "The best edifice is that in which there is least mortar," he declared. "We shall present our ideas to you in their state of native nudity." This was not among the more inspired of Saint-Simon's ideas.

Considered as a social prophet, however, Saint-Simon merits the most respectful attention. The transition from political anthropophagy has indeed been longer than he hoped. And men still may marvel that the soothsayers meet without laughing. A cynical generation has faltered in the generous faith in continuous progress of a definitely ameliorative quality, which Saint-Simon as much as any one inspired in the nineteenth century. The *progrès des lumières* has brought conceptions of psychology and social habitudes which ill accord with the patterns in which Saint-Simon thought. Yet he was the true herald of trends of thought and action which, formed in the nineteenth century, bid fair to be major sequences in the twentieth.

A generation ago, the sympathetic Weill could write that Saint-Simonism was dead. The last decade has produced more appreciations of his work than the preceding century.

"Scarcely a party or a school," declare two recent appraisers,[1] "has not borrowed something of doctrine or at least of phraseology" from Saint-Simon or his immediate followers. These discernible "influences"—upon the national workshops of 1848 and upon Marxian socialism—upon the scientific study of society and such movements as Social Catholicism—upon Carlyle and Mill, de Vigny and Dumas fils, de Lesseps and Renan, Bismarck and Lenin—suggest episodes in the genealogy of ideas which it would be fascinating to narrate. The prescience of Saint-Simon must, however, seek its verification in the more general movement of events. It is perhaps significant that after a relapse into religious traditionalism alternating with aggressive naturalism, the search is begun anew in the western world for ethical formulations, congruent with the scientific view of the universe. Industry has not failed to increase its social esteem and its dominance over the minds and habitudes of men. And in its growth it has given rise to institutions of self-organization, such as Saint-Simon dimly foresaw. The growth of industrial banking, of investment trusts, of vast industrial integrations and conglomerates, of rationalization schemes, of standards committees and arbitration agreements, of professional business administration and of avowals, at least, of "service" as the *raison d'être* of business—these phenomena have been proceeding with such terrific speed that their significance for the internal equilibrium of the state is even less clearly apprehended than their external importance. Many are disposed to recognize with the neo-Saint-Simonians in France that "despite wars, and in the midst of wars, there continues to grow, confusedly and as a city in the clouds, a cosmopolitan world of production and of exchange." But economic cosmopolitanism implies and de-

[1] Preface by Bouglé et Halévy to their edition of the *Exposition* (Paris, 1925).

pends upon a continued rise of industrial administration toward a rôle of public responsibility which must alter fundamentally the internal basis, structure and functions of the state. Our minds are not yet ready to grasp this. Yet we may believe that the capitalistic socialist state of Saint-Simon's predictions is more plausible in the days of the Young plan than it could possibly have seemed in the days of Chateaubriand and Charles X. Historians are now wont to cover themselves with self-reproach. It may not be their task to appraise the reality, the degree, the rapidity of such tendencies as these. But it is precisely our inadequate ideas of what is going on around us that most powerfully govern those actions we can control. Saint-Simon described our condition a century ago: "Marching almost with closed eyes, along a road we do not know, we fancy ourselves sometimes neighbors of what is far away, and more often think far distant what is close at hand."

A few weeks after the publication of *Nouveau Christianisme*, Saint-Simon died. Conscious to the last, he continued to elaborate aspects of his ideas, and to discuss the details of a periodical, *Le Producteur*, that was being founded to expound them. He believed that his critique of Christianity would rally large numbers of the Catholic clergy and churchmen to assist in effecting a rapid transition to the industrial and scientific system; he was happy in the belief that he had at last done something. "Remember," he said to Rodrigues just before he died, "to do great things it is necessary to be passionate." As the philosopher of the line of Charlemagne brought his laboratory experiment to a close, his friends, overcome with mystical devotion to their master, hastened to spread the doctrines which had been the fruit of Saint-Simon's passion for glory and the good of man, while they altered them, in conformity with their understanding of the law of progress.

THE FALL OF CONSTANTINOPLE
SYMBOLICALLY CONSIDERED

by

Louise Ropes Loomis

XIV

THE FALL OF CONSTANTINOPLE
SYMBOLICALLY CONSIDERED

SINCE the days of the Hebrew prophets who lightened their captivity with rhapsodies and visions, men
have taken cities as types of different kinds of human life
and their downfall as the defeat of the particular kind of
life they typified. To the prophets Babylon was the great
harlot, "the golden cup in the Lord's hand that made all
the earth drunken." [1] The wrath of Jehovah smote her and
she became a desolation. Jerusalem, on the other hand, was
the place of peace and fulfilment of happiness. Her destruction signified the removal of peace and happiness to the
world of ideal things to come. Athens, in her turn, seemed
to Greeks like Pericles and Thucydides "the school of
Hellas," where beauty and freedom were loved as nowhere
else.[2] Her decline was the setting of the sun upon the world.[3]
Imperial Rome ruled the nations as judge and lawgiver "to
enforce the ways of peace." [4] Her capture by barbarians
meant to the fifth century the sinking of civilization in a
welter of violence. Babylon, Jerusalem, Athens, Rome and
a few more,[5] they are still to us, ages after, imperishable

---

[1] Jeremiah, LI, 7.

[2] Thucydides, II, 40, 41.

[3] Hypereides, Funeral Oration; extract in Botsford and Sihler's Hellenic
Civilization, 611.

[4] Vergil, Æneid, VI, 852.

[5] *E.g.* Sodom, Sparta, possibly Venice. Paris in recent times is such a city
and, probably, New York. London has never assumed so sharp and concise
a form in the general mind. There is, for instance, no adjective "Lon-
donian" to denote a special quality of person produced in London, equivalent to Athenian, Spartan, Roman or Parisian. The word "Londoner" implies nothing as to character, merely the fact of residence in London.

symbols of a life that we either love or hate. A modern poet dreams of building Jerusalem

> "In England's green and pleasant land."

There have been other cities, equally great, perhaps, and famous, which have never in Western imagination taken on this symbolic character. Damascus, Alexandria, Milan, Augsburg, Bruges, all rich and busy hives of men, they have not seemed to epitomize so clearly one peculiar way of life, to be reducible, as it were, to one prepotent personality, distinct from any other city. Most of these cities also have suffered no overwhelming catastrophe that brought into contrast the vigorous thing they had been with the bleak thing they became and so made it easier to perceive the essential, distinguishing quality about them.

There is a third and smaller group of cities, of which Troy may stand as an example, which might have become symbols and did not. Troy, according to the early Homeric poets, was a city that counted on its strength and favor with the gods to condone a crime and for that reason perished in blood and fire. Taken thus simply, Troy was an emblem of sacrilege meeting due vengeance. But her story was told again by later, more sensitive Athenians, who saw not only the one guilty pair but also the crowd of heroic defenders on the walls and the watching, agonized women. It was told yet again by an Italian to whom Troy was the nursery of the mighty ancestors of Rome. So the significance of the city in literature became confused. She was either wanton or superb as one chose to regard her. Given one interpretation alone, she might have been symbolic; given two apparently contradictory interpretations, she could not be, for a symbol must above all be consistent, presenting a single aspect.

Christian Constantinople might, it would seem, have been

one of the first group of cities. Her august foundation, her long dominion, her cruel fate set her on an eminence above the other cities of her time. She was the New Rome that had added Hellenic culture and Christian faith to the old, imperial magnificence and for centuries had restrained and taught the pagan hordes of the East, until at length they had broken down the walls of Theodosius and Justinian and laid her waste.

In 1453, there were men in the West who saw her in this light. On July 12, Aeneas Sylvius wrote to Pope Nicholas V from Graz: "What terrible news is this that has just been brought in from Constantinople! My hand trembles as I write, my mind quakes with horror. I can neither be silent for indignation nor speak for grief. I am ashamed to be alive and wish that we had all had the luck to die before this happened. * * * The city which has stood since Constantine eleven hundred years and more and has never fallen into the power of infidels, has in this unhappy year been sacked by filthy Turks. Rome also was sacked, 1164 years after her foundation, by Athlaric, king of the Goths. But he gave orders not to violate the temples of the saints, while the Turks will undoubtedly vent their rage on the churches of God. I mourn for the temple of Sophia, the most famous in the entire world, now destroyed or defiled. I mourn for the countless basilicas of the saints, built with wonderful art, now lying either ruined or polluted by Maumeth. What shall I say of the innumerable books in the city, not yet known to the Latins? Alas, how many names of great men will now be lost! This is a second death for Homer, a second oblivion for Plato. Where now shall we look for the mighty works of philosophers and poets? The fount of the Muses is dry. * * * See, what I feared has come to pass,—one of the two lights of Christendom is put out, the seat of the

[245]

Eastern Empire overthrown, the whole glory of Greece in ashes!"[1]

Three days later Lauro Quirini, the Venetian humanist and patrician, was writing in a similar strain from Candia, bewailing the downfall of the imperial city, the triumphant conqueror of provinces, the strong fortress of the Roman Empire. "Her citizens, descendants of the Romans, have been slain before their fathers' eyes, her noble maidens, gentle boys, gracious matrons, holy nuns have been seized, violated, cut to pieces. Her grand and gorgeous temples, wonderful to behold, have been shockingly defiled, her sacred objects of devotion foully polluted." Not Troy nor Carthage nor Jerusalem nor Saguntum suffered so brutal or so piteous a defeat. "For as this city was nobler than the rest, so is her fate more fearful. * * * Over one hundred and twenty thousand books, as I heard from the reverend cardinal of Russia,[2] have been destroyed. * * * The literature is perishing which once illumined the whole world, giving it salutary laws, holy philosophy and other goodly arts that are the refinement of human life."[3]

Other men of letters had similar visions of the glory that was being extinguished and tried to arouse a sense of the disaster in the popular mind of Europe. The death of Nicholas V, Platina thought, was perhaps hastened by his distress at the loss of Constantinople.[4] Cosimo de' Medici told his friends that nothing more tragic had happened for many

---

[1] Aeneas Sylvius, Briefwechsel, ed Wolkan, Abt. III, I (Fontes Rerum Austriacarum, Abt. II, 68, 1918), 199-201.

[2] The title given to Isidore of Kiev, papal legate to Constantinople when she fell.

[3] Lauro Quirini, Epistola ad Nicolaum Quintium, Bib. Vaticana, Cod. Lat., 4137, 211-212. The text is slightly different from that published in Agostini's Historia degli Scrittori Veneziani, 1752, I, 220 ff. Quirini met at Candia the refugees who escaped or were ransomed from the Turks.

[4] Platina, Nicholas V; Muratori, Rerum Italicarum Scriptores, III, pt. I, 1913-1923, 337-338.

centuries.[1] Here and there someone wrote an elegy in classic meter to deplore the passing of the city of Constantine.[2] Nor was it only scholars who felt the loss of one of the "eyes" of Christendom.[3] The Genoese captain and his seven hundred men, who came of their own accord in January, 1453, to offer their services to the city in peril, the Venetian seamen, who stayed to fight on her walls when her plight grew desperate, did so, we are repeatedly told, "per honor de Dio et per honor di tuta la Christianitade." [4]

But there were others who knew that the glory of Constantinople was no longer what it had been and were not disposed to concern themselves keenly about its disappearance. To many artists and students she had already lost her ancient prestige as a treasure-house of beauty and knowledge. Byzantine painting and carving, which had supplied the models for the earlier Middle Ages, were old-fashioned and outgrown to the generation of Donatello and Ghiberti and Benozzo Gozzoli. Byzantine styles in architecture were not now admired. Santa Sophia was undeniably a marvel,[5] but for the most part Western visitors seem to have walked about Byzantine streets with little of the old sense of jealous awe that Luitprand and the Crusaders felt. Even some of the humanists fancied apparently that they had obtained from Constantinople everything important that she had to give and were now able to dispense with her. They

[1] Poggio, Bracciolini, De Miseria Conditionis Humanae, in his Opera, Basle, 1538, 88 ff.
[2] The manuscript of such an elegy, once in the city library of Augsburg, is now in the Staats-Bibliothek at Munich, Cod. Lat., 3586, 219. The text was printed by Wattenbach, Anzeiger für Kunde der deutsch Vorzeit, 1877, n. 12.
[3] Aeneas Sylvius, op. cit., 129.
[4] Nicola Barbaro, Giornale, as quoted by Schlumberger, Le siège, la prise et le sac de Constantinople, 176, n. 2. Cf. also 45 and 95.
[5] Vide, for example, the description by the censorious observer, Ubertinus Pusculus in his Constantinopolis, III, 506-520, printed in Ellissen's Analekten, pt. 3, 1857, supp., 52.

mentioned the catastrophe casually in their letters or not at all.[1]

More serious still as affecting Western public opinion was the decay of Constantinople's political and military dignity. For a century she had been a constant suppliant for Western aid against the Turk. Her envoys had been petitioners at the courts of popes and kings. Travelers to the Bosphorus had come back with humiliating stories of her degradation. Bertrandon de la Broquière, for example, the equerry of Philip of Burgundy, wrote in 1432 a vivid account of his "voyage d'Outre-mer." The Greek boatmen who brought him to Pera treated him with abject respect as long as they mistook him for a Turk and assaulted him furiously when they discovered he was a Christian. The Greek emperor was paying an annual tribute of ten thousand ducats to the Sultan. The Turks within the walls of Constantinople were not subject to imperial jurisdiction. "And, as I said, if by chance a Christian slave escapes from the house of the Turks and reaches Constantinople, the Emperor or his servants are obliged to give him up to the Turks." [2]

In 1436, the delegates from the Council of Basle reported the state of nervous depression in which they found the Byzantine population. A special service of prayer for the preservation of the city had been held in Santa Sophia, attended by the Emperor and the people barefoot. The white-haired patriarch had lain in an agony of entreaty before St. Luke's portrait of the Virgin, while the crowds

[1] Guarino Veronese, who had studied at Constantinople in his youth and who at this time was getting up a memorial to Chrysoloras, alludes not once in his extant letters to the event. Sabbadini, Epistolario di Guarino Veronese, II. Francesco Filelfo, who had also been a student in Constantinople, wrote a letter of congratulation to Mahomet II, printed by Dethier, Monumenta Hungaricae Historicae, XXI, pt. 1, 703. Poggio took the calamity as a starting point for a long, moralizing dialogue on the misery of the human lot. Op. cit., 88-131.
[2] Bertrandon's book was printed in Paris in 1872, edited by Charles Schefer. Quotation from a selection given by Schlumberger, op. cit., 6.

[248]

thronged around him with storms of tears and cries. Unless some help comes from the West, the writers insisted, it is certain that "this city will shortly fall into the hands of the Turks."[1] Letters like these were meant to awaken pity in the influential persons who heard them read at Basle. It seems likely that they also produced disdain for a people too weaklivered to protect itself except by unmanly appeals for deliverance.

But beside the widespread impression of Greek incapacity in war there were other notions current in the fifteenth century that tended to disfigure the picture of Constantinople in the Western mind. There were the ugly memories of animosity and misunderstanding running back to the Crusades, growing partly out of the scorn of feudal warriors for traders' habits and morality. The humanist Matteo Palmieri told Cosimo de' Medici that it was only for humanism's sake that he grieved over the city. "If you recall the character of the Greeks, their manners, customs, deceitfulness, indolence and greed, you will think they deserve every punishment. Our Cicero first described their disposition and habits quite clearly in his oration for L. Flaccus. As for their faith, religion, attitude toward other Christians, what these have always been is best evinced by the ruin of the Christian armies that went out to recover the Holy Land and were destroyed through their intrigues. * * * So tight is the grip that cowardice and avarice have on them that even when they were immensely rich in gold and silver, they would not spend a coin on the protection of their city. I presume they left a gorgeous booty for the Turks, for it is reliably reported that vast treasures were discovered in the city, far greater than is generally supposed. But always when

[1] Letters of Symon Freron and John of Ragusa to Cardinal Juliano at Basle, March 5 and 10, 1436. Bib. Laurentiana, Strozzi Ms. 33, 103, 104. Several letters describing fully the tension at Constantinople are printed in Cecconi's "Studi Storici sul Concilio di Firenze," 1869.

they were in trouble they came beseeching the aid of the popes, begging others for the help they could very easily have given themselves." [1]

A revolting portrait of this other Constantinople, this type of pusillanimity and greed, is drawn by the humanist, Ubertinus Pusculus, of Brescia, a strict Catholic. He was in the city for some months before its fall, watching its last torments with harsh and unrelenting eyes, and then came home to write his epic, "Constantinopolis," an unbroken recital of sins culminating in well-merited doom.

> "What other land
> Ever begat such sons? No man ranked high
> Who drew no income from the public fisc
> Or who was not a burden on the state.
> The finest prize was life in idleness
> Without a hardship. He who earned his bread
> By toil or prowess had a wretched lot.
> Dice had become the fathers' chief concern.
> Senators hung upon the tables, spent
> Their nights within the playhouse, pausing not
> Till past midnight. Then weary, dull with sleep,
> They gravely sought their homes, as solemn-eyed
> As if they'd been debating things of weight
> Or next day's dawn might force them to decide
> To fight a desperate battle with the Turk.
> Vile lucre buys a Greek for any crime.
> Judges make sale of laws; no place is sure
> For justice. Sight and sound of holy faith
> And grace of uprightness and love of good
> Are absent from the stale ways of the town.
> To celebrate the festal days of saints
> The craftsmen, all the populace, in fact,
> Throng to the markets, drive their knavish trades.
> Never or rarely do they pass within
> The sacred doors of churches; all things else
> They set before the worship due to God." [2]

[1] Poggio, *op. cit.*
[2] Ubertinus Pusculus, *op. cit.*, II, 125-147.

The crowning turpitude of the Greeks, the one which stripped the glamour from the image of their city, was, of course, their obstinate disagreement with Rome in religion and their failure to carry out the promises made at the Council of Florence. "Twice now," said Matteo Palmieri, "they have professed the Catholic faith in councils and have then repudiated it." [1] Ubertinus makes this matter the main burden of his poem. "You," he says, addressing the city, "sham;

> You feign a wish to join the Latin fold.
> You send your envoys to the Pope and swear
> To pay him honor; only ask a hearing
> And friendly judgment, if you prove your case.
> You come and argue, are reduced to silence,
> Acknowledge right the Latin, Roman creed.
> Florence is witness, witness too Eugene,
> The universal father, and your king,
> Illustrious John, likewise your patriarch,
> Who now lies buried in the Tuscan town. * * *
> You pay your reverence to the Pope and make
> Your peace and vow your faith, accept his rules
> And mutual pledges. Answering your prayers,
> A fleet sails o'er the sea to keep the Turk
> From crossing Helle's strait."

An expedition is also organized in Hungary

> "To win you back your lands from Turkish hold,
> Kill and drive out your foes, make you once more
> Imperial and mighty to restore
> The lofty trophies that your fathers built,
> The glorious triumphs and the ancient realm.
> For you were called New Rome and rose upon
> The strength of Rome, the heiress to her sway." [2]

[1] Poggio, *op. cit.*, 89.
[2] Ubertinus Pusculus, *op. cit.*, I, 144-173.

But Sultan Murad defeated the Hungarian army, where-
upon Emperor John and his councilors concluded to side
with the Turk in the future against Western Christendom.

"Then thro' the city flew the wild report:
'The pledge is broken with the Pope; the laws
Of Rome are nothing more to us!' The tongues
Of ignorant mobs hooted the Latin name
With curses; everywhere resounded sneers
At Latin heretics. If some good man,
The city's patriarch or some pure priest,
Protested in God's name, who rules the world,
That Roman laws still bound you, he was made
A mock and laughing-stock."
                         "O perfidious race
Of Greeks! What cruel Fury drove you straight
On toward the abyss, possessed you to your fall,
O men of Greece, that you should dig the gulf
In which you sank your land, your cherished homes,
Your wives, your children?" [1]

As a result of their doubledealing the Greeks soon found
themselves estranged from Rome and at the mecry of an
enemy more formidable than ever. Once more they made
overtures to the Pope who forgivingly sent his legate

"To see what path could bring the Danaans back
To the good shepherd's fold, set up again
His just and righteous laws." [2]

But even then the Emperor smuggled off a messenger to
Mahomet with the offer of an alliance. Only when that messenger returned with the news that Mahomet was pushing
his preparations for an advance on the city was the tardy
ceremony held that consummated the union with the West
and fulfilled the pledges made at Florence thirteen years
before. The majority of the Greeks still defiantly refused to
participate. Therefore the holy Constantine, "the city's

[1] Ubertinus Pusculus, *op. cit.,* I, 544-552; II, 517-522.
[2] *Ibid.,* III, 489-490.

father and founder," refused to intercede for them when the day of terror dawned.

> "Thou couldst not lift thy voice
> Nor pray to God to turn from his just wrath
> Against a race who spurned his own command
> And said no law divine bound them to heed
> The Pope of Rome, the shepherd whom God set
> Himself o'er all the world." [1]

Therefore God held back for a month the breeze that might have blown the Venetian ships from Tenedos to save them.[2] "Our Lord," says the Venetian eye-witness, Nicola Barbaro, "issued the bitter sentence against the Greeks, namely, that it was his will that the city of Constantinople should fall that day into the hands of Mahomet, thus fulfilling a prophecy of St. Constantine that a victorious enemy would come one day from the East." [3] Regarded from this point of view, the fall of Constantinople was a sign of the inevitable retribution that waits on a renegade people.

As a matter of fact, after the first shock of horror at the news of the sack and massacre,[4] the leaders of the West, both religious and secular, seem to have abandoned all idea of rescue or recovery and to have turned their minds to the consideration of how much they themselves had lost by the disaster and when Mahomet might be expected to invade their territories. The Florentine merchant, Jacopo Tedaldi, sent word that the Venetian loss amounted to fifty thousand

---

[1] Ubertinus Pusculus, *op. cit.,* I, 64-69.

[2] *Ibid.,* IV, 1024-1033.

[3] Quoted by Schlumberger, *op. cit.,* 277 and n. 1. Barbaro mentions the so-called equestrian statue of Constantine, on a column near Santa Sophia, with an arm outstretched pointing toward Anatolia. It seems to have been a statue of Justinian threatening the East.

[4] The news came first in some cases in exaggerated form. *Vide* the letter written from Venice on June 30 to the Pope to apprise him that Pera as well as Constantinople had been taken and that every Christian in both cities of six years old and upward had been put to the sword. Martene and Durand, Thesaurus, I, 1826.

ducats and the Florentine to twenty thousand in accounts.[1] "The conquest filled all Christians with consternation," wrote Machiavelli in his History of Florence, "but especially the Pope and the Venetians, who both imagined they heard already in Italy the crash of Turkish arms."[2] The crusade which was preached by popes, prelates and princes with varying degrees of earnestness for the next ten years had as its advertised purpose not the reinstatement of Constantinople in her old grandeur but the preservation of Europe from a doom like hers.

"The fate of all Christendom, blessed father," cried Quirini, cutting short his laments over the past, "is at stake, not, as T. Livy says, the right of Rome or of Carthage to issue laws to the world. The question now is whether Christ's name shall be adored in the land or Mohammed's. . . . Mahomet now possesses, alas, he possesses Constantinople, the seat of empire, which by its situation and command of every resource can easily subdue the world. Before this his power, though great, though, so to speak, enormous, was yet ill-organized and internally divided. Now it is well consolidated under the protection of an almost impregnable fortress."[3] "Mahomet," wrote Tedaldi, "is consumed with ambition to become a greater conqueror than either Alexander or Cæsar. He asks where and what is the situation of Venice, how far it is from terra firma and how it can be reached by sea and land. . . . He talks of nothing but war. He says that he intends to fix his capital at Constantinople, because he can have wonderful ships built there. . . . He has taken Constantinople, the strongest city of Europe."[4] "The Turk," said Aeneas Sylvius, "now holds his sword over our necks. The Black Sea now is closed to us,

[1] Tedaldi, Informations . . . de la prise de Constantinople par l'empereur Turc, Martene and Durand, *op. cit.*, I, 1823.
[2] Machiavelli, Istorie Fiorentine, VI; Opere, 1796, II, 255.
[3] Quirini, *op. cit.*, 212-213.   [4] Tedaldi, *op. cit.*, 1824.

the Tanais is become inaccessible. The Wallachians now must obey the Turk. Next his sword will penetrate to the Hungarians and then to the Germans." [1] "The city, like a kind of door," exclaimed the Florentines talking to Cosimo de' Medici, "will furnish an entrance for the Turks to overrun the other countries of Europe." [2] Philip of Burgundy was convinced that "if we wish to keep our faith, our liberty and our lives, we must go against the Turks and defeat their forces before they grow still stronger." [3] Christian Constantinople had become suddenly Turkish Constantinople, an object no longer of esteem or of scorn but of fear.

Yet even the excitement over the Turkish menace was shortlived, "starting up quickly and as promptly subsiding," as Platina put it. [4] Aeneas Sylvius doubted the motives of even Philip of Burgundy, "the only Christian prince," he remarked ruefully, "who showed himself a genuine foe to the Turks." He might have wanted to avenge his father, whom the Turks had once held in captivity, he might have wanted to save his soul, he might have wanted to get himself talked about. [5] Alfonso of Naples toyed a while with the idea of a crusade. Frederic III composed a letter to Charles VII of France, inviting him to join. A hairy comet, an earthquake, a sickness were interpreted as divine warnings of the enemy's approach. But Mahomet's spies, who had assured him before his march on Constantinople that the princes of the West were too absorbed in their own wars and rivalries to combine against him, had read Europe rightly. [6] Constantinople, whatever one felt about her, was after all remote. Only Hungary and Venice took the field

[1] Aeneas Sylvius, Briefwechsel, 201.
[2] Poggio, op. cit., 88.
[3] Aeneas Sylvius, Commentarii de Suo Tempore (Frankfort, 1614), I, 24.
[4] Platina, Calistus III; Muratori, op. cit., III, pt. I, 341.
[5] Aeneas Sylvius, Commentarii, 22.
[6] Ubertinus Pusculus, op. cit., II, 153-290.

to guard their possessions. The crusade ended in the fiasco at Ancona.

If any Western city might have been expected to display some sympathy for Christian Constantinople, that city was Florence. Years before she had brought the gentle Byzantine, Chrysoloras, to teach Greek in her university, and ever since she had been the center of the Greek revival. She had entertained the illustrious train who came to the council of union in 1438. Cosimo de' Medici had portraits of the Byzantine emperor and patriarch on the walls of his private chapel.[1] Florentine merchants, as Tedaldi reported, had lost large sums by the disaster. In 1454, a Messer Marco Castranselmo, a resident of Constantinople, arrived in Florence, bringing relics that had belonged to the Emperor, a cross made from the wood of the True Cross, pieces of the Savior's robe, of the sponge offered to him on the cross, of the bread of the Last Supper, and a Greek copy of the Gospels said to be as old as Constantine. The Signori voted to pay Messer Marco one thousand broad gold florins for these objects. "The said relics were placed in Santa Maria del Fiore with great reverence, escorted by a beautiful procession of all the religious and the companies of the city and the Signoria and the College and all the officials and the Duke of Calabria. And the book was deposited in the Palazzo with great solemnity."[2]

Considerable enthusiasm was evinced at first for the crusade. Money was contributed and many men took the badge of the red cross. "Solemn processions were also held, so that nothing was lacking publicly or privately to show the general resolution to be foremost among the Christians with counsel, money and men to support the enterprise. However," continues Machiavelli, "the crusading fever was somewhat al-

[1] They are still there, of course, in the Palazzo Riccardi.
[2] From the anonymous "Memorie della Città di Firenze dall' anno 1418 sino all' anno 1459. "Bib. Vaticana, Barberini Cod. Lat. 4812, 52-54."

layed when the news came" of the Turkish defeat at Belgrade. "For the alarm felt by the Pope and the rest of Christendom at the loss of Constantinople being thus relieved, they proceeded less ardently with their preparations for the war." [1]

When, some seven or eight years later, Pius II and Bessarion were making their supreme effort to start the crusade on its way, the Florentine envoy came alone to the Pope to say that his city, "the school of farsighted men," saw no object in fighting Turks merely to hand over their empire to Venetians or in jeopardizing the safety of their merchants who were now living and trading again in Constantinople. A crusade was expensive anyway and nothing was harder than inveigling money out of Florentines. Let the Turks and Venetians go on fighting. "Their forces are equal to one another and the Venetians will not crush the Turk nor the Turk the Venetians. The war will drag on a long while and both parties will perhaps be ruined. Then they will allow us to enjoy some peace." [2] Turkish Constantinople and Turkish trade were all that the farsighted Florentine now saw when he looked eastward.

So Christian Constantinople passed from the horizon of Europe, leaving a blurred and ambiguous image behind her, of little value as an incentive to bring armies to her relief. Memories of her grandeur still survived, arousing here and there spasms of compunction over her fate, but in many minds these memories were obscured by others of discord, betrayal and contempt. So her fall was recorded, sometimes as the destruction of a noble queen among cities, sometimes as the collapse of a decrepit fraud, as it seemed to Gibbon. [3]

[1] Machiavelli, *op. cit.*, VI; Opere, II, 259.

[2] Aeneas Sylvius, Commentarii, X.

[3] Even the Greek historians described it from opposite points of view, depending on their attitude toward the union with Rome, their subsequent relations with the Turks, etc. Phrantzes, the Emperor's confidential min-

The catastrophe itself became one of the landmarks of history but the significance of it remained doubtful. Like the fall of Troy, it was part of two conflicting visions of the one city. Babylon, Jerusalem and the rest, their meaning was plain and they were transmuted into immortal symbols that every man could read and understand. But Constantinople faded to a dim and enigmatic ghost of the past, far off by her Golden Horn. Was either of the conflicting visions of her true to fact or were both perhaps true together? The student of Byzantine history may decide that question, but no student can make her living and vital again in the imagination of Western Europe, to be grasped and held there as another undying symbol of human character and destiny.

---

ister, furnished Gibbon, as everyone knows, with most of his charges of Greek cowardice, incapacity and spite.

THE ECONOMIC DETERMINATION OF HISTORY: ITS VALUE, STATUS AND LIMITATIONS

by

Harry Elmer Barnes

XV

THE ECONOMIC DETERMINATION OF HISTORY: ITS VALUE, STATUS AND LIMITATIONS

1. Socialism, Marxism and Economic Determinism

THE time has now come when Socialism, Marxism and the economic interpretation of history should be dissociated in the discussion of open-minded persons, though of course we should recognize the historic fact that Marx is the most important figure in the history of Socialism and also the man who did more than any one else to call attention to the neglect of economic factors in the study of history. Socialism may well be vindicated, even though much of the specific Marxian economics may be shown to be fallacious and though the economic interpretation of history cannot be demonstrated to be impregnable.

It is a sufficient justification for Socialism if it can prove to fair-minded people that the present régime is unnecessarily wasteful and oppressive and can offer reasonable assurance that a system of production for service can actually be established and will notably improve human well-being. Therefore, there seems to the writer to be no reason whatever why the devotee of Socialism should cling frantically to the economic interpretation of history as something which must remain impeccable, lest the whole fabric of socialistic philosophy and practice might fall in ruins before him.

Personally, the writer accepts the socialistic critique of the existing economic order, but maintains a highly tentative attitude of amiable scepticism with respect to the possibility of establishing complete economic democracy. Therefore, what he will have to say about the economic interpretation of history is in no way connected with any fervid emotional desire to defend to the limit the program of contemporary Socialism.

2. *Criticisms of Theory Thus Far Inadequate*

Perhaps the first point which we should like to make in regard to the question of a critical examination of the economic determination of history is that the great majority of the critiques produced up to the present moment have been incomplete, irrelevant or both. In most of the criticisms of the economic determination of history the Marxian view of history has been confused and identified with the Marxian system of economics and with the hedonistic calculus which Marx took over from Bentham and the classical economists. This is distinctly true of the latest and one of the most elaborate of the critical analyses of the economic determination of history, namely, the thorough and scholarly book by Dr. Bober. Though this is entitled *Karl Marx's Interpretation of History* it covers practically the same field as O. D. Skelton's *Socialism: A Critical Analysis*. It is in no sense a specific study of Marx's views of history, but is rather a thoroughgoing and exacting critical analysis of the whole Marxian system of economics.

It scarcely needs to be pointed out that the economic determination of history in no way stands or falls with the Marxian economic dialectic. Marx regarded the economic interpretation of history as an integral part of his system. Yet the real core of Marxian economics: the labor theory of value, the class struggle, the expropriation of the capitalists, and the establishment of the socialistic commonwealth, is in no sense dependent upon the validity of the economic interpretation of history. It goes without saying that it is equally

[262]

true that the economic interpretation of history can stand or fall entirely independent of the tenability of the Marxian economic analysis or Marx's adaptation of Bentham's felicific calculus. Therefore, when one has disposed of the labor theory of value, or of the Marxian psychology to the effect that man is a cold and calculating intellectual machine dominated in his conduct solely by considerations of self-interest, he need not imagine that he has thereby and incidentally settled the fate of the economic determination of history.

3. Need for Intensive Study of Many Factors

The earlier criticisms of the economic determination of history have not only frequently been invalidated because of their identification of this theory of history with Marxian economics; they have also, for the most part, been naïve because they were worked out prior to, and in ignorance of, the formulation of the processes and principles of cultural and institutional development by the cultural anthropologists and social historians. Such a book as Clark Wissler's *Man and Culture* is of greater importance as a preparation for a critical study of the economic interpretation of history than all the solemn treatises on historical methodology and economic theory ever published. Hitherto, it has been regarded as a sufficient critique of the economic determination of history to show that essentially the same system of economic production and exchange does not invariably produce an identical type of society and culture among all peoples, irrespective of the cultural background out of which this particular economic system developed or into which it is introduced.

With the cultural anthropologists and historians there would be no such assumption whatever. They would recognize that society is a complex variable, made up of numerous and complicated elements. Any sensible view of determinism could not well mean that a single dominant factor in the social and cultural complex would always produce an identical result in each and every type of cultural complex. Rather, the critical student would at once recognize that the influence of any element in civilization is bound to be conditioned in a highly specific and particularistic fashion during the process of its development in any cultural area.

For example, though the economic factor might in every case be the dominant one, it could scarcely be expected that the same system of technique in manufacturing would produce identical cultural results in Scotland, Spain, Russia, India, Japan, and Togoland. The thoroughly up-to-date student of cultural phenomena, even though he believed in the validity of the economic interpretation of history, would never expect to discover similar economic processes producing identical cultural responses in every society, however different the cultural complexes which existed. Therefore, when investigating the problem of economic determinism, we should at once give up the expectation of discovering identical cultural systems as the outgrowth of similar economic processes, and should concentrate our attention upon a very careful and intensive study of the interrelations between the economic and other factors in any cultural complex. It is also well to bear in mind the highly differential reaction of economic elements upon the other aspects of civilization.

Not every non-economic phase of civilization is affected to the same degree by the economic factors. Government or law much more directly reflects economic forces than art or religion, for example.

In other words, in our future studies of economic determinism, we should follow the example set by Boas and the critical ethnologists and by Vidal de la Blache, Richthofen and the regional geographers. Boas and his followers demonstrated that the facts in regard to cultural evolution could only be discovered upon the basis of intensive studies of specific cultural areas, and Professor Lowie has shown that such studies do not confirm that simple and lucid synthesis of cultural and social evolution, characteristic of such works as Lewis Henry Morgan's *Ancient Society*.

The regional geographers have likewise pointed out the essential futility of attempting to settle the question of geographical determinism by broad and vague generalizations in regard to environmental influences of a world-wide scope. They insist that scientific insight in regard to the question of geographical factors in history can only be secured upon the basis of highly intensive studies of the interaction between geographic and other elements in specific and unified geographic regions.

Much the same orientation must be given to the future study of economic factors in society. We must pass from efforts at large scale and sweeping generalizations to a very careful study of the interaction of economic and other influences in each cultural area. The results obtained from a quarter of a century or more of such monographic studies might well serve as the basis for a tentative verdict as to the validity of the doctrine of the economic interpretation of history.

It is quite obvious that the samples selected for study should be taken from every stage of economic development, drawing upon anthropology and history for types of society and cultural complexes differing from those of our own day. The writer would suggest in passing that the vast mass of material assembled by Frédéric Le Play and his associates in their monographic studies of the families of workingmen in relation to their geographic and cultural surroundings is probably more important as the basis for testing the economic interpretation of history than all the work done in

[265]

the field of economic analysis by Marx and his subsequent followers. Those interested in a realistic approach to the economic determination of history would have done far better to have confined themselves to a critical examination of material like this gathered by Le Play than to have given themselves up to theoretical discussions, the analytical dialectic of the Marxian system and the controversies it has engendered. The economic interpretation of history can be tested by investigation, not by argument.

It might be well also to insist that the validity of the economic interpretation of history does not necessarily mean exclusively the soundness of the particular view of economic determinism expounded by Marx. It is quite true that, as Dr. Hansen contended, Marx's own interpretation was far more comprehensive and subtle than most of his critics and followers have realized; yet, it can hardly be maintained that the economic interpretation of history must be regarded as completely identical with the Marxian version. Further, it is probably best to abandon such a dogmatic formula as that of economic determination and to adopt in its stead the more scientific and contemporary conception of the economic conditioning of civilization. The conception of conditioning does not necessarily commit one in advance to the expectation or necessity of confirming a particular hypothesis, and gives at once a more objective and scientific tone to the whole discussion.

In the light of the above criticism and qualifications relative both to the defense and the criticism of the economic interpretation of history, it would seem that we may almost say that the whole subject today presents a virgin field for the cultural anthropologist, historian and economist. Most of the theoretical work which has been done on this topic up to the present time may be set aside as of little relevance, though we have achieved much in the way of massing of concrete materials in field and monographic studies and in the formulation of the laws and principles of cultural evolution by the cultural anthropologists and historians. Neither the exponents nor the critics of economic determinism have thus far been in possession of either the technique or the information essential to a definitive defense or critique of the doctrine of the economic determination of history.

4. *Classic Instances Cited Against the Theory*

We might call attention briefly in this regard to certain classic instances brought up by opponents of economic determinism in their effort to discredit this doctrine. The non-pecuniary and almost anti-capitalist psychology of certain of the ancient Greek city-states, and the absorption of such Greeks in æsthetic interests and activities, are often offered as a refutation of the economic interpretation of history. Before any such contention could be regarded as conclusive, however, it would first be necessary to undertake an intensive analysis, for example, of the Athenian cultural complex in the age of Pericles, and to discover how far the æsthetic ideals of the Greeks grew out of their general mode of life and to what degree the latter was related to the nature of the economy of Attica.

Another case is that of the early and medieval Christians. It has been held that the Christian philosophy of life and the primarily religious interests of the Middle Ages offer another definitive refutation of the economic interpretation of history. Before we can accept this, however, it would be necessary to see how far the growth and success of Christianity were linked up with the economic and social conditions involved in the decline of classical civilization and the decay of Roman imperial, provincial, and municipal institutions. We should have to inquire as to what extent the success of Christianity was due to the fact that it offered com-

[267]

pensation for progressively less favorable economic and social conditions here on earth.

An economic history of Monasticism would also be highly relevant in the way of examining the degree to which the ideals of Christianity were able to withstand the conditions of economic prosperity. Likewise, it would be necessary to examine the manner in which the ideals of Christianity have been modified by and adapted to changing economic conditions. Saint Jerome, Saint Anthony, Saint Francis of Assisi, John Knox, Chancellor Day, Pastor Bigelow, Sherwood Eddy, and Bruce Barton all regard themselves as equally sincere, authentic, and literal followers of the doctrines of Jesus of Nazareth.

Perhaps the most powerful argument against the economic interpretation of history is that which Ernest Troeltsch and Max Weber have launched in their contention that the capitalistic revolution did not produce Protestantism, but rather that the Protestant ideals constituted a powerful force in bringing about the rise of modern capitalism. Before one could accept this hypothesis, however, it would be necessary to inquire to just what extent the early Protestant ideals grew up out of changing social, political and religious conditions which were, in differing degrees, associated with the economic transformations between the period of the Crusades and the discovery of America.

It will not be necessary to emphasize the fact that modern dynamic psychology has definitely silenced one type of opposition to the economic determination of history, namely, the protestation of non-economic motivation by those who have been conspicuously successful in various types of economic enterprise. The mechanism of compensation explains for all time the irrelevance of this type of critique of economic determinism.

In short, we are today in no position whatever to pass any

final judgment upon the matter of the validity of the economic interpretation of history throughout the development of man and his culture. We are only just coming to be in a position to be able to begin a really scientific and adequate study of the problem.

5. *A Tentative Theory of Historical Causation*

Certain readers might legitimately inquire as to the nature of the theory of historical causation which is held by the writer. In general, he would state that he is opposed to the espousal of any cut and dried or dogmatic formula of historical causation. As has already been stated, we feel that the "laws" of history are something which will require much future study before they can be formulated in even a tentative fashion.

In a rough and general way, it may be held that the chain of historical causation is something like the following: We have as the two constant factors in history the geographical environment and the original nature of man, but these relatively unchanging factors are so involved with other conditioning influences that their interaction is continually varying in nature and content. The original nature of man, reacting to a given form of environmental stimulation, will produce a specific outlook upon life. This will control the degree to which science and technology can develop and will affect the forms which their evolution will take. Technology will, to a large degree, determine the nature of the economic life which will exist in any given epoch or area. The economic factors will exert a powerful conditioning, and sometimes a determining, influence upon the other institutions in society: social, political, juristic, religious, ethical, educational and literary. Marx's view of historical causation differed from the above, in that he began with the technological factor rather than with the nature of man and his physical environment and the outlook upon life produced by the interaction between the two. This would not, however, necessarily invalidate his contention that technology determines economic institutions, while the latter determine politics, law, religion, etc.

But the historic process is not so simple as we may have implied above. Cause and effect are continually acting and reacting upon each other. A few mechanical inventions may alter the economic and social life of mankind so completely as to transform the dominating psychology of any epoch. Again, certain psychological and religious factors may at times be so strong as to obstruct the dictates of economic advantage and material prosperity. The Greek absorption in metaphysics and æsthetics, for example, seems to have prevented them from making any extensive application of their scientific discoveries. The skein of historical development is a tangled one, and it is a profound historian who can solve the problem of cultural causation in one country in any single period of human development, to say nothing of being able to formulate a universally valid and applicable interpretation of history.

Much the same criticism may be directed against the dogma of fixed and invariable "economic laws" applying with uniform pertinence and relevance to all peoples in all stages of culture. Laws can be formulated only on the basis of many observed repetitions of phenomena under identical circumstances. Obviously, human history furnishes no such data with respect to the genesis of culture as a whole or the economic aspects of culture in particular. There are few or no cultural complexes or patterns of economic behavior and achievement which repeat themselves or reproduce themselves with completeness and fidelity. Even approximations of repetition and duplication may be due to the operation of new and strange factors. As the cultural anthropologists and historians have proved, through their famous principle or process of "cultural convergence," identities in the form of institutions do not necessarily prove an identical origin or course of development. Cultural similarities may be quite as much the product of accidental or fortuitous convergence as of identical development through conformity to immutable laws of evolution. Perhaps no one has summarized this view more concisely than Muller-Lyer, even though he does not himself accept it in full:

> Since culture is constantly developing fresh phases, since nothing repeats itself—excepting for the case, which we need not here consider, of the progress of backward peoples—and since no link in the great chain of causality is like the previous one, except possibly in external appearance and that delusively, the inference of analogy fails; we cannot say that this condition of culture has already existed once, and that therefore we may expect the same results again. In the process of the development of culture, circumstances are constantly changing; thus history teaches us nothing concerning the economic laws of development.

Another obstacle in the way of formulating the laws of economic development lies in the fact that the economic evolution of mankind is not yet a completed process. Economic evolution is now going on more rapidly than ever before. Hence, even if we could discover many identities and repetitions in the economic life of the past, we would scarcely be warranted in enunciating rigid universal laws, for we could not be sure that the developments of the future would not completely upset and refute all generalizations based upon the past.

The critical evaluation of the conception of rigid and invariable laws of economic development does not, of course, mean that one need accept the hypothesis of chaos and absolute arbitrariness in the development of civilization in the past, which forms the assumption, tacit or explicit, of the conventional anecdotal and episodical political historians.

We may well recognize very definite tendencies in the economic development of certain times and of specific culture-areas in the past, a knowledge of which may serve as a very great aid to our understanding of the nature and significance of history. Yet we should not confuse a local or temporary trend with a universal and cosmic law.

6. *Economic Determinism and Contemporary Society*

The general cultural, social and psychological results of the Industrial Revolution in Western society present an admirable opportunity for testing, in a specific period of civilization, the validity of the economic determination of history, namely, the thesis that other aspects of civilization are determined by the economic processes which prevail at the time. It can scarcely be denied that the facts to date afford a large degree of confirmation of Marx's thesis, though it was unquestionably the development of rationalism and science since 1500 which made possible the technological revolution that established contemporary capitalistic enterprise so firmly. It is, of course, possible to accept the Marxian doctrine of social causation as applied to Western society since 1800 without implying in any way the adoption of the socialistic program of social reform.

In regard to society at large our institutions have come to be based in large part upon the new economic order and its processes. Population growth has paralleled modern industrial evolution. The foundations of social classification and the social hierarchy conform rather exactly to the economic differentiation of society. Our social interests are primarily bound up with the economic interests, real or supposed, of each class. Pecuniary standards dominate in our social outlook. There is little doubt that social values have taken on the pecuniary coloring of the capitalistic order, the bourgeoisie desiring to acquire more wealth and power, and the proletariat attempting to check this and to capture industrial processes for its own use.

Government remains, as it has always been, fundamentally a struggle between economic classes, but this conflict has now become primarily one between the capitalists and the proletariat, with the intermediate group tending as yet to side with capital in most industrial states. In some of the more archaic states, economically considered, like Hungary, the landlords still control politics. In most of the Western states the capitalists have come to dominate. In Russia we have the proletariat temporarily in the saddle. In certain countries like England there is still an essential deadlock between the older agrarian interests, capital and the proletariat. Not only domestic politics but also international relations have come into conformity with modern industrialism. The basic motivation of international relations in recent years has been the effort to secure raw materials and markets, and it is not without reason that contemporary diplomacy has been variously denominated as "dollar diplomacy," "oil-burning diplomacy" and "rubber-neck diplomacy."

Law has shaped itself up in harmony with the outstanding aspects of modern industrialism. Where the bourgeoisie have come to control, the theory of a natural order based upon unlimited competition has furnished the cornerstone of juristic theory and practice; so much so, in fact, that Justice Holmes once accused his colleagues on the United States Supreme Court of attempting to project Herbert Spencer's *Social Statics* into the Constitution of the United States. The protection of private property, the perpetuity of contracts, the obstruction of state interference in business affairs and the imposition of special disabilities on the proletariat have been the outstanding features of bourgeois jurisprudence. Where the proletariat have come into control, the situation has been reversed and legislation has been

[273]

passed expropriating the capitalistic and agrarian owners and proclaiming a régime of coöperation or of communism. Without passing judgment upon the question of which procedure, if either, is preferable, it may be remarked that in either case legal concepts and procedure have adapted themselves very closely to the dominating economic ideals and interests.

Religion has not escaped from the contamination of the new industrial age. As Veblen pointed out nearly a generation ago in his *Theory of the Leisure Class*, the "pious observances" of the capitalists are little more than a phase of the "pecuniary taste" and "conspicuous waste" of the wealthy. Certain psychologists have since suggested that they may also be a manifestation of psychic compensation for the dubious economic ventures of week-days. The capitalists have in most places been able to insure the interpretation of religion among the middle classes in such ways as to emphasize the sanctity of private property and the perpetuity of the capitalistic system. The Church is still primarily a mechanism for capitalistic propaganda. Several American writers of prominence have openly and frankly created "a Wall Street Christ." The Reverend Doctor C. Everett Wagner has well declared that a very popular trend in modern religion "rings the cash-register," contending further that it is a "movement of sanctified commercialism, peculiarly a product of the twentieth century." He allies himself with "the many clergymen and laymen who are thoroughly disgusted with Big Business declaring dividends on religion." Bishop Charles Fiske of the Episcopal Church protests in the same spirit that "America has become almost hopelessly enamored of a religion that is little more than sanctified commercialism. It is hard in this day to differentiate between religious aspiration and business prosperity." We recognize with due credit and admiration the brave resistance to the commercialization of religion by such organizations as the Federal Council of the Churches of Christ and the late Interchurch World Movement, but the Federal Council is not, unhappily, representative of the dominant trends in contemporary bourgeois religion. On the other hand, in a régime of proletarian domination, supernaturalism tends to be discarded and a secularized religion based upon the communistic dogmas comes to supplant it. When the proletarian leaders retain Christianity they represent it as primarily a program of secular economic revolution, a point of view vigorously maintained by Upton Sinclair in his *They Call Me Carpenter* and by Bouck White in his *Church of the Social Revolution.*

Ethical questions and solutions have not remained apart from economic considerations. The capitalistic groups have been fiercely determined to retain the supernatural and conventional theory of ethical judgments and standards, which represent morality as almost wholly a matter related to religion and sex—a moral man being one who is formally affiliated with an ecclesiastical organization and whose sexual conduct in public is externally correct. This theory is highly convenient to the plutocrat, as the reprehensible practices associated with the theory of business enterprise thereby escape condemnation, and he usually has the pecuniary resources to obscure his sexual dereliction unless he is uncommonly stupid and unlucky. A person like Mr. Sinclair of the oil scandals is deemed much more "moral" than the Countess Cathcart. The reformers, on the other hand, incline to minimize the significance of supernatural standards and sexual criteria in ethics, and contend that capitalism, waste and economic oppression are the really serious forms of immorality. Moral standards, they maintain, must be secularized and socialized. They contend that books like Stuart Chase's *Tragedy of Waste* or *Your Money's Worth*

[275]

reveal a much more serious type of immorality than the classics by Ovid, Petronius, Boccaccio, Casanova, Zola or Frank Harris.

The economic classes in society have not failed to recognize the importance of capturing the school system in behalf of their cause. Capitalistic states base their education, as far as possible, on subjects perpetuating the old "humanities," which in no sense bring up the dangerous problems of property and economic justice. As social progress has more and more produced the necessity of devoting some attention to the social sciences, the vested capitalistic interests have endeavored to give the instruction therein such a slant as to emphasize the sanctity of private property and the perfection of the present scheme of things. In the especially precarious field of economics there has been an effort to divert attention from the description and analysis of the contemporary economic order and to concentrate pedagogical activity upon instruction as to how to administer more profitably the present system of business enterprise. The risky nature of pedagogical insistence upon straightforward presentation of the facts regarding the existing state of economic and social affairs has been indicated with an ample display of clinical material in the Reports of the American Association of University Professors, in Upton Sinclair's *The Goose Step* and *The Goslings,* and with withering irony in Thorstein Veblen's *The Higher Learning in America.*

Not only do the capitalists insist upon conventional safety in all instruction pertaining to the existing economic and social system; they are also extremely sensitive in regard to formal moral correctness, as they recognize the invaluable service of conventional moral codes in maintaining capitalistic respectability. Hence, there is little toleration of any effort to offer instruction in scientific ethics or to suggest that the whole problem of ethics must be given a broad social

[276]

and economic setting. There has been a concerted attack on scientific sociology as especially dangerous in this regard. The slightest deviation from conventionality in doctrine or practice is immediately pounced upon and branded as "free love." A professor of ethics was congratulated because on a questionnaire his students rated fornication as a more serious crime than murder, while eminent sociologists have been fiercely attacked, and at times dismissed, for merely submitting questionnaires to ascertain the views of the younger generation on sexual matters. A popular teacher in one of the larger school systems was recently dismissed for allowing a student in an advanced class to read and construct an English theme about the restrained and generally critical discussion of the newer morality contained in George Jean Nathan's *The Land of the Pilgrims' Pride.* The bourgeois group rarely stop to reflect that by bringing women into industry and gradually breaking up the home they have done more to disrupt the earlier monogamous family life than all the exponents of "free love" in human history.

When the industrial proletariat control the educational system or specific educational institutions they likewise see to it promptly that the schools become a powerful adjunct of socialistic or radical proletarian propaganda and devote themselves to the task of training up young labor unionists, Communists or Syndicalists. As yet the proletariat have been far less successful than the capitalistic groups in developing an effective control over education.

Art thoroughly reflects the age of contemporary materialism. The new technology has made possible a new type of massive architecture, most notably exemplified by the metropolitan skyscrapers. These same technological advances have led to the remarkable standardization of architecture and many other phases of art where products can be duplicated and produced on a vast scale and far more cheaply than by the old individualized methods of handicraft manufacture. It is not surprising that the New York *Evening Post* of March 19, 1928, carried as a prominent news item the following announcement: "Artist Aims to Be the Ford of Statuary." The article continued: "A combination of Henry Ford and Benvenuto Cellini was found in New York today. He is Simon Moselsio, a Russian sculptor, who follows the Detroiter in the use of quantity production and the Florentine in personally attending to every detail of manufacturing. He works in four materials—porcelain, wood, marble and bronze. Just now he is producing in quantity tiny bronzes, with the result that statuary may soon adorn any smoking stand, mantelpiece or whatnot where Americans keep their objects of art." Nor can one overlook in this regard the growing importance of the movies and the radio as a method of producing a type of highly standardized visual art and music.

Contemporary art has tended to specialize on *motifs* usually associated with some aspect or another of present-day industrial society, and not infrequently eulogizes by implication the achievements of the bourgeoisie. Then, the great financiers and industrialists use their pecuniary resources to acquire the great masterpieces and to endow metropolitan art museums, standing before the public as the real patrons and connoisseurs of art. How far they actually are in many cases from any real appreciation of the artistic spirit and values may be seen from the naïve surprise and indignation once expressed by one of the great American industrialists when the trustees of the Dresden Gallery refused to sell him the Sistine Madonna at any price which they chose to set upon this work! When the laboring classes dominate society, art is immediately drafted into the service of the proletariat, as the example of Russia affords illuminating proof. In such cases the themes of art become even more frankly materialistic.

Journalism has long since become a class affair, but the superior pecuniary power of the capitalistic press and their capacity to attract remunerative advertising have enabled them to present a better range of entertainment for their readers and to print papers of a far more impressive physical appearance. Therefore, the proletariat have usually failed to support the papers of their class with adequate loyalty—a serious handicap to proletarian propaganda.

Finally, literature shadows forth the economic stratification of society. The non-fiction work is given over more and more to the description and analysis of questions connected with modern industrialism and to the plans for conserving, mitigating or destroying it. Fiction, likewise, is in part devoted either to the eulogy or the criticism of capitalistic institutions and practices. When not so employed it chiefly provides diverting entertainment for the leisure class or pictures thinly veiled Utopias where the author portrays a better world in which to live.

The most extensive effort to present an economic interpretation of contemporary industrial civilization has been executed by Mr. Upton Sinclair in his various books: *The Jungle, King Coal, Jimmie Higgins, The Profits of Religion, The Goose Step, The Goslings, Mammonart, The Brass Check*, and *Money Writes*. While we cannot avoid admiring the courage, industry and information possessed by Mr. Sinclair, the work should be done over with less indignation and rather more humor and irony, a task partly executed by Thorstein Veblen, unfortunately in a literary style likely to render his works permanently obscure.

It goes without saying, of course, that, though we should be certain that we are correct in the above discussion of the effect of economic factors on modern life, this would in no sense prove or disprove the universal validity of the hypothesis of economic determinism.

It may be well in this connection to call attention to the view of Mr. G. D. H. Cole, to the effect that in an economy based upon production for service rather than private profit, economic determinism would no longer hold good. In other words, Socialism should terminate the validity of one of the chief socialistic dogmas:

In short, if economic classes and class-conflicts are done away with, the Marxian thesis will no longer hold good, and economic power will no longer be the dominant factor in Society. Economic considerations will lose their unreal and distorted magnitude in men's eyes, and will retain their place as one group among others around which the necessary social functions are centered. For the artificial material valuation of social things, which is forced upon us by the actual structure of present-day society, it will become possible to substitute a spiritual valuation. When once we have got the economic sphere of social action reasonably organized on functional lines, we shall be free to forget about it most of the time, and to interest ourselves in other matters. The economic sphere will not, of course, be any less essential than before; but it will need less attention. Always associations and institutions, as well as people, need most attention when they are least "themselves." Our pre-occupation with economics occurs only because the economic system is diseased.

7. *Karl Marx and Social Science*

Karl Marx's position in the history of historiography is in no exclusive sense linked up with the question of the validity of the economic interpretation of history as a universal key to the development of human culture. As a formula, the dogma of economic determinism certainly serves to explain more of human history than any other single concept of historical interpretation. To have been the foremost figure among those who have developed this most useful instrument of historical interpretation is certainly enough of an achievement to satisfy any reasonable follower of Marx. Marx's contribution to history has not been exceeded by that of any other worker in the field, and his place in historiography is likely to be much more thoroughly appreciated a century hence than it is now.

While recognizing all of this, it is the opinion of the writer that Marx's greatest contribution to social science is to be found neither in his systematization of socialistic theory nor in his doctrine of historical interpretation, but rather in the impulse which he gave to the study of institutional economics which has been forwarded in our day by men like Sombart, Weber, Webb, Tawney, Hammond, Veblen, Mitchell, Hamilton, Douglas and others. In this type of economic analysis the historical point of view is, of course, a dominant one. Hence, Marx's contribution to the historical orientation in social science is by no means limited to the dogma of the economic interpretation of civilization.

BARON VON HOLSTEIN, THE DARK FORCE OF THE GERMAN FOREIGN OFFICE

by

Maude A. Huttman

XVI

BARON VON HOLSTEIN
THE DARK FORCE OF THE GERMAN
FOREIGN OFFICE

OF THE statesmen who directed the foreign policy of Germany during the fifteen years after Bismarck's retirement the least known [1] and yet the most influential was the Chief Councillor in the Foreign Office, Baron Friedrich von Holstein. At the time of his retirement in 1906 Maximilian Harden bitterly arraigned him, but detailed accounts of this *Eminence Grise* were not available to the public until his colleagues [2] began to publish their memoirs after the close of the World War. They all bear witness to the power and machinations of the man who Bismarck said had "flecks on the inner iris." The recently published documents of the Foreign Office,[3] too, afford plenty of evidence of his responsibility in shaping the policies of his country. Holstein's room in the Foreign Office communicated with that of the Secretary of State and here he sat, from early morn until late at night, like a great spider spinning webs for his victims.[4] He had his spies in every capital and carried on cor-

---

[1] "*Er ist so klug, sich in der Welt gar nicht zu zeigen, so dass viele kaum von seiner Existenz eine Ahnung haben*," Waldersee, *Denkwürdigkeiten* I, p. 286.

[2] *E.g.* Hammann, Eckardstein, Alexander Hohenlohe, Waldersee, Tirpitz, Schweinitz, Eulenburg (both his memoirs and Haller's biography based on his letters and diaries), William II. In December, 1925, the *Berliner Tageblatt* published the revelations of Holstein's speculations on the Stock Exchange, and this called forth a series of magazine articles from Harden and others.

[3] *Die Grosse Politik der Europäischen Kabinette. The British Documents* also contribute evidence.

[4] "*Er kam mir immer vor wie eine Spinne, die in irgendeiner dunkeln Ecke sitzend, alles beobachtet und ihre Opfer nicht aus dem Auge lässt.*"

respondence with each embassy, often with underlings over their superiors.[1] He intrigued men into office and a great number of ambassadors owed their fall to his whims.[2] No wonder "many an ambassador who had grown gray in the service of the State trembled before him. . . . German ambassadors who came to Berlin might be kept waiting for days before seeing him and some were never admitted to his presence, owing to some personal pique of Holstein."[3] He took no more than a month's holiday each year revealing his address only to a trusted few. Before going off he would lock up the archives of his department and his superiors were put to serious inconvenience if they needed a document.[4]

He avoided society, but occasionally entertained a few choice friends at Borchardt's famous restaurant.[5] The Kaiser wrote of him, "I tried in vain for a long time to make his acquaintance. I invited him to meals but he always declined. Only once did he condescend to dine with me at the Foreign Office; he appeared in morning coat and explained that he did not possess a dress-suit."[6] Although he was a recluse he kept in touch with society through Frau von Lebbin, his political Egeria,[7] who met all Berlin at the house of her friend, Frau von Schwabach. That he lived in perpetual fear of some sort was apparent, for he always carried a loaded revolver, and took pains to talk of his daily practice

---

Prince Alexander Hohenlohe "Eine graue Eminenz," *Deutsche Revue*, Jan., 1919.
[1] Harden, *Zukunft*, Aug. 18, 1906. *Cf.* Hammann, *Der neue Kurs, p.* 67.
[2] Harden, *Köpfe*, I, pp. 130-131; "Holstein" in *Das Tage Buch*, Jan. 16, 1926, p. 86. *Cf.* Waldersee, *Denkwürdigkeiten* II, pp. 260, 316, 340; III, p. 183.   [3] Hohenlohe, *op. cit.*   [4] Hohenlohe, *op. cit.*
[5] He was a gourmet and got the nickname of the "oyster lover." Inviting Philipp Eulenburg to dine he suggests choice vintages and delicacies of the season.
[6] *Ereignisse und Gestalten,* p. 83.
[7] To this devoted friend he willed his papers. After her death they passed into the hands of Paul von Schwabach and it is generally believed they are now in a strong box at Bleichröder's.

in shooting.[1] His unwillingness to be photographed exceeded a normal dislike and he permitted it only as he was retiring.[2] His charm was incontestable. Hammann[3] considered him as fascinating as Philipp Eulenburg, who possessed an incredible gift of enchanting and enthralling.[4] Alexander Hohenlohe, who became his bitter enemy, says that he had seldom met anyone who was so strangely fascinating and he confessed that he had all he could do to keep from falling under the influence of the magnetic force that seemed to emanate from him.[5] He loved nature, was kind to the poor and considerate of underlings.[6]

Hammann describing his first impressions says: "I was a total stranger to Holstein, the Great Unknown. * * * As I crossed the threshold of this sinister custodian of profoundest secrets, I could not but feel like the student in Faust. * * * Like all who came into contact with Holstein, I got the impression that he was a highly gifted man. His distinguished way of conducting a conversation and his vivid manner of expressing his ideas inspired one with respect for his mental vigor. A strong will and the warning, Take care! seemed written on his face, with its short, aquiline nose and deep-set, darkly gleaming eyes. In spite of the extraordinary graciousness with which he received the inexperienced newcomer into the concern, I still had the feeling, perhaps because of what I had heard previously about his sinister character, that there was something fundamentally abnormal and morbid about the man.[7] But it was quite evident to me that

[1] Eulenburg suspected the reason for his never having a resident servant was his fear that a servant might be bribed or might rob or murder him. Haller, *Aus dem Leben des Fürsten Philipp zu Eulenburg*, p. 376.

[2] An enterprising newspaper man did once get a snapshot of him as he was leaving the Foreign Office; Hammann, *Wille und Weg*, Jan. 15, 1926, p. 499.

[3] Chief of the Press Department of the Foreign Office, 1893-1917.

[4] *Bilder aus der letzten Kaiserzeit*, p. 15.   [5] *Op. cit.*

[6] The Bismarcks' brutalities were notorious.

[7] As a young boy he had seen his father burned to death and the memory of this tragedy haunted him all his life.

with due caution for his peculiarities there was a tremendous deal to be learned from him." [1]

Eulenburg too has left a portrait of him. "If you * * * had known Holstein personally and as well as I did, you would have shared Bismarck's opinion that he was gifted, but always to be held in check, for he was mad. As a matter of fact, Holstein can be judged fairly only if the pathological elements in his nature are taken into consideration. He suffered from political chimeras. * * * Another most dangerous pathological characteristic was a sort of passion for killing. Bulow and I often called him 'the marten,' for that animal never stops until it has killed every fowl in the chicken-house." This passion could be aroused if he believed someone had failed to return his bow. He would start on an endless persecution of "the enemy." Eulenburg says his friendship for Holstein was based on his "great admiration for his fine mind, his deep knowledge, political and literary, his incontestable gift for divination," and on his "very deep sympathy for this self-tormented, shy and probably timid soul." [2]

His instinct was for indirect methods, even when direct ones would have served as well, and this tendency led him to ascribe devious motives to others.[3] He stooped to the basest means and considered them justified by his patriotic ends,[4] for he "loved Prussia and the Empire like a mother, like a bride." [5] In spite of his "abnormal characteristics and excesses," [6] Holstein was considered an honorable servant of the State until 1925, when it transpired that he had been divulging political secrets for thirty years to his bankers who were buying stocks for him.[7]

[1] *Der neue Kurs*, pp. 57-58. *Cf.* Esternaux, *Wille und Weg*, April 15, 1926.
[2] Haller, *op. cit.*, pp. 376-377. *Cf.* Hohenlohe, *op. cit.*
[3] Hammann, *The World Policy of Germany*, p. 120.
[4] Besides employing spies he wrote anonymous letters and articles.
[5] Harden, *Köpfe*, I.   [6] Hammann, *Bilder*, p. 40.
[7] The revelation was made by the *Berliner Tageblatt* in December, 1925.

Holstein's whole career was a will to power.[1] In early days he had often groaned, says Harden,[2] "Just once to have power of achieving, just once, with only a human arm, to turn or to stop the wheel of the world's destiny." Power, not its appearance, and power concealed from the world, was what his soul yearned for. And this "man of the dark"[3] came to wield a power such as no official in a modern State has possessed. Bülow declared, "Since Bismarck's retirement, from the non-renewal of the Russian Reinsurance Treaty . . . to the handling of the Morocco Question . . . nothing of importance has been done in our foreign policy in which Holstein has not had a hand. The end of his moral responsibility dates only" from "June 19, 1904."[4] Although France under Richelieu had its Père Joseph, *l'Eminence grise*, the public knew him and he would gladly have accepted a red hat from the Pope. Holstein "evaded all official responsibility,"[5] and refused both Hohenlohe's and Bülow's offers to make him Secretary of State. To the end, he held no higher position than that of Chief Councillor in the Foreign Office.[6]

Baron Friedrich von Holstein was born into an old Mecklenburg family in 1837. Trained for the Law when his own wish was to become a soldier, he early deserted his profession for that of Diplomacy. In 1860 he began his career as attaché in Petrograd and soon came to see a good deal of Bismarck,

Eckardstein (*Persönliche Erinnerungen an König Eduard*) says a few people had always known that Holstein speculated. Since 1925, there have been many conjectures as to the reason. Was he buying silence about his private life? Certainly he needed large sums for his net work of spies. *Vide Das Tage Buch,* Jan. 2, 1926, for an anonymous article and Jan. 16 for one by Harden; also *Wille und Weg,* Jan. 15, 1926, for an article by Hammann.   [1] There seems no evidence that he was a reader of Nietzsche.
[2] *Zukunft,* Aug. 18, 1906.
[3] Harden, (*Köpfe* I, p. 127) says Bismarck so called him.
[4] Hammann, *Bilder,* p. 34. *Cf.* Haller, *op. cit.,* p. 379.
[5] *Ereignisse und Gestalten,* pp. 83-86 for the Kaiser's complete judgment.
[6] It was with difficulty that Hohenlohe, his son says, persuaded him to accept the title of Excellency.

who was Chief of the Prussian Legation. He held posts at various embassies [1] and in 1871 Bismarck found a use for him at Versailles. In the same year, when Count Harry von Arnim was sent as Ambassador to Paris, Holstein was appointed his Second Secretary.[2] A few years later Bismarck instituted legal proceedings against von Arnim for the recovery of missing documents, and Holstein was a witness for the State. The public was disgusted when it learned that the Secretary had systematically spied on his chief.[3] Harden reports Bismarck as saying after 1890, "I had Holstein to thank for the Arnim Scandal. If he had not from the beginning poisoned the springs from which I drank I could have gotten rid of the talented comedian without an open conflict." [4] As for Holstein, the trial seemed to leave an indelible mark on his soul "and it is not impossible that it bore its part in embittering his nature." [5] He once said in referring to the trial that the Bismarcks had burned the mark of Cain on his forehead as though he were a convict.[6]

In 1876 Holstein was back in Wilhemstrasse, where he was to remain for thirty years, and a brilliant career seemed opening. He was an intimate at Bismarck's house. When Herbert became Secretary of State he wanted his father to make Holstein Under-Secretary, but the Prince refused. Holstein was useful as a tool for underground work,[7] but

[1] In London and Washington he acquired his perfect English.
[2] Waldersee at the Embassy considered him "a very uneasy soul, very vain and not thorough. His gigantic desire to do everything led to his achieving really nothing at all. But he speaks and writes French extraordinarily well." *Op. cit.* I, p. 156.
[3] Eckardstein, *Erinnerungen,* I, pp. 22-23. *Cf.* Hohenlohe, *op. cit.* For the trial *vide Der Arnim'sche Prozess.* Bismarck discusses the trial in *Gedanken und Erinnerungen* II.
[4] *Das Tage Buch, loc. cit.,* p. 83.
[5] Hohenlohe, *op. cit.*
[6] Reibnitz, "Fritz von Holstein," *Querschnitt, Jahrg.* 6, 1926.
[7] Waldersee, *op. cit.* I, p. 286. Bismarck said, *"Er möchte wohl, kann aber nicht. Er hatte Ehrgeiz grosser Stils, doch zu wenig Augenmass und war eigentlich mehr Arnims Schuler als meiner. Nur im Souterain zu brauchen . . . auf der inneren Iris hatte er immer schon Flecke."* Harden, "Das Tage

not for an important post, and Bismarck thought fit to warn the young Prince William to avoid Holstein.[1] As he was retiring, Bismarck remarked to a friend, "they must try to get rid of Holstein. He knows the business and will . . . immensely impress the new people, will get his hand on everything and only produce confusion."[2] Schweinitz had noted in 1887 that Holstein was a peculiar, malicious person, using the press to injure people, and two years later he avoided the Foreign Office on account of Holstein.[3] The Old Chancellor believed his handy man had worked for his fall and in 1894 he urged Hohenlohe to get rid of Bötticher, Marschall and Holstein or "they will intrigue you out of office as they did me."[4] Whether he was right or not,[5] it is certain that for years Holstein lived in constant dread of Bismarck's return and labored indefatigably to prevent a reconciliation between him and the Kaiser.[6]

With the disappearance of Bismarck from Wilhelmstrasse the "Era of Holstein" began, for, as Harden puts it, after Bismarck went "the magician's apprentice had no master"[7] and he became the "spiritus rector"[8] and the "evil genius"[9] of the Foreign Office. The new Chancellor, General von Caprivi, was inexperienced in foreign matters. He could not expect much help from his Secretary of State von Marschall,

---

Buch, loc. cit., p. 88-89. Harden denies Bismarck ever said Holstein had Hyena eyes.   [1] Ereignisse und Gestalten VI.

[2] Harden, Das Tage Buch, loc. cit., p. 93.

[3] Denkwürdigkeiten, II, pp. 349, 389.

[4] Thimme, "Bismarck und Kardorff," Deutsche Revue, May, 1917.

[5] For conflicting testimony vide Harden, Köpfe, I, p. 101, and Waldersee, op. cit., II, pp. 56 and 136.

[6] Haller, op. cit. Harden (Das Tage Buch, loc. cit., pp. 88-89) states that Bismarck knew that Holstein had set spies on him and his son.

[7] Köpfe, I, p. 104.

[8] So called by Hammann and the Kaiser.

[9] Eulenburg's title for him. When Eulenburg wrote to Holstein that the direction of Germany's policy had passed into his hands after Bismarck's retirement, Holstein replied: "It is true that I feel myself the de facto Director of the Political Division" (of the Foreign Office). Haller, op. cit., pp. 194-195. Cf. Harden, Das Tage Buch, loc. cit., p. 86.

for he too was new to the business. The industrious and gifted Holstein with his infallible memory and knowledge of the archives must have seemed a godsend. It soon began to be said that both Chancellor and Secretary were completely in his hands.[1] Caprivi's first important act seemed to prove it.

On the eve of retiring, Bismarck had been busy with the details of renewing the Russian Reinsurance Treaty. The Kaiser approved and Russia was eager to sign. It was believed by Holstein that Herbert Bismarck remained in office a week after his father's departure in order to see the renewal through. But Holstein had decided that the treaty of which he disapproved should not be extended. When Herbert asked for the papers, he was informed that the Baron had them in his possession and a stormy scene followed in Holstein's room.[2]

Holstein succeeded in persuading Caprivi not to renew the Reinsurance Treaty[3] on the ground that the terms might make it impossible to fulfil treaty obligation due to Austria-Hungary and Rumania. He insisted that "nothing tangible can be expected from it and if it becomes known we shall be discredited as false."[4] "If we do at this time extend the clause dealing with the Straits, we do so on the assumption of secrecy on the part of Russia in a matter which, if disclosed to England, would drive a wedge of distrust between England and Germany.[5] . . . It is Russia's interest to be indiscreet, for as soon as there is the bare suspicion of this matter, all the world, that is, our other friends, will leave us. We shall then be restricted entirely to our Russian con-

---

[1] Waldersee, *op. cit.*, II, p. 137. There seems little doubt that Holstein inspired the "Uriah Letter" in 1892.

[2] Hammann, *Der neue Kurs*, p. 36. *Cf.* Harden, *Köpfe* I, pp. 102-103.

[3] Hammann, *World Policy of Germany*, pp. 46, *seq.* Harden, *Das Tage Buch*, loc. cit. p. 86.   [4] Harden, *Köpfe* I, pp. 100-101.

[5] *Die Grosse Politik*, VII, pp. 22, 48-49. Hereafter this collection of documents will be referred to as *G. P.*

nection. . . . Then Russia will be in a position to set the
conditions for our further relations to her." [1] It is true
that Marschall and Schweinitz [2] both voted against renewal and that Caprivi became convinced that such
a treaty "would lay a mine beneath the Triple Alliance to
which Russia might any day put a match," [3] but the driving
power in the whole decision was Holstein, who did not
share Bismarck's *cauchemar des coalitions* nor his belief
in the value of this wire between Berlin and Petrograd.

When William II dropped the pilot he thought he was
now master of the ship, but he deceived himself. [4] Below
stairs was a group with Holstein at their head that guided
the ship at will. They would have been powerless, however,
had they not had the assistance of the Kaiser's friend, Philipp
Eulenburg, [5] who not inaptly has been called "the Ambassador of the German People to the German Emperor." He
was in constant communication with the Kaiser and kept
Holstein informed of the advice he was giving their Sovereign. [6] Holstein had a keen eye for the Kaiser's weaknesses
and once in his exasperation he compared William to the
Emperor in the Second Part of Faust and predicted his fall
and the establishment of a German Republic. [7]

The public had no notion of the influence of these men on

[1] Holstein's note of March 28, quoted by *Vindex Scrutator* in *Der rote
Tag*, Nov. 4, 1920. For Holstein's alleged fear that Bismarck might betray
the existence of the treaty, cf. *Der neue Kurs*, pp. 32-33.

[2] Ambassador to Russia.

[3] *G. P.* VII. p. 31. Cf. *The World Policy of Germany*, p. 45. Vide *G. P.*
VII, p. 7, for statement of Berchem, Under-Secretary, that "so complicated
a policy" cannot be continued without Bismarck, with his prestige and
"magical influence."   [4] Haller, *op. cit.* pp. 73-74.

[5] *Ib.* p. 178, where Bülow writes Eulenburg that Holstein "knows that you
are the corner-stone without which everything would fall to pieces."

[6] Eulenburg's *Aus 50 Jahren* (1923) and Haller's biography, *Aus dem
Leben des Fürsten Philipp zu Eulenburg-Hertefeld* (1924), based on letters and diaries contain a wealth of material and abundant evidence of
Eulenburg's restraining influence on the Kaiser and his relations with Holstein. In 1866 Holstein opened correspondence with Eulenberg at the Munich
embassy, vainly endeavoring to keep it concealed from Eulenburg's chief.

[7] Hallen, *op. cit.*, p. 168.

national affairs until the *Kladderdatsch* began its campaign
against them. Week after week it directed the shafts of its
bitter wit against the *Austernfreund* [1] the *Spätzle* [2] and
Graf Troubadour. At first general readers had no idea of
what persons these nicknames represented, but the Foreign
Office knew well that they stood for Holstein, Kiderlen-
Wächter and Eulenburg, then the Prussian Minister in
Munich.[3] The reasons for the attack were presently given in
the fable entitled "The Three Men in the Fiery Furnace,"
which ran as follows: "There was once upon a time a king
who had many true and honorable servants. But there were
three who were not wholly upright and they did much evil
behind his back, for they slandered many of his most loyal
servants, so that they were removed from office and thrust
out of the palace. These disloyal officials were called Insinuans, Intrigans and Calumnians. The worst of them,
Insinuans, was probably the most dangerous, for he saw the
king more often than did the rest and also he played the
lute in masterly fashion and sang to it melodies that be-
witched the king." [4] At last a plain man arose who contrived
that the three evil-doers should be cast into a fiery furnace.
Holstein, who hated the faintest glimmer of publicity, was
in torment and bent all his energies in a vain effort to discover the author.[5] The campaign finally ended after Kiderlen wounded one of the editors of the paper in a duel. It
had been a long agony for the "Man of the Dark" [6] at the
Foreign Office, only less horrible than the Arnim Trial.

In 1894 Caprivi made way for a Chancellor more to the
Kaiser's liking. How far Holstein was responsible for his

[1] *I. e.* Oyster-lover.
[2] The name of a favorite dish in Swabia, the part of Germany from which
Kiderlen came.   [3] Hammann, *Der neue Kurs,* p. 59.
[4] Eulenberg was a poet and his singing gave the Kaiser great pleasure.
[5] He suspected Herbert Bismarck and, later, Count Henckel von Donners-
marck, both of whom refused to fight when he challenged them.
[6] Bismarck's expression. *Köpfe,* I, p. 127.

fall is a question,[1] but when he heard of his removal he offered his own resignation, believing that Bismarck was to be recalled. Fortune, however, was kind, for the Kaiser appointed Prince Hohenlohe, over whom, according to his own son, Holstein exerted an almost hypnotic influence.[2] During the first years of the new chancellorship "this eccentric person, highly gifted, possessed of encyclopædic knowledge, but misanthropic and full of whimsical suspicions, was able most easily to exercise his influence," [3] but he did not sway Hohenlohe as he had done before Hohenlohe became Chancellor. It must have been a bitter pill when Hohenlohe paid a visit to Friedrichsruh, for Holstein's fear of the Old Chancellor's return to power amounted to an obsession. He complained also about this time that the Kaiser listened too much to aides-de-camp and acted without consulting his Ministers. There was danger to the Fatherland in such habits. As deep an objection to them, however, lay in Holstein's dread that they might interfere with his own determination to move the figures on the political chess-board.

Holstein had two desires: to prevent a further strengthening of the Franco-Russian Alliance and to fix Russia's attention on the Far East. Therefore Germany joined France and Russia in the shortlived East Asiatic Triple Alliance in 1895 [4] which indirectly lost Germany her friendship with Japan. In the same year through Holstein's influence Germany missed the chance of coming to an understanding with England over Turkey. Salisbury suggested an Anglo-German Agreement dealing with the question of the partition of Turkey, which was bound to arise if the Sultan's rule ever broke down. Holstein was convinced that Salisbury's real

[1] *Haller* (*op. cit.*, p. 169) believes that Holstein had an important part in bringing it about, as does Alexander Hohenlohe.
[2] *Op. cit.*
[3] Hammann, *The World Policy of Germany*, p. 58.
[4] Hammann, *The World Policy of Germany*, pp. 54-59. Bismarck called it a "leap in the dark" due to a "straining after prestige."

purpose was to embroil Europe while England stood apart. Accordingly Hatzfeldt, the German Ambassador in London, was soon forbidden to discuss the project further.[1]

Holstein insisted [2] that he had nothing to do with the Krüger Telegram, but since he was always consulted in matters of importance it is hard to believe that he knew of it only as a *fait accompli*.[3] At all events he always called it a great mistake and charged it to the Kaiser's account. As the year wore on his vexation with his Sovereign increased. "It would be hazardous under any circumstances for a 'Kaiser to be his own Chancellor,' but with this impulsive and unfortunately quite superficial *Herr* . . . it is utter ruin." [4] Holstein even attempted to get the Chancellor to force the Kaiser to keep his hands out of politics.[5] From the very beginning he feared the Naval Program would arouse apprehensions abroad and he considered Tirpitz a mischief maker.[6]

In 1897 Bülow became Secretary of State and in some quarters it was "hoped that since the Kaiser is now beginning [7] to see Holstein in a clear light . . . Holstein will retire of himself." [8] But instead of being dismissed as the Kaiser [9] desired, Holstein became more potent while Bülow was Secretary and Chancellor than at any time during his career.[10] It was between 1898 and 1905 that he was instru-

---

[1] *G. P. X. Cf.* Haller, *op. cit.*, p. 179, for Hatzfeldt's opinion of Holstein's reasons.

[2] Harden, *Köpfe*, I, p. 105.

[3] Haller (*op. cit.*, p. 191) suspects him of refraining from preventing it in hopes it would compromise the Kaiser.

[4] *Ib.* pp. 184-185.   [5] *Ib.* pp. 185 *seq.*

[6] *Ib.* p. 213; *cf.* Harden, *Köpfe* I, p. 136.

[7] In spite of Bismarck's warnings the Kaiser came to consider Holstein "a pearl."

[8] Waldersee, *op. cit.* II, p. 399.   [9] Hammann, *Bilder,* p. 33.

[10] In a conversation with Hammann in 1925 the author asked why Bülow kept Holstein so many years when he had no illusions about him. Hammann replied that "there was a skeleton in the closet" and that Mühlberg believed Holstein threatened to reveal it. Hammann brought out his diary showing the record of a conversation in 1906 with Mühlberg and Bülow. The latter

mental in rebuffing England when the question of an Anglo-German Treaty repeatedly came up, and in disregarding Rouvier's suggestion for a Franco-German understanding about Morocco.

Joseph Chamberlain had conceived the idea of an alliance between England, Germany and America, already bound together by similarity of race, religion and mentality. Such a partnership might attract Japan too, and would solve the problem of World Peace. After many confidential conversations with Hatzfeldt, he told him in March 2, 1898,[1] that England was going to abandon her policy of isolation and was looking about for allies. Germany and England had no insurmountable colonial differences and if Germany would join England she would support Germany if attacked. He was prepared to work for an Anglo-German Treaty and Parliament would undoubtedly accept it. To prevent any danger of fear in Germany over antagonizing Russia he suggested that concessions be made to placate that country. He closed with the observation that if England were unable to effect this alliance, an understanding with France and Russia was not an impossibility.

It is not our purpose to discuss fully these or the later proposals for an Anglo-German Treaty. We shall merely try to point out the motives behind Holstein's attitude toward them.[2] The German Foreign Office showed a reserved and

---

acknowledged that Holstein was capable of anything, even treason to serve his ends. *"Wir sollen mit einem Raubenmörder durch einem dunklen Wald fahren; schadet nichts ihm die Livree zu geben—mit ihm Komödie spielen bei Sommer dann 'Rausschmeissen."* Hammann objected that *"man könne dem Kutscher . . . wohl die Livree geben, man soll ihm aber nicht noch den Dolch in die Hand drücken."* Another reason given was the fear that if dismissed he might divulge State Secrets. In 1895 Eulenburg had written "we cannot possibly do without Holstein's genius."

[1] Eckardstein, *op. cit.* I, pp. 292, *seq.* and Hatzfeldt's reports of March 29, April 1, 5, 7, 23, 26, in *G. P.*

[2] Eckardstein (*op. cit.,* I) has a lively account and documents are to be found in *G. P.,* XIV. There is no trace of these negotiations in the *British Documents,* for they were privately conducted.

hesitating disposition toward the English advances. Not unnaturally Germany feared to disturb her good relations with Russia [1] and Holstein believed that England's deliberate purpose in these proposals was to compromise Germany with Russia. He must have been strengthened in this conviction when the Tsar, in answer to the Kaiser's notification of the proposals, wrote that England had made a similar approach several months earlier to Russia, in the hope of destroying the friendship between Russia and Germany.[2] Hatzfeldt could not talk Holstein out of his belief that Salisbury was thoroughly dishonorable and full of sinister designs against Germany, who was to be used to pull England's chestnuts out of the fire. Holstein really desired an alliance with England ultimately but considered the time not yet ripe for it. It was an article of his political creed that England would never settle her differences with France and Russia. Germany, therefore, need not hurry to come to an agreement with England and could, meanwhile, take any tone she chose. He was obsessed with the idea that England must discover that Germany was the only possible ally before she would be willing to pay a proper price for Germany's friendship.[3] He was equally opposed to any treaty with Russia which might jeopardize good relations with England. He was clinging to the old policy of the "Free Hand."

This was the line of reasoning that prompted Holstein's unreceptive mood toward the English proposals for an alliance in 1898. He did not, however, object to special agreements and on September 26, 1898, an Anglo-German Treaty dealing with the Portuguese Colonies was ratified. This was

---

[1] Upon examination they seem to have rested chiefly on the good personal relations between the Kaiser and the Tsar.

[2] *G. P.*, XIV, p. 243. *Vide* Holstein's memorandum of August 20 for his fear that a general treaty might involve Germany in a war with Russia in which France would join, and for his fixed idea that Russia wanted a war with England and France one with England or Germany.

[3] He never forgave Salisbury's remark "you want too much for your friendship." *Vide* Hatzfeldt's reports of May 12 and 14, 1898 in *G. P.* XIV.

followed by the Samoan Treaty of 1899 [1] and the Yang-tse Treaty of 1900. But in 1899 Germany had again failed to seize England's offer to come to an understanding over Morocco.[2]

In 1901, a few days before the death of Queen Victoria, Chamberlain again broached the subject of an alliance between England and Germany. He told Eckardstein that "the time of England's splendid isolation" was over. She was ready to settle questions of World Politics, especially those touching Morocco and Eastern Asia, with one of the existing groups of Powers. He and the Duke of Devonshire preferred the Triple Alliance. If it were impossible to come to an understanding with Germany, England must ally herself with France and Russia, even at the cost of great sacrifices in Morocco, Persia, China, etc. He added certain confidential proposals, some concerning Morocco.[3]

Holstein's suspicious nature and his devotion to theories never were more striking than in his reception of Eckardstein's report and throughout the subsequent negotiations.[4] He still believed a general treaty with England involved danger of war.[5] "Threat of an understanding with France and Russia absolute humbug. We can wait. Time is on our side." [6] England would never make a favorable treaty with Germany until she felt herself in a tight place [7] and Germany would not pull chestnuts out of the fire for her. Holstein considered Salisbury capable of immediately [8] repeating to Russia any offer Germany might make with the inquiry,

[1] *Vide G. P.* XIV, p. 600 for Holstein's high-handed behavior during the negotiations.
[2] *Ib.* XVII for the documents relating to this offer. *Cf.* Eckardstein, *op. cit.* II, pp. 106-107, 117, 123 *seq.*
[3] *Op. cit.* II, pp. 235 *seq.* The conversation took place at the Duke of Devonshire's, where they were both guests. Hatzfeldt was ill and Eckardstein had charge of the Embassy.
[4] *G. P.* XVII; Eckardstein, *op. cit.* II. *British Documents* II.
[5] Eckardstein, *op. cit.* II, p. 26.   [7] *G. P.* XVII, pp. 22-23.
[6] Holstein to Metternich, Jan. 21.   [8] *G. P.* XVII, pp. 33 *seq.*

[299]

"What do you offer?" [1] therefore the offer of an alliance must not come from Germany. The German people would need convincing that a treaty would not be exclusively valuable to England.[2] Later Holstein issued a new dogma. Instead of making a treaty with Germany, England should join the Triple Alliance. "The way to Berlin lies through Vienna." [3] No wonder that Hatzfeldt told Eckardstein that he did not blame him for not wanting to struggle any longer with "that great paradise of fools in Berlin." [4]

Holstein became desperately nervous that England might construe something into a request for an alliance.[5] He repeatedly forbade Hatzfeldt and Eckardstein to give the English anything in writing.[6] On October 31, Holstein went into the whole subject of an Anglo-German alliance very frankly with his old friend Valentine Chirol who had come over expressly to investigate the situation in Germany. After declaring that Germany had no need of a *rapprochement* Holstein said, "I am one of those who believe that the current of the age will, however, little by little, and perhaps only when I am gone, bring . . . Germany and England together." But, he said, so long as Salisbury was at the rudder there could be no question of an alliance.[7]

On February 8, 1902 Eckardstein [8] dining at Marlborough House saw Chamberlain and Paul Cambon in a long and close conversation and caught the words "Morocco" and "Egypt." Two years later the Entente Cordiale between France and England was published.[9]

[1] Exactly what the Kaiser had done in 1898!

[2] The popular opinion was that Germany had been betrayed or outplayed by England in every agreement since 1890.

[3] *G. P.* XVII, p. 283.   [4] Eckardstein, *op. cit.* II, p. 290.

[5] Eckardstein had never told him that it was his suggestion on March 16, that led Lansdowne to make his proposition of that date for a defensive Anglo-German Alliance. *Vide op. cit.* II, pp. 280-281. Cf. *British Documents,* II, pp. 86 and 87.   [6] *G. P.* XVII, pp. 70-71.

[7] *Ib.* XVII, p. 101; *cf.* pp. 106-9.   [8] *Op. cit.* pp. 376-377.

[9] For a severe criticism of Holstein's failure to meet England's advances 1898-1901 *vide* Eugen Fischer, *Holsteins Grosses Nein.*

Germany's Morocco Policy of 1905 was another child of Holstein's brain.[1] He instigated the plan for the Kaiser's visit to Tangier,[2] that melodrama which was to serve as a German *acte de présence*.[3] He disregarded Rouvier's repeated offers to come to an understanding over Morocco and so lost another chance of a friendly disposal of that apple of discord. He forced France to agree to a Morocco Conference and Algeciras became for Germany the Olmütz that he had wished to avoid. During the Conference he had his own way until it was evident that the "infernal mischief maker"[4] was willing to wreck it. Then Bülow assumed control of the negotiations.[5] He decided to part with Holstein and on April 5, 1906 he told Hammann[6] that he had accepted Holstein's offer of resignation. At last the despot of Wilhelmstrasse was dethroned.

We are wont to think of Russia under Nicholas II as a country driven by dark forces. The study of Baron von Holstein proves that Germany too had her dark force. A psychiatrist is needed for a thorough analysis of Holstein's personality but the historian can estimate only too easily his baleful influence on World Politics. It was a calamity that he was in power when England wished to make a general treaty with Germany. When Holstein's *bête noire*, Salisbury, had gone and Germany began to show her desire for England's friendship, Sir Edward Gray displayed as unreceptive an attitude as had Bülow, 1898-1901, under Hol-

---

[1] *Vide G. P.* XX for the documents. Eckardstein, *op. cit.* III, has much valuable material.

[2] Hammann, *The World Policy of Germany*, p. 149.

[3] Holstein broke with Hammann because of the latter's refusal to assume a belligerent tone towards France in the official press, *Bilder*, p. 35.

[4] King Edward used this expression during the Crisis. *Vide* Eckardstein III, p. 122.

[5] Hammann, *Zur Vorgeschichte des Weltkriegs*, pp. 148-150.

[6] *Ib.* p. 151. Holstein had during his career offered his resignation eleven times. He had no intention of actually resigning and never suspected that Bülow, who fell ill on April 5, was responsible for the acceptance of this offer. *Vide* Hammann, *Bilder*, p. 38.

stein's influence.[1] In 1901 the Spirit of the Pities must have wished for "a man of facts not theories, who is never tied to his dearest private convictions when in action, and who never is in danger of practicing 'program politics.' "[2] After 1907, the year of Eyre Crowe's Memorandum,[3] the Ironic Spirit must have smiled to see an English Holstein shaping England's policy toward Germany.

[1] *Vide British Documents* III, pp. 364, 370 and *G. P.* XXI pp. 445, 453.
[2] Spengler's ideal statesman, *Der Untergang des Abendlandes* II p. 548.
[3] *British Documents* III.

HISTORY AND THE SCIENCE OF SOCIETY

by

Joseph Ward Swain

XVII

HISTORY AND THE SCIENCE OF SOCIETY

S HORTLY before the war, a French historian was able to speak of "the *malaise* from which history is now suffering"; and in more recent years the symptoms of this discontent have been multiplying on every hand. New interpretations of familiar events in history are being put forward; criticism of the older historians is spiced with contempt; treatises upon the theory of history appear with increasing frequency. Yet though the "old history" is clearly dead, the nature of the "new history" which is to supplant it remains a matter of controversy.

In the old days, history was a type of literature, and was honored as such. But in the middle of the nineteenth century, when all men bowed down before the great god Science, historians, too, forsook their former sanctuaries to run after the new power which was to redeem and restore the world. Nor can they be blamed for so doing. The same haste to hail the new lord of the world was shown by everyone: literature became "scientific," art became "scientific," and we even heard of the "religion of science." In fact, the new enthusiasm for science was the creation of literary men rather than of the scientists themselves: a few hundred persons may have read and understood the treatises of Dalton and Darwin, Helmholtz and Kelvin; but many thousands were converted to the new faith by the glowing pens of such writers as Taine and Zola, Renan and David Friedrich Strauss, or of a whole host of lesser lights in the next generation—all of whom knew little or nothing about science—

or by the writings of such philosophers as Herbert Spencer. Even the influence of such scientists as Huxley and Haeckel was due to their literary ability much more than to their scientific achievements; and Mr. H. G. Wells, though trained as a scientist, was really a man of letters after all. Historians were therefore only following their literary confrères when they turned to science; and how could they help doing so? It was confidently asserted by the accredited oracles of the day that scientific knowledge was the only type worth having, that the methods of natural science were the sole key to the truth, that the word "scientific" was synonymous with the word "true": if history was not "scientific" it was not "true," or even a worthy branch of knowledge; it was a sham and an imposture. Historians therefore hastened to agree with the commonalty of educated men that one must be a scientist or nothing, and they loudly proclaimed that they, too, were scientists with the best of them.

At first historians made this claim because they followed the fashion of the day and, like other literary men, wished to do obeisance to its ruling deity. Times have since changed, and the younger literary critics are now beginning to talk of "that quaint Victorian faith in natural science"; but the efforts of historians to be "scientific" are redoubled. This very persistence is worthy of note, and perhaps we shall be in a position to understand it better if we investigate what "science" does beyond proclaiming "the truth." In the nineteenth century, science was put forward by its literary advocates as a new revelation concerning the eternal verities, in rivalry with the Christian revelation and possessing the great advantage that its precepts were demonstrably true. But this attitude has largely passed, and science is now praised for its utilitarian value. Where once we heard much of the "warfare of science and theology," we hear instead of "science remaking the world." By learning the properties of things, scientists are able to make use of them and to do what they wish with them. It seems to be for such practical purposes that scholars are now seeking to establish history as the science of society. If only we knew as much about society, they say, as we do about coal and its by-products, we should be able to do as many things with the one as we can with the other. It is well known that many of those who are most earnest in their efforts to establish history as a science are also deeply interested in radical social programs. They hope that their studies may enable them to find the means of realizing their social ideals.

When, however, the historians come to state exactly what they mean by "scientific" history, their difficulties begin. Many, including the less ambitious ones, are wont to declare that by "scientific" history they mean "critical" history: they claim that they are scientists because they make every possible effort to get their facts correct. Such efforts certainly deserve all praise, but it is difficult to see what is "scientific" about them. Surely the ability to copy a text correctly is the virtue of a stenographer rather than that of a scientist; and the criticism which the historian applies to his sources resembles that which a lawyer applies to the testimony of a witness in court more than anything else. Unless we merely mean that it is correct as to fact, there is nothing "scientific" about the conventional variety of critical history.

In the early days a few ambitious writers endeavored to make history into a science by proclaiming laws or formulæ which would explain it. Buckle, Taine, Karl Marx, and a number of others in the middle of the century, attempted thus to account for the course of human development. In our own day the German writer Oswald Spengler has made an ambitious effort to perform the same feat, and lesser efforts have been made by other scholars. But in general such attempts have not been conspicuously successful, and have usually received rather scant attention from the professional historians. These scholars have preferred to leave the task of formulating general "laws" to the sociologists. It is perhaps well that they should do so, for, after all, the "science of society" is sociology, and if the laws of society are to be formulated, the sociologists seem to be the men to do it.

II

It makes very little difference to us here, however, whether those who do this work call themselves historians or sociologists. It is more important to know whether or not it is humanly possible to create a science such as these men dream of, which would enable them intelligently to guide the course of social development. A little reflection will make it evident that the difficulties which have hitherto prevented the satisfactory establishment of such a science are fundamental. Even if it were possible to achieve complete accuracy (which it is not) the science of society could never become a science exactly comparable to those dealing with physical nature, and could never be made to yield such certain and such satisfactory results. Comparisons between the two fields of study are therefore bound to be misleading.

One reason for this is the fact that the scholar's relation to human society is necessarily very different from the scientist's relation to nature. The scientist is, of course, a part of physical nature, just as the scholar is a member of society; but his relation to it is not so intimate or so emotional as the scholar's to society must be. It makes no earthly difference to the natural scientist how his problem works out, but it may make all the difference in the world to the social scientist how his works out. The only answers which he will accept are ones making adequate provision for himself, his

[308]

friends, his social class, and the various groups to which he is loyal: it is vain to expect him to commit *hari-kiri* if he finds that he or they are the cause of society's woes. This peculiar position of the social scientist would seem to explain the fact that, in spite of all their talk about "objectivity," our present social scientists have as yet presented us with little more than their own ancient beliefs and prejudices writ large.

But the difficulty facing those who would establish a science of society lies much deeper than mere "prejudice" of the common or vulgar variety: it seems to be inherent in the nature of society itself. In the long run, the reason why a given society has certain institutions and is organized in a certain way rather than another is the fact that the people who make up the society in question deem those institutions and that way of organization the best ones available. It may be that they think so only because of their ignorance and stupidity; yet the fact remains that their ideas and beliefs in regard to religion, economics, the family, politics, and the like, are the basis of the institutions organizing their collective life in these various fields. The institution itself is an idea, and exists only in so far as this idea is entertained in the minds of men. A society is a group of persons held together by common ideas, and primarily by common ideas in regard to their institutions. The study of society is thus largely reduced to a study of these ideas and their application; or, as some writers have put it, sociology is a *Geisteswissenschaft*—a science dealing with ideas, not with material objects. From this it follows that anything tending to change these ideas must change the society at its very foundations, and, inversely, that if the institutions are to be changed, these ideas must first be changed.

At this point the sociologist enters upon the scene. What is the effect of his activity? He studies institutions, he promulgates new ideas in regard to them, and in so far as his work is effective at all, he changes people's views in regard to these institutions. His society is therefore changed, and soon his description of the institutions in question is no longer accurate. But he cannot foresee what the effect of injecting his new idea into the minds of his fellow citizens will be, for that particular experiment has never been tried. No scientist knows what will happen the first time he performs an experiment—or else there would be no real need of his performing it at all. The importance of his work lies in the fact that he assumes that the second time he treats the same material in the same manner, the same results will follow. But, for the social scientist, there can be no "second time," because, as has just been pointed out, every experiment necessarily and fundamentally changes the nature of the materials experimented upon for all time. Every effort consciously to guide society must always be a first experiment, whose outcome no one can foretell. The position of the social scientist of today is not fundamentally different from that of the Utopian of old.

The error of those who speak of a "science of society" lies in their assumption that there is a universal and unchanging human nature at the bottom of society, upon a study of which they hope to base their science. It is, of course, undeniable that there are many elements in society which are widespread and fairly constant, and it was these that attracted the attention of the scholars who first conceived the idea of a science of society. But the assumption that these fundamental qualities of man and of society are as eternal as those of physical matter is denied by experience and contradicted by the Darwinian Theory. Human society is not comparable to a complex machine, and blue-prints showing how it works today will not remain accurate for long. We cannot draw up an air-tight system of sociology which will

last forever, merely by seeing to it that every part is correct
—any more than similar efforts were successful in the case
of the celebrated "One Hoss Shay," or in that of its great
prototype, the theological system of John Calvin. The teachings of science are popularly supposed to hold true forever,
but such perfection can never be achieved even by the very
best sociology.

There is also the problem of the application of scientific
knowledge to society, supposing such knowledge were really
in existence. The natural scientist deals only with objects
which he is free to treat as he wishes: if he discovers a
process enabling him to remold inanimate matter, or even
plants and animals, into new forms which are closer to his
heart's desire, he rarely meets with active opposition. But
should the social scientist discover a means of changing and
improving society, the efficacy of which was admitted by all
of his colleagues, it is by no means certain that he could
persuade his fellow-citizens to adopt it: they might not wish
to be improved in that particular direction. Animate and
inanimate things are under the scientist's control, but men
are not—unless he is a dictator. And though we have seen a
superfluity of dictators in recent years, it is extremely doubtful whether humanity would long tolerate a dictatorship of
scientists and sociologists.

It is to be feared that those who seek to redeem society
through the social sciences have not yet completely emancipated themselves from the older view that "science" is a
revelation from on high, and that they consider themselves
its accredited interpreters, set off from the rest of the human
race. They aspire to a rôle comparable to that of the clergy
in a theocracy, and if they were in power they would quickly
turn to those methods of government which have made
theocracies odious in days of yore. A régime of blue laws
would come into being—not those of today or those of Puri-

tan New England, but laws equally irksome and leading to equally regrettable consequences. For the type of mind which created the old blue laws is very similar to that which would create the new. In his bad points as in his good ones, the man who turns to social science for the amelioration of society is a worthy grandson of the Puritans—in his very real desire to improve the world, in his high seriousness, in his assurance, in his intellectuality, in his contempt for those who disagree with him, in his democratic talk coupled with snobbish behavior, in his denial of the doctrine of free will coupled with a conviction that he can, by his own free will, recast human society. In America, at least, the social scientist inherits far more from John Calvin and Jonathan Edwards that he does from the great physical scientists. His hands may be those of Esau, but his voice is the voice of Jacob. Science is one thing, but sociology is quite another.

III

It is not true, however, that all sociologists think of themselves as drawing blue-prints to show the workings of the social machine. One of the founders of the science of sociology was Herbert Spencer, and ever since his day the science has retained the evolutionary character which he gave it. It may be that many sociologists seek to imitate the physical scientists by discovering, through analysis and experimentation, "how society works"; but others merely endeavor to "explain" society by showing the evolution which has brought it to its present state. Such sociologists are really historians, though they may write their histories on a much wider scale than the one adopted until very recently by the professional historians. It is their purpose to write histories of society which shall include every aspect of social life. According to the suggestive title of a rather ponderous German book, sociology is identical with the philosophy of history. The writers who follow this line of thought differ greatly from the analytical sociologists discussed above, and therefore deserve a separate treatment; and this treatment can also be made to include historians in general.

This desire to explain the present by the past, or to seek an understanding of things from a knowledge of their origins, is a manifestation of the "historical-mindedness" which has spread so widely during the past half-century. Yet this historical-mindedness is by no means new. It is to be found in very ancient times, and among the most primitive peoples. From one end of this country to the other there are rocks, cliffs, and other features of the landscape whose names, and perhaps whose very existence, are popularly explained by the deeds—no doubt imaginary—of some Indian brave of long ago. There are numerous stories in the Old Testament which similarly explain the landscape of Palestine by the alleged deeds of the patriarchs. Examples of the same thing could be drawn from the mythology of every people. Nor do the mythologists stop with explaining the landscape. With every primitive people there is a whole class of myths, which folk-lorists call ætiological, whose purpose is to explain the origin of current social customs and institutions. Thus religious rites are often explained as imitations of some great event in the past: the Bacchic orgies of Greece were supposedly a rehearsal of the fate of Bacchus when he was torn asunder by the Titans. Political institutions are explained by stories concerning the alleged founder of the government. The tenth chapter of Genesis explains the existence of the different peoples with whom the Hebrews were acquainted by tracing their descent from Noah. History is thus made to explain the present.

Of course we can hardly say that the stories thus told are true, in our sense of the term; but they are believed to be true by the persons who tell them and by those who hear them; they are therefore just as effective as they would be if they really were true. They fulfill their function of explaining how men came to be as they are and to act as they do, just as history does for us today. History is mythology, save for the fact that we believe it to be true. History is mythology which is believed, mythology is history which is not believed; and the two shade off into one another by imperceptible degrees. What was once history is now mythology, and sometimes the reverse is true. Moses was once history, then he became mythology, and now he has apparently got at least one foot within the pale of historicity again. On the other hand, what is history for one man today is mythology for his neighbor, and persons on different intellectual levels find different mythologies credible. But whatever their status in the eyes of the critical historian, these myths are important and interesting to those who believe them because they seem to explain the present world by depicting its origins and history.

It thus appears that historical-mindedness, in its rudimentary forms at least, is fairly universal among mankind. But two developments in modern times have contributed much to the spreading of this type of thought. One of these developments was the rise of the genetic or evolutionary philosophy which was taught by the *philosophes* of the eighteenth century and which reached its culmination in Darwinism. This new philosophy was of course compelled to lay the greatest emphasis upon history, and it called for a much fuller history than had ever been written before: whereas the antique myth-makers had been satisfied with an account of the first origin of things, the modern evolutionary philosopher requires their complete history from the beginning to the present day. The great prosperity enjoyed by historical studies during the last fifty or seventy-five years was in large measure the consequence of this philosophical view of the world.

The other new development was the elaboration of critical methods for the study of history, which has made writers far more certain of their facts than they ever were before. This "scientific" criticism has purged history of many of the fables and legends with which the narrative of human events was once adorned; but it does not follow that criticism has also made it possible for historians to give a truly objective account of any single event in the past. Criticism may enable a historian to get his facts correct, but it takes more than facts to make a history. Every historian must add to the facts in various ways, and, as will presently appear, it is just these additions which make his work important.

In the first place, no historian can tell everything that happened, or even everything that is contained in his sources —unless these sources are so scanty as to render his whole picture guesswork. How, then, is he to tell which facts to put into the narrative, and which to leave out? Some historians introduce facts because they are dramatic or amusing, but the "scientific" historian generally gives only those which are "logically" important in the series of events he is narrating. Thus one set of facts will loom large in a political history, another set in an economic history, and still another in a social history; and the events which are emphasized in one history will be ignored in another. But by what standards are we to judge between these histories? Or again, approaching the matter from a slightly different point of view, it may be pointed out that the observer perceives only isolated facts. The historian must string these into a connected narrative, and he must therefore have a thread to string them on. He may believe that he observes the thread as much as he does the individual events. He does not: he creates it for himself. But how does he create it? And even when the thread is ready, which fact is to come first and which second? Chronological order may be followed in most cases, but what is to be done when two events take place contemporaneously in distant places? Again a "logical" arrangement is necessary. And finally, the historian must explain why things happened as they did. Every event in history had many causes, and each person who took part in it acted from different motives. The historian can give only a few of these, and the question must arise, which ones is he to select? The answer to these three questions is simple. He selects and arranges his facts, his thread, and his causes in conformity with the logic of his own philosophy of life.

This selecting and arranging must be done by even the driest of "scientific" historians; but when philosophy becomes the guide of history, can we say that history is objective? Realizing the incompatibility of a philosophy of history and an objective statement of the facts, many historians in the later nineteenth century announced that they would exclude all philosophy from their writings. But the effort was vain: the more philosophy was cast out by the door, the more it flew in by the window. As a matter of fact, the history which is not based on philosophy cannot be written. We have already seen that men were led to the study of history by a certain philosophy—that of evolution. With the best will and the best criticism in the world, they could not rid themselves of this philosophical presupposition —and if they had done so, they would have ceased studying history. Or, if they did not study history because of their belief in evolution, they did so for some other philosophical reason, which was equally bound to destroy the objectivity of their work. The effort to dispense with all philosophy in history has merely resulted in the acceptance of a philosophy that is not very carefully thought out, and therefore not very good.

[316]

Thus we see that the actual work of the historian does not consist simply in chronicling events; it includes selecting, arranging and interpreting them in the light of a certain philosophy. As a matter of fact, any number of such selections and arrangements can be made. By selecting different facts, and arranging them differently, any philosophy can be made to seem imminent in history. Each historian can, must, and does read his own philosophy into the events he describes. Even though the archives of the Recording Angel were open to all historians, and not a single fact in all history were in dispute, historians would never agree as to how the story should be written. A history is more than a chronicle of events: it is the historian's personal confession of faith as well.

IV

But do these considerations indicate that history, or rather, philosophy backed and illustrated by history, has no practical value? They certainly do not. The truth is that the importance of certain views upon history, of a certain mythology, has long been recognized, even by practical statesmen. It was Stein, the rejuvenator of Prussia, who conceived and founded the greatest piece of historical scholarship that ever came out of Germany, the *Monumenta Germaniæ Historica*. During the nineteenth century most of the European governments set aside considerable sums of money for similar publications. During the recent war this country was deluged with books and pamphlets of a historical nature, purporting to explain the immediate and remote origins of the conflict. The writings of patriotic historians such as Michelet, Froude and Treitschke, were factors of the greatest importance in the rise of that extravagant chauvinism which filled Europe at the beginning of the twentieth century. The so-called "Christian epic" (the Christian philosophy of history) is an item of the first importance in the Christian religion. Bolshevist leaders consider the materialistic interpretation of history one of the foundations of their social system. Politicians in this country have sometimes gained notoriety by their efforts to create an orthodox history.

In the face of evidence such as this, it would be hard indeed to maintain that histories are of no importance. But whence do they derive this importance? It hardly seems that practical statesmen have sought scientific knowledge from the historians to aid them in their tasks. In fact, they have usually shown far less interest in critical and "scientific" history, from which such knowledge might possibly be gained, than in popular and literary history. To them it seems far less important that a history be true than that it set forth an orthodox philosophy reaching the proper conclusions, and that it seem true—though the more intelligent statesmen have readily understood that, for certain classes of readers, the pomp and circumstance of critical scholarship may perhaps add to the credibility of the narrative. In its elementary forms this history which is so desired by practical men dwells especially upon the virtues and vices of various individuals and groups; but it also has its higher developments in which a real philosophy of history is worked out. These politicians know what an asset it will be to them if only they can convince the public not only that they represent the eternal right, but also that their program is the next step in the universal progress of mankind, that it is one towards which all history has aimed, that it has been foreordained by the whole course of human events. It is of course equally true that today a politician should be able also to show that his program is in conformity with all the teachings of science, and sociology will therefore be just as valuable to him as history—though not in the way that sociologists like to think. To these practical politicians, history and sociology alike are stimuli of enthusiasm, they are the fifes and drums which keep up the spirit of the army though they do not direct its course.

It will probably be most unpleasant to such social scientists as have been dreaming that they are about to become chiefs of the general staff suddenly to awaken and find that they are only drummer boys after all. Yet it is chiefly as such that their services have been useful up to the present. Nor does the situation seem likely to change.

v

In an earlier paragraph of the essay, the social scientists were compared to the clergy of a theocracy, and it was pointed out that the mentality of the American sociologists is strikingly similar to that of the Puritans of old. They are merely putting the old wine of Puritanism into the new bottles of science. This inherited Puritanism explains many of their characteristics, and it gives the clue to a more fundamental reason why their hopes are bound to be shattered, and why mythology may prove more effective than science.

The similar mentality of the Calvinists and the social scientists is well illustrated in one of their fundamental philosophical presuppositions—their opposition to free will. The social scientists usually inveigh against the freedom of the will in language which would warm the cockles of the heart of Jonathan Edwards, or even of John Calvin himself, if anything could work that miracle. The modern writers maintain, of course, that their belief in determinism is an expansion of the scientific doctrine deduced from the mechanism of physical nature: but one cannot help suspecting that they really inherited the doctrine from their Calvinistic grandfathers, and later found new proofs of it in the writings of the natural scientists. Yet it is to be feared that those who thus follow their sires in pouring contempt upon the doctrine of free will do not understand it in all its bearings. Our Puritan forebears were not talking about the conservation of energy or the laws of matter and motion, nor did they oppose free will to the reign of law: its alternative was the grace of God. The basis of the argument lay in the contention, by the Calvinists and other determinists, that man of himself can do nothing for his own betterment, and that salvation comes only through the grace of God; the Arminians and other advocates of free will, on the other hand, held that man unaided can do much to improve his state. It is obvious at a glance that, notwithstanding their theological disquisitions, the social scientists do occupy the same fundamental position as the Arminians, for they believe that man can improve his position by his own devices, *e.g.*, by science. The social scientists, to be consistent in their opposition to free will, should insist that "science" is the result of revelation, not a great human achievement.

It is not the purpose here to argue the doctrine of free will at length; but, leaving metaphysical subtleties aside, we may well ask, what do the defenders of free will really mean? When a doctrine persists after being confuted as often as this one has been, it probably stands for something important in the minds of its advocates. The proponents of free will do not mean to insist that human conduct is necessarily erratic, or incomprehensible, or even unpredictable; but they do insist that it is important, and it would seem that, in the final analysis, they merely wish to lay emphasis upon the importance of ideas in determining a man's conduct. There is a school of thought today—apparently of Calvinistic ancestry likewise—which pictures man as being actuated entirely by his "instincts," and which declares that ideas, especially general and abstract ideas, are "rationalizations" after the event—the dust in the road after an automobile has passed. To this modern version of the ancient doctrines of original sin and total depravity, the advocate of free will is opposed. For him, ideas are a real force in the life of an individual or of society, and in the history of a people. The instincts are there, to be sure, and they certainly are very powerful forces, just as many ideas are clearly *post facto* rationalizations. But this is not the whole story. In the long run ideas are creative forces. The laws of momentum and the conservation of energy have no terrors for persons holding this point of view: the details of the psycho-physical parallelism between ideas and brain-cells are a technical matter for psychologists to work out. If they cannot do it, so much the worse for them.

When we turn to the study of history it is difficult to see how the importance thus attributed to ideas can be denied. Even the so-called economic interpretation of history is in reality a theory as to the importance of ideas in human development. When all the vague mysticism about "economic forces" is boiled out of this theory, what remains is the assumption that individuals and society are dominated by ideas on economic matters—not by men's methods of making a living, but by their ideas regarding the best way of doing so: they are often right in these ideas, but sometimes they are mistaken. Even according to this interpretation of history, men's ideas are therefore of the utmost importance—though this particular doctrine, in its extreme form, would seem to postulate that men never think of anything, or at least never "mean business" in regard to anything, except economic matters—or, in other words, that they are all perfect embodiments of the "economic man" of the classical economists. Those persons, too, who talk of "science remaking the world" must emphasize the importance of ideas in history ("science" is a set of ideas) and, in spite of themselves, they are therefore committed to the theory of free will, as this is here defined. As a matter of fact, historians have generally tended to believe in free will, just as sociologists have tended to be determinists.

If ideas do enjoy this great importance in real life, it would seem that the social scientists, in their efforts to ameliorate society, should devote themselves to making people want the new and better system to prevail, rather than to devising formulæ by which a Mussolini might perhaps make them good and beautiful and happy against their wills. A wide-spread desire for a Utopia, and a particular one at that, is more important than a trick for suddenly bringing it to pass. There are many ways of bringing about this desire, but, as was shown above, historians may do their bit in stimulating it. The study of history, by itself, cannot create a Utopia, but it may convince historically-minded persons that a particular one is desirable—just as the preaching of sociologists may convince others of the same thing, or the preaching of clergymen convince others, or that of philosophers others, or that of poets still others.

But this preaching is not necessary only for those who would effect reforms. It is equally essential for those who merely want to keep social life going at all. Every form of social life sets limitations upon individuals to which they submit, sometimes because they are forced to, but usually because they think it desirable to do so. Some way must therefore be found to lead them to this happy state of mind: it has been remarked by someone that the art of government is largely the art of propaganda. And in this propaganda, history usually plays a part. It is true that many persons, perhaps most persons, are indifferent to appeals based upon history: but in every society there are enough historically-minded persons, who take their philosophy of history seriously, to insure the existence of such a philosophy. It makes little difference whether this philosophy be the mythology of primitive peoples, or the "Christian epic" of the Middle Ages, or the nationalistic history of the nineteenth century, or the "new history" (whatever form this may eventually assume) of the twentieth century: the essential point is that it be believed and that it lead historically-minded persons to accept those ideas which are the basis of their social organization. Because of the part that it thus plays, we might say that a philosophy of history is a social institution.

In times of great social change, this philosophy of history, like so many other social institutions, is very apt to break down. The new society which is emerging will rest upon different intellectual foundations, and the old ones will be subjected to severe criticism, along with the history which justified them; a considerable body of new knowledge will probably have arisen out of the changes that are taking place, and this will have to be assimilated into the new history; new values will be set upon old facts; the new basis of society will have to be justified by a new arrangement of the facts of history, and a different philosophy of history will gradually be produced for the new age.

This process is going on today, as is witnessed by "the *malaise* from which history is now suffering." No one can say what our philosophy of history is. One critical historian will entertain a certain view of things, while his colleagues entertain others. But it is important to note that his wife will hold a very different view, the nature of which will depend upon whether she derives it from our high Tories or from those cheerful souls who are at present engaged in "debunking history." His brother will have learned still another theory of history at the Kiwanis Club. The daughter in college will learn a different theory—probably

[323]

enlightened and liberal history of the "Political and Social" sort. The son of the family, in the grades, will be instructed in still another version, which the Mayor's historical adviser has thought would be good for him, though whatever history the boy really knows will probably have been derived from "thrillers" in his magazine. The laundress will perhaps entertain still another philosophy of history, which she has deduced from patriotic penny-dreadfuls, from literature recommended by the clergy, or from a stump speaker's version of Karl Marx. It has always been the case, of course, that history has been rewritten for every grade of intellect; this was the case with the Christian epic or the nationalistic epics of modern times; but these various accounts were merely different versions of the same thing—they all came out the same way in the end, and there was a close kinship between them. But today the different versions come out differently: the poor historian described above will find little kinship with any of his family—save perhaps with his daughter. This situation will probably not continue forever. As affairs settle down again after the great social upheavals of the last generation, a greater agreement will probably arise between different members of the group.

A new philosophy of history is therefore sorely needed today, but we have no formula for creating one. About all that the individual historian can do is to go ahead and tell the truth as he sees it. The pragmatic views in regard to history which are here set forth will not justify a writer in departing a hair's breadth from the truth as this is available: to be effective a history must be believed, and in the long run, to be believed it must be true according to all the critical standards of the day. When he has once made sure of his facts, however, the historian may then arrange them as seems best, and perhaps he will hit upon an arrangement which will be meritorious. It seems hardly probable that at the present moment any one man can construct a philosophy of history which will last for long: our knowledge and our philosophy are changing too rapidly. But every good point that is made today is a contribution to the "new history" which will someday appear. An effective philosophy of history, like any other social institution, is the result of countless experiments, and the work of countless collaborators: it was thus with the Christian and nationalistic epics, and it will be thus with the epic of the "new history." Gradually, by the time-honored method of "fumble and find," a new philosophy of history will grow up which will be convincing and important to the new society which shall have grown up with it.

The historical research of the past fifty years has given us more facts than we know what to do with, and while many facts yet remain to be discovered, especially on the fringes, we apparently have learned most of those which can be learned by our present methods of research. Our task today is to make sense out of the facts we already know, just as the philosophical historians of the later eighteenth century made sense out of the facts assembled by the erudition of the preceding hundred years. The current demand for a "new history" is really a demand for such a new philosophy of history. This will come sooner or later, and we can only hope that it will be a good one. But we need not fear. If the coming civilization is a good one, it will produce a good philosophy of history to back it up. There are many tests by which we may judge a society or an age, and one of these—by no means the worst of them—is to judge it by the history in which it believed.

JOHN LOUIS VIVES
HIS ATTITUDE TO LEARNING
AND TO LIFE

by

Lynn Thorndike

XVIII

JOHN LOUIS VIVES: HIS ATTITUDE TO LEARNING AND TO LIFE

JOHN LOUIS VIVES was born at Valencia on the eastern coast of Spain in 1492, the year that Erasmus became a priest. Of his teachers there he most frequently mentions and praises Antonio de Nebrija who brought Italian humanism to Spain in 1507, and is called by Vives "the restorer of the Greek and Latin languages among the Spaniards." He was, however, less a grammarian and stylist than a critic, philosopher, historian and cosmographer, and not unacquainted with law, medicine, and theology. This breadth of scholarly interest he seems to have transmitted to Vives who shows a wide acquaintance with the literature of varied fields of learning.

In 1509 Vives went to the University of Paris, and most of the remainder of his life was spent outside Spain in the Low Countries, England, or at Paris. He thus to some extent followed in the footsteps of Erasmus. In 1512 he came to Bruges. Here he wrote a number of pious works which he commonly sent to Spanish counts or bishops. His *Triumph of Christ* was couched, however, in the form of a Platonic dialogue. For a time he taught Aristotelian philosophy at the University of Louvain and wrote treatises on the history of philosophy and against the pseudo-dialecticians. At the same time he engaged in more purely literary pursuits, writing for example an introduction to the *Georgics* of Vergil and *Declamations* on such classical themes as Sulla. In 1521-1522 he wrote and published a commentary on Augustine's

City of God, which at first had no sale but ultimately ran through many editions and was at least once placed upon the Index. Thus far Vives had been supported mainly by his pupil, the youthful archbishop of Toledo, and by Catherine of Aragon.

After the untimely death of the former he was left so poor and was also so sick of teaching boys that he decided he would rather do anything else (yet he is regarded as a great name in the history of pedagogy) and in 1522 determined to go to England, obtaining letters of introduction from Erasmus. There he tried teaching a girl instead and became the tutor of princess Mary Tudor, for whom he composed one of his educational treatises. He returned to the continent in 1524 to get married. He wrote Erasmus from Bruges that he has subjected his neck to the yoke of a woman which does not yet seem heavy to him but that God knows how it will turn out. All his friends, however, are much pleased with the match. He returned again to England, where he taught at Corpus Christi College, Oxford, and received the doctorate in civil law. When Henry VIII's divorce case came up, Vives sided with his patroness, Catherine of Aragon, and after an imprisonment of eight weeks was released by the king only on condition that he quit the realm. He withdrew to Bruges and we find him later on at Paris in 1536 and Bruges in 1538. He died before he was fifty in 1540. The amount of reading and writing he accomplished within that time is remarkable.

Of his works some are available in English translation. The *De institutione feminae christianae* was so issued as far back as 1592 under the title, "A Verie Fruitfull and Pleasant Booke Called the Instruction of a Christian Woman." [1] It has recently been further celebrated by J. W. Adamson in *Vives and the Renascence Education of Women*, London,

[1] Translated from the Latin by Richard Hyrde, London, 1592.

1912. Foster Watson published other writings of Vives on pedagogy in his *Tudor School-Boy Life*, 1908, and Vives *On Education*, 1913. The work of Vives on the subject of poor relief was issued in English translation by Margaret M. Sherwood in 1917. We shall here, however, be chiefly concerned with Vives' two longer Latin works on the corruption of the arts and the transmission of disciplines with some use of other treatises by him. The *De causis corruptarum artium* has sometimes been ranked with the *Novum Organon* of Francis Bacon as an onslaught upon scholasticism and medieval studies, but it does not seem that Vives intended the book as especially an indictment of the middle ages. The evils which have corrupted the arts often go back to ancient times. In the *De tradendis disciplinis* he reviews the books which have been written in various fields and gives lists or advice as to what to read. The work therefore bears a certain resemblance to the *Didascalicon* of Hugh of St. Victor in the twelfth century. The estimates, appreciations, and criticisms of past authors which Vives gives show remarkably sound judgment as well as omnivorous reading, and may be regarded as one of the most convincing and truly encouraging indications we possess of an intellectual advance by the early sixteenth over the preceding centuries. In this connection the estimate of Schott in the old *Bibliotheca Hispaniae* (1603-8), may well be recalled. Reckoning Erasmus, Budé, and Vives as the triumvirs of the republic of letters in the early sixteenth century, he makes Budé excel in genius or ingenuity, Erasmus in facility (*dicendi copia*), Vives in good judgment.

Of Vives' Latin style we cannot say as much. He is given to excessively long Latin periods, made up of innumerable brief phrases or clauses separated by commas, and is not infrequently guilty of tautology. His word order in these long mazes is sometimes difficult to follow. Too often he becomes oratorically repetitious of one idea. He has another common humanistic failing of excessive citation or quotation of classical authors. At times, however, his style is excellent and his words well worth repeating. Especially in his literary criticism and characterization of past authors is he apt to be terse and meaty.

We may commence our brief survey of his attitude towards various fields of learning and the authors therein by noting his position concerning the Latin language and its use as a medium of learning. Since it has spread through many nations and almost all the liberal arts are written in it, since its vocabulary is abundant, refined and augmented by the ingenuity of many writers, while it is smooth in sound and possesses a certain gravity which is not rude and wild, as in some tongues, but such as a brave and prudent man would employ who had been born and educated in a well administered city—for all these reasons it would be a crime not to cherish and preserve it. Should it be lost, great confusion would follow in all branches of learning, and great dissent and aversion among men because of ignorance of one another's languages. (*De tradendis disciplinis*, III i, *Opera*, 1782, V, 299.) Almost prophetic words these! as the Protestant Revolt was opening, as state churches were about to take form, and the national literatures of the sixteenth and seventeenth centuries in the modern languages were beginning to develop.

What was Vives' conception of the nature of true learning? In his treatise on the life and character of the scholar (*De vita et moribus eruditi*) he is far from accepting any narrowly linguistic or philological definition. "For what are languages except utterances?" he asks, "or what does it matter, if you take away the subject-matter, whether you know Latin and Greek, or Spanish and French?" Dialectic and rhetoric, too, he regards as instruments of the arts rather

[332]

than arts themselves, "and they are transmitted better by nature than by a master." As for philosophy, it is largely a matter of opinion and conjecture. But erudition consists of four things, natural talent, judgment, memory, and study. He adds a word against the literary controversies and mud-slinging of his day. "It is most disgraceful for us that thieves and panders live on better terms with one another than men of learning do."

As the foregoing paragraph suggests, Vives looks back rather critically on the preceding period of Italian human-ism, with whose origins and course he shows a fair acquaint-ance. "The memory of their fathers and ancestors began," he says, "in Italy to recall the study of the languages through the disciples of Peter of Ravenna the Latin and Emmanuel Chrysoloras the Greek." Among these disciples those of the greatest name were Leonardo of Arezzo, Filelfo, Lorenzo Valla, Guarino of Verona, and Niccolo Perotti. These were followed by Pico della Mirandola, Hermolaus Barbarus, Politian, and others. Such men were called orators because they spoke Latin more learnedly than others, but in Vives' opinion they hardly deserved this designation since they were intent upon restoring the languages from the depths of barbarism. Moreover, they limited themselves to eulogies of the arts and of princes or to invectives against their oppo-nents, and did not argue cases. Intent on the choice of words, they neglected phrasing and diction. And just as a century before them men read Cicero and the other Latin authors merely for the sense without noticing the words, so these early humanists, intent on words, passed over the diction unnoticed. They would use the same style in writing of great or small matters, joyful or sad, humble or sublime. They employed one style alike in letters, orations, works on rural life, treatises of natural science, works of morals.

The penchant for literary criticism which Vives showed in

the preceding passage he further displays at the expense of the humanists in his treatise on letter-writing. Petrarch, although he appeared like a star in darkest night after the long medieval interval which had elapsed since the days of Symmachus and Sidonius Apollinaris, is prolix and in many places morose and difficult and brings with him too much of the rust and mould of his age. Gasparino (da Barzizza 1359-1431) came considerably later. His letters deserve praise chiefly as being the first of the truly humanistic period. Then came Leonardo of Arezzo who still lacked refinement, then the two Filelfi, father and son, whose language was freer from mistakes but whose thought was inane and insipid and whose composition not sufficiently pleasing. Poggio was a garrulous trifler and Aeneas Sylvius was "happy by nature, infelicitous in his art. Aegidius Calentius and Campanus are not to be scorned, though the latter composed mostly for show. Sabellicus is always *sui similis* in abundance, facility and agreeableness." Pomponius Laetus was so intent on keeping his Latin pure that he refused to learn Greek. Pico's thought is weighty, his diction chaste. Politian is easy to understand, but too eager to please, and offends the puritanical and learned by his levity and lewdness. He also shows off too much and is abusive towards those of whom he disapproves, thus teaching the young the two serious faults of boastfulness and bitterness. Hermolaus Barbarus is braver and more cultured but more obscure. Marsilius Ficinus, the philosophaster—surely an appropriate epithet—mingled with these writers like a duck with swans, and composed letters in which he disputed about Platonic questions in an inelegant and labored style. Francesco Pico lacked genius, though superior to his uncle as a letter writer in some respects. Turning to the German humanists, Vives says that if Rudolf Agricola had revised his epistles, they would have rivalled those of the greatest among the ancients, for there was great

[334]

solidity and sanity in his erudition and sharpness in his judgment. Reuchlin's letters fell stillborn from the press. Christopher Longolius had good natural talent but corrupted it by indulging in imitation to an excessive degree. He has a Ciceronian wording with little accompanying sense and uses grand phrases for small matters. Erasmus and Budé are superior to all contemporary writers and equal to those of the two previous generations of humanists. Erasmus is facile and lucid. Budé delights in a new and unusual kind of diction which it is easier to admire than to imitate.

From this taste of Vives' pungent literary criticism we may turn to his discussion of rhetoric. (*Corrupt. art.* IV, 2, 3, 4, etc.) He found the instructions of the ancients in this subject unsatisfactory, and did not agree that the quoting of poetry in an oration was a bad practice. He also attacked the slavish imitation of Cicero that was current in his own time, agreeing with Erasmus that conditions had changed so that one could not today adequately express himself in Ciceronian phrases. Vives further complained that the men of his age not only collected phrases from the ancients to repeat but were mere apes of them in their matter and argument as well.

In his *Commentary on the City of God* Vives suggests that contentious dialectic is an invention of the devil. Elsewhere he complained that two years out of three were devoted to the study of dialectic at the University of Paris, and barely one year to natural science, ethics, and philosophy. Indeed, many men were nothing but dialecticians their whole life long. He also represents disputations as having declined. Their aim used to be the truth and the presentation of all sides of a subject, with winning as a spur only in the case of the young. Now all is sacrificed to the desire for victory, success in scholastic disputation bringing pecuniary rewards later, and the debates are staged theatrically before the public, into whose eyes the disputants throw as much dust as they can. Vives also holds it against them that they are always clamoring, "To the point, to the point, stick to the point!" (which must have been rather detrimental to classical allusions) and that orations of from five to seven hours length such as the Greeks and Romans used to delight in are no longer possible. But to the modern reader this may seem in their favor and hardly a sign of degeneration. Had Vives lived a little longer, however, the sermons of Calvinistic divines might have sated his yearnings for lengthy orations. He further criticizes the dialecticians for neglecting good authors such as Plato, Cicero, Seneca, Pliny, Jerome, and Ambrose, and attacks the Scotists and followers of Occam in particular. He ridicules the common medieval division of Old and New Logic, for which he says there is no more reason than that of the Old and New Digest, apparently in ignorance of the historical fact that medieval men at first possessed only the *Praedicabilia, Categoriae,* and *De interpretatione* which make up the *Logica vetera,* and that the Prior and Posterior Analytics and the Topics were introduced later and so known as the New Logic.[1] Vives also attacks the Aristotelian Categories and Interpretation. The Prior Analytics are in his opinion a beautiful and elaborate instrument of reasoning but of little use because overloaded with superfluities. The Posterior Analytics are learned, acute, and full of good things, but impinge on the preserves of psychology in treating of "opinion," error, and ignorance. Lorenzo Valla's attack upon the Aristotelian dialectic does not at all meet with Vives' approval, however. He censures it in crushing style in a passage at the very close of the third book of his work on the corruption of the liberal arts.

History was a subject for which Vives showed more love than he did for dialectic. The Egyptian priest was right who

[1] A similar explanation of course applies in the case of the Old and New Digest.

called the Greeks mere children because they had no record of the distant past. The study of history makes boys men, while men who know no history become puerile. 'Tis time's testimony and truth's torch, a never-failing delight, and of incredible utility in life and all learning. We enjoy fiction because it bears some semblance to fact. Without history no one would know his father or ancestors or his property rights, or what land he dwells in or how he got there. In public life and administration it is even more essential. Some say that it is useless to study history because conditions are ever-changing, but human nature does not change. The art of medicine is largely a historical collection; moral philosophy profits more from examples than precepts; and Christian theology is in great part composed of Biblical history, the lives of the saints and martyrs, and the history of the church as an institution. In fine, while Vives would not detract from other studies, history seems to him the supreme discipline, giving birth to or nourishing and increasing all the other arts. In both his work on the corruption of the arts and that on the transmission of disciplines Vives decries military history and the study of past wars. He makes a plea for intellectual history when he says that it is unworthy to record the works of our passions and not also those of our reason and deliberation. He would have the dates and famous names of history learned in childhood, judgment applied to the facts and these converted to use in life by the adult.

Vives accepted a mythical origin for history, giving Abraham, who was supposed to have received it from the sons of Seth, precedence over the Egyptian priests or Cadmus. He recognized, however, that Greek history was very fabulous until one reached the time of reckoning by Olympiads. But he probably read this in his Greek classics, just as he had read the Abraham myth in Josephus. He regarded

Philostratus's Life of Apollonius of Tyana as a blasphemous figment, but deplored the pious fraud manifest in Christian lives of the saints, the authors of which make the saint do what they think fit. He also regretted that the saints' lives and acts of the apostles and martyrs were presented in such inferior literary form to those of the Alexanders and Hannibals of pagan antiquity. The Greek historians often exaggerated grossly but not to compare with such medieval works as the *Gesta Romanorum, Golden Legend,* and Walter Burley's *De vita et moribus philosophorum.* On the other hand, Vives seems to have over-estimated the reliability of Diogenes Laërtius and Suetonius. He also took the trouble to condemn the romances which were so popular in his own century. Of recent and medieval historians, properly so classed, he speaks in somewhat varying tone in the two main works we are following. In the work on the corruption of the arts he laments that "our Latin historians" lack the style of a Livy, Tacitus, or Thucydides. In the treatise on the transmission of disciplines he has to admire the wording and elegant diction of the medieval historian Saxo Grammaticus (c. 1200). Again in the former work he rather ungraciously concedes that such medieval historians as Froissart, Monstrelet, Commines, and Valera Hispanus are a little better than the *Gesta Romanorum* and *Golden Legend,* but adds that they often omit important matters and lay stress on trifles. But in the latter treatise at the close of his list of historical writers in Greek and Latin he half apologizes for omitting those who have written the history of some small nation or single city such as Flanders, Liège, or Utrecht, or who have written in the vernacular languages like Valera Hispanus, Froissart, Monstrelet and Commines, "many of whom," he continues, "are no less worthy to be read and known than many of the Greek or Latin authors." Among Latin historians he names such medieval writers as Bede, Hermann the Lame, and Otto of Freising. He gives the national historians of his day a sharp blow, stating that each author writes about his own nation and exalts that people with no eye to the truth but only to the national glory, for which he is ready to extenuate and excuse almost any offense and to defend all the blots that really rest upon it.

Vives complained that mathematics was not taught at Paris as the ancient statutes required. In his reading lists to which we have already referred he did not admit any medieval writers until he reached the subject of mathematics, when he mentioned Sacrobosco, Jordanus Nemorarius, Thomas Bradwardine and others. He rejected the art of astrology, although he did not doubt that the stars have much influence on our bodies.

The book devoted to medicine in Vives' work on the corruption of the arts is brief and rather weak. In treating the subject again in his treatise on the transmission of disciplines he admits that he does not know much about it, and most of what he says is commonplace. His notion, already mentioned, that the art of medicine is largely a historical collection shows a more favorable attitude to the medical lore of the past than is at present in vogue. More modern in tone is his advice that there be separate men for medical research and contemplation apart from practitioners. He shared the common belief of his time that the medicinal virtues of herbs vary not only with the species of plants but with the season of the year or time of day when they are gathered, the ground where they grow, the age of the herb, and the condition of its roots, leaves, or flowers.

Vives' discussion of the law contains more points of interest, at least to the layman. He realizes that laws vary with times, climes, and peoples, and that legislators are influenced by popular desires or needs. "Among us many laws favor war; in New India they oppose war; the laws of the

Lacedaemonians were entirely warlike, for which reason they are deservedly condemned by philosophers. Those regions which can hardly maintain themselves without commerce, like Belgium, have laws which greatly favor business." Vives implies that penalties have grown harsher recently when he states that whereas Solon mitigated the laws of Draco, the emperor Frederick III (1440-1493) added the penalty of hanging for theft, and that this penalty has now become general throughout Europe. He illustrates the importance which customary law still had in his day by stating that the people of Pannonia lived very amicably under their old customs without need of jurists until as a sequel to the marriage of Beatrice of Naples with King Matthias of Hungary the jurists who came in her train began to introduce the Roman law. The whole countryside was soon plunged into a turmoil of litigation and red-tape until some prudent citizens demonstrated the evil to the king and he expelled the Roman lawyers from the country. Thereupon everything went back to the old state of calm as if a violent wind had suddenly died down. Vives contends that the laws should be clear, easy to understand, and few in number, "so that anyone may know how he ought to live." But the jurists take care to make them obscure so that the people will have to have recourse to themselves as oracles. If laws become too numerous, crime can no more be avoided than can accidents when all about are traps and nets and pitfalls. He discredits those who quote law after law from memory as precedents but neglect reason and interpretation, charging that they have sometimes not read the laws which they cite but only epitomes of their rubrics. This is indicated by the fact that they often cite by its rubric a law of which the latter part is either irrelevant to their case or contrary to their contention. Similarly he objects to those who use florilegia in any fields and who know their church fathers only through Peter

Lombard, or their Hippocrates and Galen and Avicenna through the medium of compendiums.

In the fields of metaphysics and moral philosophy Vives censured the following of Aristotle exclusively of the ancients. He also attacked the metaphysics of Avicenna and Averroes. He adopted the common but exaggerated humanistic view that one could learn more of moral standards from one page of the classical moralists, such as Seneca or Plutarch, than from all the commentaries and disputations of the schools. Of the schoolmen Vives regarded Aquinas as "the sanest and least inept," but he found his treatment of ethical questions less inspiring than that of Plato, Xenophon or Cicero.[1]

It remains to note some of Vives' political principles. He was as opposed to wars and selfish nationalism in the present as he was to the coloring of historical writing by those forces. Julius Caesar who was responsible for the slaughter of so many men even apart from the civil wars was no hero to him. "But if one examines the matter with true insight," he says, "what else are all wars between men than civil wars? The Indian is bound to the Roman by no lesser bonds than is Roman to Roman, not infrequently indeed by greater ones. Such is Nature's lesson, such the command of Christ, the author and master of Nature." Many were the efforts for peace which Vives made in the third decade of the sixteenth century. In 1522 he wrote to Pope Adrian VI on the tumultuous condition of Europe (*De Europae statu ac tumultibus*). In 1525 he wrote to Henry VIII of England on the captivity of Francis I of France and on peace between Francis and the emperor. In 1526 he discussed the European disagreements and Turkish war. In 1529 he sent Charles V four

[1] A marginal heading or note in the 1785 edition of Vives' works speaks in more favorable terms of this Secunda Pars of Aquinas's Summa, stating that it is not merely equal to Aristotle's Ethics, as Vives stated, but vastly superior and moving the reader most efficaciously by its angelic and at the same time most solid clarity.

books on concord and discord among mankind, (*De concordia et discordia in humano genere*).

Vives was not one of those humanists who flattered princes and despots whether good or bad. Indeed, he affirms that no true scholar would do this, but the general public is unable to distinguish between the flatterers and the true scholars, thinking that all who use Latin are learned men; thus learning is brought into disrepute. In another passage he asserts that such fawners who foster the crimes of princes by their adulations are all too numerous in his age. "Who does not censure it? But who does not do it?" Princes ought to look forward to the sincere praise of the truly wise as to a great reward. But the hearts of princes are so often hardened against sound teaching that Vives inclines rather to try to make an impression upon the people, who, he believes, will prove more tractable and amenable to remedies and instruction. Why were there so many sages in ancient Athens and ancient Rome and in the early days of Christianity, and so few in the present age? Because in free cities there was free speech. Thus Vives seems to favor a republican or popular form of government instead of the prevailing monarchy of the sixteenth century, and to prefer liberalism to absolutism.

In conclusion we may say of Vives that he was not only not one of those humanists who flattered princes and toadied to patrons, but further that he was a true scholar and a true citizen of the world. In these respects he is even somewhat superior to Erasmus, whom he resembles in many other respects. If he does not have Erasmus' genius for sly sarcasm and ridicule of human folly, he is perhaps a man of wider reading and of deeper sincerity.

A YARDSTICK FOR CIVILIZATION

by

Preston William Slosson

XIX

A YARDSTICK FOR CIVILIZATION

CIVILIZATION is one of those indispensible words, such as "liberty," "democracy" and "progress," which have passed from hand to hand so often as to become worn with use and should be reminted by a fresh definition each time they are again put into circulation. Rousseau and many since his time have used the word in a disparaging sense as equivalent to artificial, sophisticated, remote from the life of nature. Without pausing to discuss the very debatable point as to whether the life barbaric is really simpler or less artificial than that of the city dweller, or whether we merely feel the pressure of our own conventions and are unaware of the taboo and tribal ritual which hem in the freedom of the noble savage, it will be enough to say that in this paper civilization is used in its other meaning, the realization of values through human institutions.

Popular standards of civilization are rather capricious. Some rank Spain high as a civilized nation because Spaniards are polite; others rank her low because many Spaniards are illiterate. Some rank France high because of French cooking; others can see nothing in France except the absence of American plumbing. Some judge Italy by Dante; some by the Sicilian immigrant. Some rank Japan far above the United States in culture because of her superiority in decorative art; others will rule her out of the ranks of civilization altogether as "heathen" or Mongolian. Obviously, there is not and cannot be an absolute standard, acceptable to all. To one type of decadent poet the ideal social state might be Nero's

Rome with its cushioned luxury and artistic cruelties. To one type of austere fanatic all art and luxury might seem positive evils. There is no better way to give one's imagination a cynical holiday than to conceive a group of famous eccentrics, say, for example, John Knox, Oscar Wilde, Schopenhauer, Nietzsche and Lord Dunsany, locked into a jury room and compelled to reach an agreement on any formula for progress. Probably Schopenhauer would veto the suggestions of all the rest on the ground that life itself is an evil!

There are, however, certain human values which nearly all recognize and which may serve as the common measure of the advance of civilization. This need not hinder our cherishing some special dreams of our own which other builders of Utopia do not share. Our present quest is not the sum total of human perfection, but merely a "greatest common denominator" of the values recognized by the majority. We cannot, for instance, claim Christianity, and still less any sect or branch of it, as part of our definition because the civilized millions of China and Japan would refuse to acknowledge our standard. Nor can we claim for any particular form of government, school of art, race, language tradition or social custom that those who have it are the only civilized men.

Two standards, at least, would be recognized as valid by nine men out of ten in all countries commonly termed civilized, and because there is no way of measuring their importance as against each other we may for the sake of the argument weight them as of equal significance. The first may be called "social welfare," and be taken as implying good medical and sanitary standards, public order and security for life and property, effective administration of public business, legal rights and civil liberties to protect the individual from injustice, invention and industry, a distribution of comfort among all classes, an educational system reaching all children in proportion to their ability to make use of it. Very few persons would fail to call such achievements "progress" or "civilization."

The second standard is that of individual achievements in science, philosophy, scholarship, literature, art and other creations of the human spirit. A civilization which brought wealth, health, peace and nothing more would be but a demi-Utopia. It would be a plateau, not an inspiring mountain range. On the other hand, it would be an error to lay almost exclusive emphasis on individual genius [1] and ignore the equally significant gains which civilization brings to the daily life of the millions.

We must subdivide each group. Social welfare is made up of many elements, and as it would be absolutely hopeless to reach an agreement as to which of these is most important we must, quite arbitrarily, assign them equal value. Just so a college grants the same credit for three hours of study in Greek or in business administration, without regard to the fact that half the faculty think Greek of unique importance and the other half regard it as a comparative waste of time. It is an elementary statistical principle that when a group of investigators are agreed that many factors are all important but cannot agree as to how they should be weighted, very useful results may be obtained by considering them all but considering them as equal. Most partial or biased verdicts on civilization are due to laying exclusive emphasis on one's own hobby. Thus it was natural for lovers of art to sum up ancient civilization as a Greek statue or medieval civilization as a Gothic cathedral, and denounce our own age as inferior because it produced no art of comparable worth. It was equally natural for a scientist like Alfred Russel Wallace to say that "To get any adequate comparison with

[1] As was done by Prestonia Mann Martin in her interesting book *Is Mankind Advancing?* (1910) which rated the civilization of ancient Athens as the highest in history because of its fertility in genius.

the nineteenth century we must take, not any preceding century or group of centuries, but rather the whole preceding epoch of human history." Edward Gibbon, who overvalued security in relation to liberty, thought that the benevolent despotism of the Antonine emperors was the happiest period of history, whereas a man of naturally revolutionary temperament, Patrick Henry or Samuel Adams let us say, could never be happy under any government imposed from above, even if his ruler were an archangel. As most of us can agree that art and science, security and liberty, are all true values, there is no need to dispute here as to their relative significance.

Ten tests of social welfare would command at least general assent. One of these is biological, four civic or political, three economic, one intellectual and one domestic: (1) public health, (2) security, (3) administrative efficiency, (4) civic energy, (5) personal freedom, (6) production of wealth, (7) distribution of wealth, (8) invention and applied science, (9) popular education, (10) the position of women. These may be considered in turn for the purpose of definition, as few will consider them to require much justification.

Public health, depending in part on native racial vigor but even more on medical science and a cleanly environment, can be measured statistically by the death rate, by the presence or absence of serious epidemics, and by such comparative strength tests as are already in wide use in schools and armies. This is an excellent test, for it can be made very concrete, and only those would question its validity who prefer death to life or sickness to health.

Security, public order, is an unquestioned mark of civilization. It is the elementary reason for all human government, and civilization is backward in proportion as murder and robbery are permitted. Owing to the imperfection of crime statistics this test can rest at present only in part on a quanti-

[348]

tative basis, but, as no one would question that the United States was safer than the upper Amazon and less safe than Switzerland, at least a rough classification can be made. Is safety a good? Yeats, the most famous of modern Irish poets, has put it a contrary thought in his *Unicorn from the Stars:*

When there were no laws men warred on one another and man to man, not with one machine against another as they do now, and they grew hard and strong in body. . . . But presently they thought it better to be safe, as if safety mattered, or anything but the exaltation of the heart and to have eyes that danger had made grave and piercing.

Sociologists as well as poets have deplored the passing of the struggle for existence, and their testimony is the more disinterested since the poet could make a good living among savages as a tribal bard, where the sociologist would starve to death. But there will always be adventure for civilized men who seek it, as Byrd and Lindbergh have done, and neighborhood wars are too destructive of all the economic values of civilization to be maintained merely as a moral discipline.

Administrative efficiency or "good government" can seldom be directly measured but can usually be recognized when it is present. All countries have certain public tasks to be performed, such as road making, civil law regulation of private contract, caring for the destitute and the insane, and the raising of revenues for these and other purposes. Even an anarchist Utopia would have public tasks, though they might be performed by private agencies. Hence nearly all will admit that inefficient government not only muddles public business but handicaps private effort. One has only to contrast the Prussia of Frederick the Great with the same country under Frederick William "the Fat," his immediate successor, to see the profound difference in national welfare that rulership can make.

Civic energy, or "free government," is perhaps a test more open to argument. We cannot postulate democracy as an essential part of progress, because many theorists prefer aristocracy as an ideal or as a practical working system. But all would agree that a community which merely accepts good government imposed from above, as Nigeria accepts British administration, is less advanced than a community, however its mere forms of government be organized, which can make progress by its own efforts. Public spirit and active good citizenship will always be recognized as a blessing over and above mere routine bureaucratic efficiency.

Personal freedom is also a much debated value, and there probably never will be agreement as to how far it can safely be extended. The question arises only, however, when liberty tends to conflict with some other social good, such as security or morality. Restriction beyond what seems strictly necessary is always felt as a hardship. So much even authoritarian conservatives admit. Liberals (and they are more and more taking over the definition of our social ideals) would go farther and say that the positive benefits of free thought and its expression will outweigh its risks. Both conservatives and liberals would agree that certain legal protections to the individual are necessary as safeguards against tyrannical actions by those who hold political power.

Wealth, like security, has been challenged by exponents of "the simple life" and "back to Nature" on the cogent ground that it seems to corrupt its owners more often than make them happy. But if we consider not an occasional misplaced millionaire but the whole community it is evident that wealth is simply the measure of man's control over the world in which he lives. General poverty is not a virtue, for if absence of temptation be virtue all strictly governed prisons are monasteries of saints. Poverty in an individual, a class or a nation is a misfortune comparable to ignorance and illness. It is a crippling of power, a narrowing of opportunity, a sentence to life imprisonment at hard labor. That power and freedom may be used for evil does not make them evil in themselves.

But, of course, we can all concede that the aggregate wealth of a community is not the only measure of its economic civilization. To produce is not enough; distribution should be sufficiently equitable so that all thrifty, industrious and honest persons may claim some of the benefits which industrialism makes possible. A class of wealthy wasters enthroned above an abyss of misery and insecurity is surely no Utopia.

Wealth in a growing community has a third test to meet. It should not only be considerable in amount and widely distributed but also be progressively increased by the application of scientific principles to all forms of production. All three of these economic tests, even today, can be approximately measured. We have official censuses of wealth, trade, production, use of mechanical power, and many special studies of the distribution of wealth by economists, while the patent office records are no bad index of inventive fertility.

The only generally available statistical test of education in different times and places is the literacy rate, and even this is carelessly reckoned in most countries. But the test is too significant to be ignored, for bare literacy, even if education never goes beyond that, opens the world of printed information and discussion. Other points worth considering in this connection are the relative efficiency of the schools as judged by educational experts and the proportion of the population that advances beyond the three Rs into secondary or higher education.

The position accorded to women has generally been considered an important index of social progress. A civilization that neglects or degrades half of humanity on the ground of sex is certainly to that extent inferior to one which gives to women a free and honored position. It is very largely on this account that Islamic countries and most parts of India are considered "backward" by comparison with Christendom. Brigham Young and Strindberg might dissent from this test, but their anti-feminist views are yearly held in less regard.

These ten tests are certainly relevant to the social welfare. With equal certainty they do not comprise the whole of it. But they are such tests as can either be statistically measured or estimated with a fair approximation to truth. We must leave out of account certain important values which cannot be quantitatively estimated—for instance, "morality." We can determine within a certain margin of error which community has the most *crime*, and hence it is safe to list "security" among our tests, but there is no way to tell which community has the most *sin*, a matter of personal character beyond the reach of statistics. "Happiness" also is a value for which there is no measuring rod, and the same can be said of other inward qualities such as "wisdom," "spirituality" and the like.

But we do admit a subjective element in our second group of tests, individual achievement as distinct from group standards. We can all agree that Germany has less illiteracy than Italy, but who is competent to hold the balance fairly between German and Italian music? Creation in the fine arts and in pure literature cannot be exactly judged, if only for the reason that the critic is usually a much smaller man than the artist whom he judges. Even in science, which is far more objective than art, there will never be a conclusive ranking of the nations. Fortunately there is no need to award first, second and third prizes for creative genius. It is enough that we can distinguish, in a general way, a community that "goes in for" philosophy or painting or astronomy from one which has little or nothing to show in these fields. Again, we make no attempt at precedence, and weight all kinds of creative genius as equal. Classification is arbitrary, but ten selected fields might be: (1) the mathematical sciences, (2) the physical sciences, (3) the biological sciences, (4) the social sciences, including history and linguistic scholarship, (5) speculative thought, philosophical, ethical or religious, (6) pure literature in prose, such as the novel and essay, (7) poetry and the drama, (8) the structural arts, such as architecture, (9) the pictorial, plastic and decorative arts, (10) the musical arts, and perhaps such "expression" in art as singing, dancing and acting. This list would not be complete, but would be characteristic and cover a sufficiently wide variety of creative activities to serve its purpose.

If we rate our twenty tests equally on a scale of a hundred we have five positive grades in each. The highest class—the full five points—can be awarded to a community which ranks with the best in the test considered; four points for a very creditable record; three, for a good record; two, for mediocre attainment; one, for distinctly inferior attainment; and zero for a blank record—for instance, the scholarly achievements of a tribe of savages or the personal and civic freedom of a despotism.

It would be presumption for one writer, with limited knowledge and probably many unconscious prejudices, to attempt to pass a final verdict on great civilizations of the past and present. If the task were seriously undertaken it would require the services of a corps of eminent historians, sociologists and statisticians over a decade or two. But the present paper is not seriously intended in that sense. The object is merely to illustrate the method of rating; the reader can, of course, revise all the scores in the light of his own knowledge and opinions.

Incidentally, if, at some far distant date, there should be a world bureau of statistics, giving fair and uniform data for all nations, we would have in hand a solution to the most perplexing problem of international federation, the rating of

[353]

the proper influence of the nations in world affairs. Numerical strength will not do. China and India together could come near outvoting the rest of the world if population were the only test, and highly civilized communities of small population, such as the Scandinavian countries, would be nowhere. The present legal equality of all sovereign states regardless of population, wealth and power, is even more absurd. To weigh Luxemburg or Honduras against the British Empire or the United States of America and call them equal is a triumph of legal logic over common sense. In actual practise, of course, affairs are decided by a group of the Great Powers, which are such by reason of military and economic strength. This is closer to reality, but it ignores the important cultural contributions which small states are sometimes able to make. Palestine, Periclean Athens, Florence from Dante to Michel Angelo, Elizabeth's little England, the tiny Dutch Republic, the Swiss cantons, thinly settled Norway, have counted for much more in world history than the imposing empires of Assyria, Persia, Macedonia, Tatary and Russia. In some important respects Saxe-Weimar looms bigger in German culture than all Prussia.

Let us suppose that the world bureau of statistics, using far more concrete quantitative data than the vague ratings of this paper (perhaps a combination of educational, economic and health. bureau findings) could arrive at an *index of efficiency* and multiply each population by it, the resulting product would be a rough but usually fair measure of the real importance of each nation. In spite of the inadequacy of our present censuses, several writers have already made tentative suggestions in this direction. Thomas T. Reed, a distinguished mining engineer, prepared an estimate for several countries of the output of work per person, counting human, animal and machine power altogether.[1] This was certainly no complete measure of general civilization, for agricultural countries, such as France and Italy, do not require so much machine power as industrial nations, such as England; but it was a tolerably good measure of the real labor power available in each country, and it showed that for practical purposes China was not four times as populous as the United States. On the contrary the United States had seven times the work-power of China. Here is one possible factor in the index of efficiency. No doubt many other factors besides productive power are capable of statistical treatment once the world census is established.

For the present, however, a world census is still Utopian, and we must return to our crude estimate by grades of achievement in default of accurate figures. With respect to our first criterion, physical welfare, we notice at once a chasm, both abrupt and wide, between the last half century and all previous history, due mainly to the discovery of the micro-organisms which cause disease. The twentieth century death rate in northwestern Europe, the United States and the British Dominions is half or less than half what it was in the same regions a century before or is today in most parts of the tropics. There has been a biological revolution in the later nineteenth century, perhaps more profoundly important in its effects on human life than the industrial revolution of the eighteenth century. On the other hand, it is true that most of the benefits of the new victories over death have gone to babies and young children, and that much less progress has been made in conquering the chronic ailments of old age; and also that all the modern emphasis on fresh air, pure water, sunshine, hygienic clothing, diet, athleticism and hospital care is needed to counteract certain degenerative

[1] Thomas T. Read, "The American Secret," *The Atlantic Monthly*, March, 1927.

tendencies incident to crowded city life. Yet, with all deductions, the highest health rating must be reserved for the present time and our own western civilization.

With respect to security, the second social value on our list, the best policed parts of Europe and Canada are certainly to be ranked a class or two above the United States, which has a very high theft and murder rate. On the other hand, life and property are here more secure than in the unpoliced Middle Ages with their institution of neighborhood warfare, or even the highwayman's paradise of eighteenth century England. An intermediate ranking of "three" would seem just to us, if not generous.

In administration the highest ranking would probably go to Switzerland; with Germany, Holland, England, Scandinavia clustering close to the top. Municipal graft, the lack of trained administrators in state and local politics, a tradition of extravagance and waste of natural resources are blots on the American record, too obvious to require elaboration. But if comparison be made with Russia, either Tsarist or Soviet, China, Latin America or most European monarchies of past centuries, we show up very well in the rapid and effective handling of public affairs. "Three" again seems fair.

American "civic energy" presents a better picture. We do not deserve the highest ranking, as a really vigilant public spirit would bring more voters to the polls and cause a closer scrutiny of municipal business. But there is much patriotism called out in emergencies, and a civic good will shown in huge private benefactions for the public welfare and in the work done by voluntary associations and committees in promoting the supposed interest of local communities. "Four" is probably no overestimate.

If we grant another "four" for personal freedom, undoubtedly many critics will at once protest that in the land of prohibition and Puritanism there is no freedom at all!

[356]

But these very critics are their own confutation. In Bolshevist Russia or Fascist Italy they would not be tolerated for a moment; in the United States they make their fortunes from their criticism of American intolerance. England, no doubt, permits somewhat more freedom of opinion than the United States, but nearly all other nations permit less. As for our sumptuary laws, they are numerous but poorly enforced, and they still leave untouched many human activities (such as the clothing permitted to any given social rank) which were usually subject to regulation by law or custom in past centuries.

In production, general prosperity, and industrial progress and invention, the United States of the twentieth century not only stands in the highest class but stands alone in it. Such countries as modern Britain, Germany, Canada and a few others may be placed in the fourth class (though the inequitable land system of England perhaps lowers her to the third on the prosperity-of-the-masses test). Ancient and medieval civilizations, and all countries that produce goods without the aid of applied science, must be content with a humble "one" or "two" on all economic tests.

With respect to education, our achievement is mixed. We have not wholly abolished illiteracy, as have Germany and Scandinavia, nor raised our universities to the highest academic standards. On the other hand, we give education of secondary and collegiate grade to a larger proportion of the community than any other nation, ancient or modern. "Four" would seem appropriate. And in this land of feminism and woman's rights, we can lay a fair claim to "five" for the last item in our social welfare column.

On the basis of "social welfare," then, we have awarded to the United States forty-three points on a possible fifty. But American civilization does not show up quite so well on the tests of "creative genius." If we give ourselves an average of "three" or "good" in the various branches of pure science and scholarship we are as generous as honesty will permit, and we cannot claim much more for literature. With respect to pictorial art and music we are distinctly "inferior," showing less sense of beauty, craftsmanship and rhythm than many barbarian tribes, to make no mention of the civilized nations that specialize in art and song. If this judgment be challenged, let the critic make up his own lists of the greatest scientists, scholars, philosophers, novelists, poets, painters, sculptors and musicians from all ages and all countries, or, better yet, have each list made up by a specialist in that field. If the list be long enough there will be many American names on it (especially, perhaps, in physics, biology, oratory, the short story, history, social theory, and the kind of architecture that is half engineering), but there will be small countries, even single towns, such as Athens, Florence and Edinburgh, with as many. A lenient twenty-seven in the second group of tests gives to the United States an aggregate seventy out of a possible one hundred.

As history goes, this is a very high ranking, though not perhaps more than should be expected from our extraordinary natural advantages. To score the one hundred per cent of a rounded and balanced civilization, a nation would have to rank with the best in each field. There has thus far in history been no such community. Athens and Florence, ranking at the top in literature, the fine arts and speculative thought, were not very sanitary or orderly by modern standards, usually rather badly governed (as witness their recurrent civil strife), filled with poverty and social injustice. Hohenzollern Prussia, usually well administered and with high educational standards, lacked notably in public spirit and personal liberty; too much depended on the personality of the ruler. Victorian England, renowned alike for liberty, wealth and literature, suffered from economic inequality and the lack of adequate schooling for the poor. Palestine, which reached the world's summit of religious thought and literature, contributed little to science or art. Eighteenth century Europe (before the rise of Romanticism) excelled our own time in many branches of prose literature but was barren of poetic inspiration. Thus our tests yield not only an aggregate score but also a *profile of civilization*, with alternating peaks of achievement and valleys of humiliation. In this way the strength and weakness of any civilization may be graphically depicted.

When we have rounded out our seventy per cent of social efficiency to an even hundred—a task which should absorb all the efforts of our "hundred per cent Americans"!—there will be no reason for cessation of effort. New levels of achievement can be established which will make the "best" of today seem merely mediocre. No civilization of ancient or medieval times can probably be ranked *in the aggregate* ahead of our own American civilization, because modern invention, modern medicine and modern science have rendered possible achievements which would then have been mere fantastic speculations, but it may well be that several civilizations of the past made better use of their own meager opportunities. It is no discredit to the Athenians and Spartans that they had not discovered the germ theory of disease; it is much to their credit that they emphasized athletic exercise. It is no discredit to the men of the thirteenth century that they had not the engineering technique to build a skyscraper; it is much to their credit that they could build a type of cathedral that we are still content to imitate. The greatest compliment we can pay to the greatness of the past is to surpass it, but in common courtesy we should doff our hats as we pass.

THE END